Gobi

Gobi

TRACKING THE DESERT

John Man

Yale University Press
New Haven and London

First published in Great Britain in 1997 by Weidenfeld & Nicolson
Published in the United States in 1999 by Yale University Press

Printed in the United States of America.

Library of Congress Cataloging-in-Publication Data
    Man, John.
        Gobi : tracking the desert / John Man.
            p.   cm.
        Originally published: London : Weidenfeld & Nicholson, 1997.
        Includes bibliographical references and index.
        ISBN 0-300-07609-6 (alk. paper)
            1. Man, John—Journeys—Gobi Desert (Mongolia and Chinese). 2. Gobi
        Desert (Mongolia and Chinese)—Description and travel. I. Title.
        DS793.G6M36   1999
        915.17'3—dc21   99-26761
                                                                CIP

A catalogue record for this book is available from the British Library.

The paper in this book meets the guidelines for permanence and durability
of the Committee on Production Guidelines for Book Longevity of the
Council on Library Resources.

10   9   8   7   6   5   4   3   2   1

For Timberlake

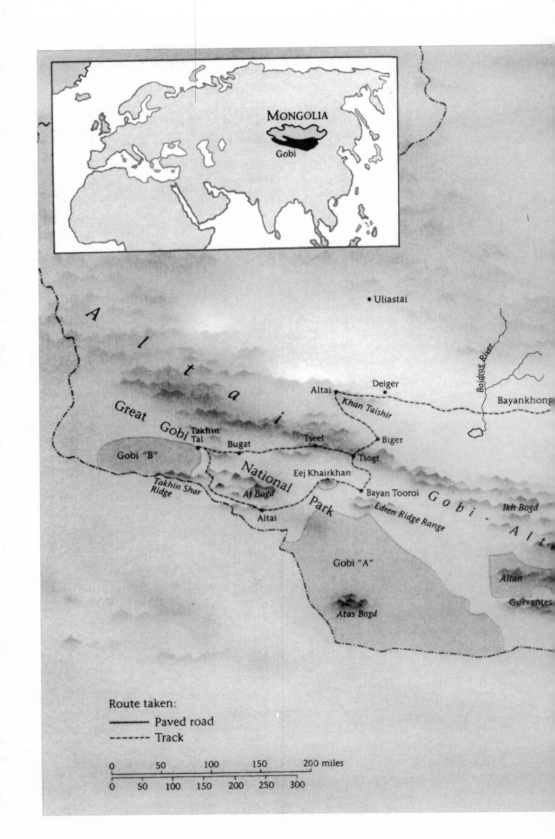

MONGOLIA

Gobi

• Uliastai

A l t a i

Great Gobi   Takhin Tal

Gobi "B"

Takhin Shar Ridge

National

Aj Bogd

Bugat

Tseel

Altai   Delger

Khan Taishir   Bayankhong

Biger

Tsogt

Eej Khairkhan

Bayan Tooroi   *G o b i*

Baidrag River

Ikh Bogd

Edren Ridge Range   *A l t*

Altai

Park

Altan

Gobi "A"

Gutvantes

Atas Bogd

Route taken:
——— Paved road
------- Track

```
0      50      100      150      200 miles
0    50   100  150  200  250  300
```

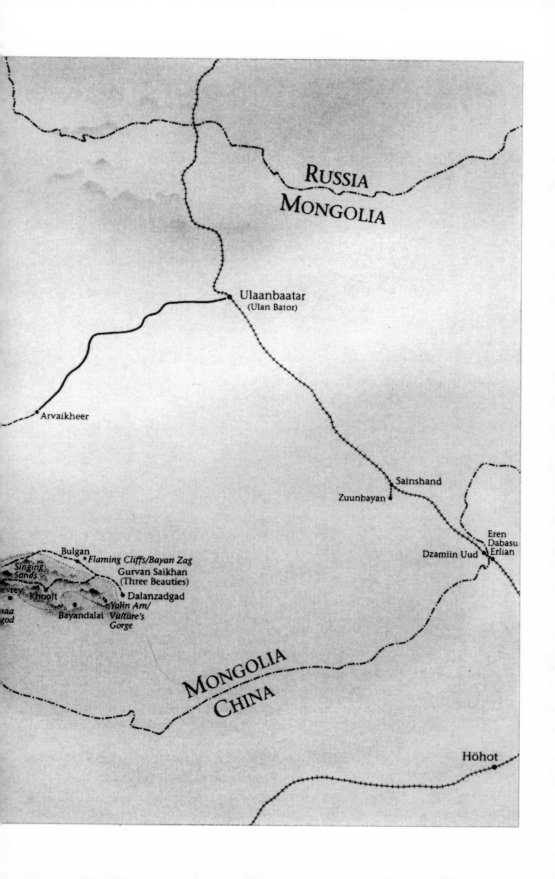

CONTENTS

ACKNOWLEDGEMENTS

At each stage of the journey from dream to experience, I was well-provisioned by friends generous with advice and information.

The idea of going to the Gobi would never have occurred to me but for the seed planted long ago by Emeritus Professor Charles Bawden, former Professor of Mongolian at the School of Oriental and African Studies, London. It was he who introduced me to the language, and his expertise guided me on numerous occasions during the writing of the book. Alan Saunders, lecturer in Mongolian Studies at SOAS, offered matching support, helping me over countless details.

My publishers took the risk with me. It is hard to find publishers willing to do that these days. My thanks to Ion Trewin; to Rebecca Wilson, for so perfectly harmonizing encouragement and criticism; and my agent, Felicity Bryan.

The journey to the Gobi National Park was only possible with the expert help of Dr. Batzhargalin Erdenebaatar, Research Institute of Animal Husbandry, ably assisted in the field by Byambatsogt. I'm grateful to Jeremy Swift for putting us in touch.

Professor Brian Windley, Leicester University, provided vital insights into the geology of the Gobi, as did Lewis Owen, now at the University of California, Riverside.

Tom McCarthy, director of the Mongolian Snow Leopard Project, was an inspiration. Through him I first felt the spirit of the Altai. I shall not count myself happy until I have seen a snow leopard in the wild. His offer of a base in Bayan Tooroi gave me something to aim for in the void. His wife, Priscilla Allen, provided many additional insights. The artist Simon Coombes, who was with Tom in the Altai, took the picture of Tom and the big cat (prints of his snow leopard painting are available from Showcase Editions, Unit 30, Knightsbridge Business Centre, Cheltenham).

Dr. C. Dulamtseren introduced me to the problems of the Gobi National Park. Dr. Adyasuren of the Ministry for Nature and the Environment described the problems of desertification. John Hare provided a context for my discussion of wild camels. Tsend and Choinjin were my guides.

Thanks also to Andrew Laurie, then working for the Mongolia Biodiversity Project in the Ministry for Nature and the Environment; Ian Sloane, HM Ambassador in Ulan Bator; Erdene Enkhsaikhan, Bizinfo, for fast and efficient help with travel and communications.

On dinosaurs, Michael Novacek and James Clark of the American Museum of National History, New York, provided essential insights. David Unwin (Geology Department, Bristol University) explained details of the 'fighting dinosaurs.' Professor Altangerel Perle, Associate Professor of Geology at the National University, Ulan Bator, was generous with his time and details of his work.

John Blashford-Snell, Julian Matthews of 'Discovery Initiatives,' and Badamochir helped with accommodation in UB. R. Sodnomdarjaa, of the Institute of Animal Husbandry, provided welcome additional research.

On the Gurvan Saikhan (Three Beauties), both the park and the mountain range, guidance came from Richard Reading (Northern Rockies Conservation Cooperative and Nature Conservation International, Jackson, Wyoming) and Siegfried Tluczykont (GTZ/ Ministry of Nature and the Environment, Ulan Bator). Thanks also to Chimgee of GTZ, Ariunaa, Tsogt, Dashzeveg, Shirav, and Sangidansranjav.

On Przhevalski horses, Dorothee Stamm, Christian Oswald and Jan van Vegter all contributed generously.

Nescor's Bob Friedline gave me my introduction to Gobi oil. Gary Parkinson guided me round Zuunbayan.

Bill Fearnehaugh filled me in on JCS work in the Gobi.

Ann Savage, who helped at a crucial moment, has my deepest gratitude.

My thanks, with my love, to my wife, for encouraging me to go (and return), and for her ready and perceptive advice.

1

Into the Void

The rains were late in Mongolia that summer. Everyone complained about it: no new grass, no fat cattle, no fresh meat. In the northern steppe-lands, fires destroyed hundreds of square miles of dried-up grass and forest. To the south, in the Gobi, the few herders who did not drive their flocks to the mountains bore the heat, the empty skies, the desiccating winds, without relief. From the high Altai in the west across 1,500 kilometres of desert to the lower lands of the east, from the edge of the northern grasslands 500 kilometres south over the Chinese border, you could count grass by the blade. Old water courses that might have brought a sudden, brief flourish of greenery contained nothing but their own pebbles, sands, earths, gravels and scurrying dust.

For me, arriving in the Gobi for the first time, there was no great surprise in this. The Gobi is desert, after all. The annual rainfall would fill no more than a coffee mug, and only then if you could find a way to prevent it evaporating. I had no way of knowing that this year was drier than the last, no warning of what awaited me.

I and my two companions had been driving southwest for three days. We were almost through the Altai mountains. It was June. Yaks grazed grassy slopes still splashed with snow. We began to descend, swaying and bouncing along a rutted track. Soon, I guessed, we would be out of the mountains, and into a vast, parched, flat place of no water and little rain, a world of sand and gravel and searing heat and air that turned the skin to biltong. I was not looking forward to the experience.

Ridge gave way to ridge, grass gave way to rock, until at last we came to the point at which we saw beyond the mountains. From a platform of gravel, I saw for the first time what I had come for: a carpet of grey, patched with the purple of drifting cloud shadow, stretching to the horizon. But that was a backdrop for a scene that confounded every

1

expectation. In one section of the sky, rain clouds gathered, and here and there dust-devils spurted upwards like spinning tops. Jutting from the desert floor was a sight to touch the soul. From beneath the gathering clouds, the setting sun shot tinted light horizontally, and spotlit a mountain. It was one mass, but made up from a set of surging hillocks and ridges that formed a family group, rising from the sea of sand like breaching whales. The base stood in shadow, made rich as plum by refracted light. The mountain was Eej Khairkhan, the Sacred Mother, sacred to Buddhists, and sacred from times long before the arrival of Buddhism. This was barren rock in a near-barren expanse, yet at that moment, with its flanks fringed with rose, the Sacred Mother was alive with colour and movement.

We stood in silence, bound by the interplay of slowly moving cloud and falling light. The clouds lapping the eastern side smeared as rain began to fall, blurring only the cloud's lower edge. It was hot enough down there to evaporate the rain before it hit the ground. Slowly, like a picture developing, a rainbow formed.

The Gobi of my imagination was all flat immensities, grim and gritty uniformity and deathly extremes. I was welcomed instead by a mountain, by exquisite radiance, and by the promise of life.

I was there in summer because the living is easy, relatively. The temperature may get up to 110 in the shade, 145 in the midday sun, but in this high, dry land, the heat does not sap the will. For six months of the year, life is much harder. The winters drive the temperature down to − 40, on whichever scale you like, because at − 40° centigrade and Fahrenheit meet. Then in the spring, when mountain and desert, barrens and grassland, north and south, all warm at different rates, air rises and flows with punishing force. Brutal cold gives way to sand-blasting gales that can flay exposed skin and strip the paint from a car.

So I came for the summer, flying in from the west, from Kazakhstan's capital, Almaty, which used to be called Alma-Ata before Russian names were displaced by post-Communist ethnic correctness. From Almaty to Ulan Bator was a new route for MIAT, the Mongolian national airline, and seasoned travellers unnerved by MIAT's ramshackle internal flights should note that this service at least was smart, clean, reassuring, with announcements in English as well as Mongolian.

Even so, I was keyed up. Leaving the snows and greenery of the Tien

Shan, looking down on a succession of empty quarters – Djungaria in northwest China, the dark grey of the Altai mountains, and finally the rolling grey-green grasslands of Mongolia – I was on the point of fulfilling an old ambition. Years ago, I had talked my way on to a university expedition to Mongolia, in the days when it was a closed world, on the understanding that I made a stab at learning the language. After a year, I had mastered some of the rudiments and several useful phrases: 'How are your pastures? Keep down your dogs!' The expedition did not happen; I had never been to Mongolia, and my scanty knowledge had become a husk. I was drawn to the Gobi to breathe life into my fossilized scattering of fact and attitude.

To begin with, there were paradoxes to be resolved. The Gobi was a barrier between nomads to the north and settled lands to the south, a void skirted by Silk Road merchants as they drove their camel trains between east and west, an empty quarter that suggested the essence of remoteness and hideous inaccessibility. Yet it was crossed often, with devastating effect, and apparent ease, by conquerors from Attila to Chingis Khan.*

It was empty, yet not empty. Down in the basement of the London Library, filed under 'Topography: Mongolia', I found an account written by a German who travelled across the country in 1913–14. It included a map – crumbling along its fold lines into a puzzle of two dozen separate rectangles – which recorded Mongolian tribal pastures. There were names everywhere, including the Gobi. It looked positively suburban.

On larger maps, it was a blank, with few settlements, none of them known to outsiders; yet everyone knows the name itself. Those under middle-age may not recall exactly why they have heard of the Gobi, but it is probably because of some schoolday memory or parental anecdote about the American explorer Roy Chapman Andrews, discoverer of dinosaur bones by the ton. His adventures in the 1920s turned the Gobi into a household name. The one particular location that shared in this general renown was the Flaming Cliffs, the spot where the Americans had unearthed dinosaur eggs, one of the greatest

* The old spelling, 'Genghis', sanctioned in the *Britannica*, is wide of the mark. The first letter is neither the soft 'g' of 'general' nor the hard sound of 'guest'. The first syllable combines the 'ch' of 'church' with the 'ing' of 'sing'. In Mongolian he only has one 'g' but it's hardened, as in 'mangle'. Academics widely agreed to add a second 'g' to correspond with Old Mongol, but modern Mongol, in its Cyrillic form, does not do this. In brief, there is no universally accepted version in English, let alone other languages, which have many versions of their own.

palaeontological finds of the century. There have been countless other finds since, making the Gobi one of the world's richest fossil sites, but nothing has eclipsed those early expeditions.

This was a subject that seized me as a teenager, me more than most. I had run my fingers over the scimitar teeth of the first dinosaur to be scientifically described, the predatory Megalosaurus, named by William Buckland, Oxford's first professor of geology, in 1824. I had followed in my imagination and reading where dinosaur studies led, from Europe to North America, immersing myself in the late nineteenth-century rush for fossils in the American and Canadian Midwest, the virulent rivalries, the foundation of America's great dinosaur collections. My first book had been on dinosaurs and the history of their discovery. Andrews' three great sweeps into the Gobi, which made a North American phenomenon global, were as much a part of my twenties as Mongolia.

As the plane dropped to meet its shadow on the grassland below, one ambition stood clear above the rest. I had to get to the Flaming Cliffs.

I had planned to travel with an interpreter, and a friend had directed me to Erdenebaatar.* He met me, guided me to a Russian minibus driven by a man as squat as a wrestler, and took me into town, past grazing horses and the tents in which half of Ulan Bator's half-million inhabitants live, past power plants and workers' apartment blocks, to the centre, so open to the surrounding hills that steppe and city interfuse. Friendship Park drifts from town to countryside. Horsemen still ride down Peace Avenue alongside new Korean buses, and gallop across the vast square where Sükhbaatar, founder of the revolution, proclaims its glories – from horseback, naturally.

As in English, surnames and place names retain old meanings. A common Mongolian name is Baatar – 'hero' – a reminder of the Mongols' martial past, when they ruled most of Asia and a good deal of Europe. Ulan Bator (Ulaanbaatar, as the Mongolians spell it) means

---

* Mongolians traditionally use only one name, though they now add a patronymic, which helps as an aid to identity, as a Christian name defines a 'Smith'. It doesn't quite work, because the father's name comes first, so on first acquaintance it seems as if you are addressing someone abruptly by their surname, military fashion. You get used to it, because most names have a familiar short form, in this case Erdene, with the finale accented. Technically the accented e is a vocative. Sükh ('Axe') combines to make the composite Sükhbaatar, but as a common name on its own it becomes Sükhe(e).

'Red Hero', the champion in question being Sükhbaatar – 'Axe-Hero' – himself. Erdenebaatar means 'jewel-hero', which just about summed him up. He had the slight shoulders of a town-dwelling intellectual, not the burly, muscular build of the herdsmen. Like many Mongolians, his looks spanned continents, with something of the North American Indian in the eyes and jet-black hair, a definite European cast to his impressive nose. Fortyish, soft-spoken, lugubrious, he was an expert in animal husbandry, vastly knowledgeable about rural Mongolia. He had travelled a lot, often, all over the country, giving him a resilience you would not guess from his build. His expertise was leavened by a restrained, dry humour. Having learned English late in life, he spoke with care, and relished new phrases.

The bullet-headed, bull-shouldered driver was called Byambatsogt. Byamba means 'Saturday' and 'Saturn', and *tsogt* is 'glorious'. He handled his Russian four-wheel-drive minibus as Chingis Khan's cavalrymen rode horses: with verve, expertise, care, and unflagging endurance. He and Erdene had worked together for years. They made a solid team.

We would tackle the furthest reaches first. The Flaming Cliffs would have to wait. They were in the backyard by comparison with the Gobi's southwest corner, an area little visited by outsiders, with few inhabitants and a wealth of wildlife. I knew of it only because an American zoologist, Tom McCarthy, who was researching snow leopards in the Altai mountains, had based himself in a national park to the south of the Altai. So vast and isolated was the area that it contained several other exotic species as well, including wild camels, the wary, graceful progenitors of the domestic breed; the world's only desert bear, so rare it was almost extinct; and far to the west, wild horses, a native subspecies recently reintroduced.

To get there, Erdene and I could perhaps have flown to a local town, Altai, named after the mountain range, and hired a car. But there were flights only twice a week, and planning was all uncertainty and question marks. The flights, the weather, a car, a driver, fuel: we could be certain of none of these things. Erdene advised it was better to take Byamba and his Russian minibus all the way from Ulan Bator.

We had 800 kilometres to go. It would take three days, if nothing went wrong. But my time was short. Every day counted. We arranged to set off early the following morning.

It was a crisp June dawn, with blue skies over the green hills that billow up to the north of UB (Ulan Bator resembles Los Angeles in very little, except that both are known by their initials). I was staying in a hostel near the centre, but nothing interrupted the view southwards to the hills, and very little broke the silence. To the right, the curlicued eaves of a Buddhist temple, now a museum, glowed in the slanting sun.

Erdene arrived. There was a problem. A spare part could not be found, until later, probably.

'We could start this afternoon, though?'

'Oh, sorry.' Erdene looked glum. 'We would be driving tomorrow. Tomorrow it is impossible to start. Tomorrow is Saturday. Byamba says Saturday and Monday are his unlucky days. If he travels on Saturday, bad things always happen.'

It seemed odd that his name was also his unlucky day, but there it was: I was to have my schedule undermined by superstition. Erdene was adamant. 'We have a saying: Chinese do everything according to money, Mongolians order their affairs according to their luck.'

'But that means two days' delay.'

'Byamba is coming. Perhaps we will think of something.'

By the time Byamba arrived, swinging the van around in front of the hostel, desperation had inspired an idea. 'Erdene, please tell him that I am very interested to hear that Saturday is his unlucky day, because for me Saturdays and Mondays are lucky days. If I travel on Saturdays and Mondays, good things always happen.'

Erdene spoke, and both laughed. 'OK! We go!' He paused, then in an aside, he said, 'About Saturdays and Mondays, this is true?'

'No. Bullshit, I'm sorry to say.'

'What is this bullshit?'

I explained. Erdene, the animal husbandry expert, was intrigued. 'What sort of bull?'

I assured him that although the species and sex were significant, the breed of bull and its health, as revealed by the quality of its shit, were not.

'Not a cow? Cowshit, goatshit, this you do not say?'

'No.'

'Ah-ha. How do you use this term? Do you say "I did bullshit"?'

'You could say: I gave him a load of bullshit.'

'Ah. A load of bullshit. And English people understand this?'

'Americans also.'

Satisfied at last, Erdene climbed into the bus, rehearsing, 'A load of bullshit, a load of bullshit.'

6

We could hardly have left instantly anyway, for there were things to do: permissions to get, food and fuel to buy, money to change – a short, sharp deal in a particular street with one of many money changers, each one laden with fat wads by the bagful.

We left, at 7.00 the next morning, with five extra twenty-litre cans of fuel, pasta, rice, Nescafé, sweets for children, bread, salami, a churn of water (screwed to the floor), and two spare wheels. Erdene and Byamba brought a tent each, but I had a vague notion that travellers in Mongolia could always rely on nomad hospitality. Besides, it was summer. So all I had was a sheet made up into a sleeping bag and an inflatable air-cushion. My main concern was for information: notebooks, dictionaries, tape recorder, maps, camera, pencils, ballpoints.

On the map, it looked an easy start, a nice clear line heading west. Erdene confirmed that the road was paved for 400 kilometres. This was good news, because Mongolia, though the size of western Europe, only has 1,600 kilometres of road. We were about to whip along a quarter of the country's road system.

Not that fast, as it turned out. Ten minutes west, where austere apartment blocks begin to give way to open areas, the road was barred by concrete blocks and pipes, for roadworks, I supposed, though there were no signs of any. This was the *only* road west, and there was simply no provision for the traffic. My first thought was that a major commercial artery had been severed.

Apparently not. Byamba bumped the minibus off the road, and headed over worn grass. There were car tracks everywhere. It seemed the road was little more than a suggestion. We were free to find our own way, and did so for twenty minutes, uphill past apartment blocks, past tents in wooden compounds, past an industrial complex, down over more grassland, under the railway line that leads westwards, and back onto the road.

The road, running in easy curves and long straights between billows of light green, had been built with Russian help as part of a programme to modernize. It was intended to help tie the country together, underpin the economy, make transport fast and efficient. But after what is called the 'transition' from Communist to post-Communist, intentions had faltered, with consequences that made the road an epitome of the country.

The first shock was as intense here as anywhere in the 'former Soviet

Union', but for opposite reasons. In Mongolia's case, there was no declaration of independence, for they had been nominally independent since 1921. The Russians simply pulled out. In 1991–2 the country lost its foreign aid, its traditional markets, and thirty per cent of its productive capacity. Cities neared collapse, with empty shelves, power cuts, queues for food, massive inflation.

To make a road is one thing, to keep it in these circumstances is another. A workforce, trucks, tar, fuel, roadrollers – these things, once routinely available as part of an industrializing economy, have been hard to come by since 1989. So in close-up, the fine strip of tarmac stretching to the horizon turned out to be potholed, and fuzzy at the edges. Progress is erratic. The traffic – a truck or car every five minutes – proceeds by slalom, weaving back and forth between holes that are not visible until you are almost upon them. Naturally, since you may have to swerve to either side, you favour the middle of the road. But the hard shoulders of gravel, pebbles and dust form a useful buffer zone between road and steppe. Confronted by a sudden, extra-large hole, Byamba would swerve off the tarmac to left or right and run along in a cloud of dust, until some new depression forced him back on the harder surface.

Even more unnervingly, to pass oncoming vehicles involved a game of chicken. Say a car appears over the rolling steppe ahead, a mile or two in front. Its driver, like yours, favours the middle of the road. For a long minute or two, you weave towards each other, until it seems that in this infinity the drivers are bent on occupying the same space at the same moment. Only at the last second do they concede that driving on the right has its attractions.

This seemed particularly perverse, given that we were driving through outer space. Westerners, culturally bound to the notion that roads are for driving on, rapidly learn that in Mongolia this is not necessarily so. There are no fences, after all. Even the tarmacked westward highway is part of the steppe. Cows, horses, goats and sheep wander across it freely. Other than the road itself and its occasional ditches and embankments, the only acknowledgement that there *is* a road is provided by a rare line of gers, the white, round house-tents known everywhere else in Central Asia as yurts. Rough signs proclaim them as 'guanzes', wayside cafés, where you can pick up tea, noodles and dumplings. In many places, there is nothing to stop you simply driving straight off the road, riding over the green as if on horseback. Sailing also came to mind. On wheels or hooves, you are free as a yacht.

So we proceeded, across a steppe so parched and pale in its greenness that it became grey in the distance. In this treeless expanse, cloud shadows mottled the plains and distant hills, now rounded, now with bare rock shouldering through.

I slept in the heat, and was awakened by sudden silence. We were at the top of a low pass, beside a huge pile of stones. It was an obo. I was familiar with the word and the concept. Obos were piles of stones marking high points. But I had never seen one before, and I was not sure why we had stopped.

Erdene briefed me. 'First, we honour the obo. Then we look after our horses.'

I was astonished to hear he had horses so far from Ulan Bator. Looking for them could wait, apparently. He led the way to the obo, a three-metre mound of small stones, pebbles, beer bottles and Coke tins, capped by a stick from which flapped a piece of tattered silk. With mounds like this, Mongolians acknowledge the spirits of any high place. Building them is an ancient shamanistic practice, long predating the first, tentative arrival of Buddhism in the eighth century. Later, large obos became foci for Buddhist ritual, but creating them remains an easy, unselfconscious part of travel, a ritual by which Mongolians assert their heritage and the network that binds them. Byamba and Erdene circled the obo three times, tossing little stones onto it.

'Now we look after our horses,' said Erdene, and joined Byamba contemplating the distant horizon, having a pee. 'Also, you can say, "I am freeing a snake." What do you say in English?'

I considered a few possibilities, but none seemed quite as graphic. So we all freed our snakes and looked after our horses together, before pressing on.

'Turn left at the dead camel'

Just beyond our first main town, Arvaikheer, the road ran out. The car wove and surged over open steppe towards the setting sun, sometimes following a main track, sometimes diverging from it. Every driver was free to select a better route, and the way westward became a sort of Oregon Trail, spreading out in a flurry of tracks. Travel became a series of transitions between the well-worn and the untried, an endless search for the smooth over the corrugated, the hard over the soft.

Other vehicles and people were few. At one point, a family was repacking baggage on their car. We stopped to offer help, receiving tea and cigarettes. Further on, a young man, running over from a ger, tried to hitch a lift. We did not pause, leaving him staring resentfully through a cloud of dust.

What of traditional nomad generosity, I wanted to know.

'Women, children, old people, OK,' said Erdene. 'But he is young. Why should he travel for free? Let him take the bus!'

In two months of travel, I think I saw two buses. I didn't fancy his chances, at 9.00 p.m.

The sun sank, night surrounded us, we plunged and swerved onwards. A jerboa, a rat with kangaroo legs, leapt through the headlights. I wondered when we would arrive at our destination, Bayankhongor, somewhere ahead in the gloom. 'It is another two hours,' said Erdene. 'Or maybe four.'

There was something odd about the darkness. Stars glittered above, but a glow silhouetted the western horizon. At first, staring out from the bouncing arc of our headlights, I thought I was seeing the refracted lights of some distant city, except that not even Ulan Bator casts a gleam over the horizon. I realized that what I was seeing was twilight. In this unsullied darkness, the western sky retained a dim aurora rendered invisible almost everywhere in Europe by lights from houses, streets and cars.

At midnight came journey's end: Bayankhongor, a single bulb drawing us in along a couple of kilometres of metalled road. Byamba knew of a hotel. We drove across a grid of darkened concrete buildings, and pulled into a yard, flanked by the hotel, a great rectangular monument to socialism and high hopes. Beside it was a ger. Other than our headlights, all was in darkness. A large dog, a hairy creature at least the size of a small lion, appeared, barking.

'Keep down your dog!' Erdene called, then in an aside to me: 'A four-eyed dog. Very dangerous.'

Keep down your dog! So it really was a useful phrase, especially given a dog of this size and ferocity. I was gratified that my linguistic labours of twenty-five years previously had not gone to waste, and embarrassed, because everyone was asleep.

There was no need for embarrassment. A small wizened lady, who apparently slept in her 'deel', the all-purpose wrap-around Mongolian national costume, appeared from the ger, collared the dog, held it while we filed inside, then followed. She was the hotel's housekeeper, and she made us welcome despite the hour.

Her ger, with four children asleep in their beds, was comfort itself: electric light, TV, radio, tapedeck, fridge and phone. She poured tea from a Thermos, offered hard curd, and rice and boiled meat. Finally, after half an hour of warmth, food and chat, she led Erdene and me into the hotel. Byamba would sleep in the bus, to ensure safety. Poor chap. He had been driving for eighteen hours.

Inside, my sympathy for him evaporated. I saw the truth. The lady's ger and the bus itself provided all there was of warmth and friendliness round here. The hotel, a place of vast spaces and pretensions, was a shell. There was no reception area, and no other guests. A single bulb lit us up an echoing stairway, and another bulb showed us to our cavernous suite, a double room for me, a fold-out sofa in what was once a sitting room for Erdene. The toilet and shower room had no light, and no running water. The old lady reappeared with a bucket and a Chinese plastic Pepsi bottle, each half-full of water. One was to flush the toilet, the other was for both of us to wash with. There was no toilet paper of course. The sheets on the bed were torn, and the blankets as coarse as hair shirts.

Did anyone ever come here, I asked, as I rinsed my toothbrush by torchlight. Oh, yes – Erdene passed on the fruits of his conversation with the lady – this hotel was not going to kick its bucket yet. It was the best hotel in town, so it had several visitors a week. Once, before transition, it had worked well. Now, it had been privatized, and the owner never came, so the lady earned what she could, doing her best.

Before falling asleep I reassessed. She really did do her best, for the hotel and her family. There was nothing to be done about the water, or the bulbs, or the toilet paper. But the torn sheets were clean, as was the tattered carpet, and there was not a speck of dust on the 1950s sideboard. Safely away from the dead shell she administered, she lived in comforts both traditional and modern.

'Erdene,' I called from my rough and ragged bedding. 'What's a four-eyed dog?'

His voice sounded hollow in the darkness. 'It has yellow eyebrows, like more eyes. So we call it "four-eyed dog".'

'Oh. Thank you.'

The lady came again at 7.00 a.m. with a Thermos of hot water brewed on her stove. We chewed on stale bread, made coffee, and were off by 7.30.

This time, the going was tougher. There were hills now, yellow as wheat in the early morning sun, the first hint of the Gobi. Hour followed hour, and landscape succeeded landscape, turning grey as the sun rose, showing flecks of chalk or darker streaks, like coal. There was a small river, which we forded, and a plain as flat as a beach, on which vehicles had etched tracks, making a trail half a mile wide. Here, between small scattered, gorse-like bushes, there were rocks that had the peculiar ability to sit right on top of the sandy soil without being buried. I wondered if they had been placed delicately to mark the way, but then saw they were scattered randomly, the result of some geological process I could not fathom.

We were north of the Gobi proper, but this was desert nevertheless, no less Gobi than the Gobi itself. Indeed, there is some debate over what 'the Gobi' is, and its extent. Unlike so many other Mongolian names, 'Gobi', sometimes translated as 'desert' or 'waterless place', does not actually mean anything. It is what it is – gravel, sand, bare earth, rock, mountain, dune, various types of vegetation, and more. Mongolians like to say there are thirty-three types of Gobi. I have seen it written and heard it stated as established fact, but I have a feeling that it's just one of those neat, surprising aphorisms, like the twenty different types of snow in 'Eskimo'. Having already seen a dozen types of Gobi, I knew there must be many more, surely many more than thirty-three. If you cross-correlate mountain, hill, plain, river, dry river-bed, spring and outwash plain with stone, rock, sand, gravel, pebble and soil; and hardness, softness, colour and size; and plants and wildlife, from mouse to snow leopard; and domestic animals – if you combine all these variables you have enough to define a hundred, a thousand different types of Gobi.

The Gobi seemed to be already all around me. That, though, is a moot point. Back in Ulan Bator, I had tried to define the extent of my subject with the help of a desert ecologist, Dulamtseren. I found him in his office, in the Institute of General and Experimental Biology, a place that belied its grand title: bare rooms, a skeleton staff, echoing corridors, all reflecting the poverty imposed by lack of funds and once-rampant inflation. A wizened 64-year-old, born in the western Gobi, Dulamtseren insisted that 'the Gobi' not only included the area the size of France straddling Mongolia's southern border, but also another huge slab of desert right up against the Russian border.

'But' – I glanced at the huge wall map, the only thing in his office besides his desk – 'there are lakes there.'

'Yes, but the surroundings are all Gobi.'

Others insist the Gobi flows only from the flanks of the Altai mountains. Some would include the eastern Altai, known as the Gobi Altai. Others would say you could include the *southern* slopes of the mountains perhaps, but not the peaks, and not the northern slopes. Later, in the eastern Gobi, a guide would insist that our surroundings, a desolate region of dunes and gravelly undulations, were not part of the *real* Gobi. I stared round at the wasteland, and asked why. 'This is my home,' he said. To him, the 'real' Gobi was the opposite of home, somewhere over the horizon, not a place or a landform, but a state of mind.

To my eyes, the area approaching Altai was Gobi, and like almost all the Gobi, both desert and yet more than desert. From the top of each rise, the grey surface acquired a patina of green in the distance as the minute flecks of grass merged together. When we stopped to see to our horses, I saw this was not merely a hint of life, it was the basis of life itself: pasture. Every few yards there were horse and camel droppings. And every hour or so, two or three camels, shaggy with shedding wool, or a small herd of horses, or a distant ger, provided further proof that even this apparent wasteland was home for some, sometimes.

We hit rising ground, a gentle but long haul up a ridge, and our minibus revealed a limitation. Byamba swung round, halted, and opened the bonnet. We had overheated, and needed to face into the wind to cool down. This enforced pause would become a regular feature of travel uphill. It wasn't just our bus; it was a fault common to most Russian vehicles in these desiccated regions. Sometimes, breasting a pass, you see several trucks all facing the wind, their bonnets agape.

Then down, past hills with a strange pink tinge, and into a deep gorge with a flat floor, both formed by flood waters in the not-too-distant past. Rocks were eroded into soft pillow shapes and holes five or six metres up in the cliff sides, drilled out by swirling debris. The bumps and dents all bore witness to the size and power of the floods that occasionally swept down along the path we were taking to the Baidrag river. It turned out we were on a track, though if there had been any other travellers this way recently, winds had blown away all traces of their passage. Ahead, spanning the river, just beside a thirty-metre crag that punctuated the junction of tributary and main stream, was a well-made bridge, carried for a good 200 metres on posts, and up the bank beyond, a little community of gers and brick shacks, with several guanzes.

'You are the team leader,' said Erdene, as we rolled across the planking. 'Which one do you choose?'

'Let's take the end one.' It had a satellite dish, which made it look more civilized than the others.

'Perhaps the middle one is better.'

So much for leadership, and just as well. The dried-meat dumplings were excellent, and I had another chance to get used to salty tea.

After lunch, heading west, we skirted jagged peaks, their strata buckled and twisted, smoothed off here and there into table-tops. Around us, slabs of rock thrust through the desert floor like the remains of ancient temples. Then we were in a plain washed pale green by tenuous pasture, where two gers and a herd of goats stood against a trembling mirage. They seemed to be rooted in puddles.

A vehicle of some kind appeared ahead, a truck. It was the first vehicle we had seen in five hours' travel, and the first I had seen on desert as smooth as this. It was belching smoke. In fact – I became concerned as we got closer – it looked as if it was on fire. Since Erdene and Byamba made no comment, I doubted my own judgement; then, turning, saw the truth. We, too, seemed to be on fire, throwing up a pall of smoky dust that stretched a hundred yards or more behind us.

The truck, pursuing its own path, went past us a kilometre away. Far beyond its column of dust, pale in the distance, ranged the Altai mountains, the barrier to the Gobi proper.

In the late afternoon, Byamba spotted houses: Delger, the centre of the local 'sum', a sort of sub-county. Perhaps we could refuel. Besides, he had a friend there. We swung towards it, over a surface flat as pavement, through a world of mirages and drifting cloud shadows. Delger's houses, with a separate palisade for gers, hovered in a limbo an unknowable distance away. It turned out to be about four miles.

Disconcertingly, as we approached, the mirage off to one side did not evaporate. It was a real lake, a big one, though not on the map, and for a moment I dreamt of throwing myself in and downing draughts of cool water.

'Byamba says it is salty,' said Erdene. 'You cannot drink it. They must use a well here.'

Byamba drew up by a house, asked a question, and returned with a brief shake of his head: no fuel, no friend. We paused only by the well, capped by a hand-pump, where Erdene and Byamba filled our churn with clear, cool water before heading on into the setting sun.

Gradually, we edged towards the Altai mountains. High up near the toothy ridges, snow still lodged in dimples and crevices, descending between rounded flanks in scrolls and squiggles that reminded me of the beautiful Mongol script abandoned (but not forgotten) in 1941. The flanks divided and subdivided as they descended, forming lower slopes like pleated skirts.

For two hours we drove over untracked plains, then on over rolling dune-like landscape.

'How far to Altai?'

'I don't know. We are lost. Perhaps you know where we are.'

I had once worked briefly in the Amazon, where you can be genuinely lost within yards of a trail or river, unable to see the sun, unable to tell north from south. That's unnerving. Out here, 'lost' had a different meaning. We could see for ever. The sun was ahead of us, the Altai mountains something between fifteen and thirty kilometres to our left. We were making about thirty kilometres per hour, give or take a few. But where *exactly*? I had no idea.

There are only two ways of discovering your position accurately: by knowing the area intimately, or combining an accurate map (there are excellent Russian ones, if you can find them) with geopositioning devices that derive your position to within metres by radio and satellite. With inaccurate maps and no GPS, being 'lost' is a common experience, overcome by stopping and asking – a problem for foreigners travelling without help, but of no great concern to Mongolians. When Tom McCarthy, the American zoologist, once asked for directions, the herds-man pointed at the horizon and said, 'Go that way, and turn left at the dead camel.' In a place with no name and no salient features, a dead camel is as good as a signpost. People and places are found by hearsay. Right now, without anyone to ask, we were not exactly lost. We just had no clear idea where we were.

At last, as the day died, we hit a dirt road, which turned into a paved road, which led into Altai. This town, capital of Gobi-Altai 'aimag' or province, has some stature: a grid of paved streets lined with slender trees, a museum, two hotels. Ours, enticing foreigners with 'Hotel' in Latin script, had new chocolate-box frescoes of ibex and snow leopards, a disco, and at least two other guests. This was luxury. The light and airy room, with its yellow floor, had a working toilet, and toilet paper, and a shower, with glacial water that came straight off the mountains. As the dust flowed dark around my icy feet, a jet of meltwater blew off my scalp and numbed my brain.

I recovered over supper in the disco. They opened the kitchen for us, cooking up rice and dried meat, serving German beer and Chinese Pepsi.

I hadn't seen much from China. It was odd: both economies had been liberalized, and China was not far away. It would surely be easier to drive south over the Gobi than north over mountains.

'All things made in China are terrible!' said Erdene. 'The coats, the boots are cheap, but they fall apart. The Russians make better things.'

It was a fair comment, given the depth of Russian involvement in Mongolia over the last seventy years. Mongolia's nominal inde-pendence had been guaranteed by Russia. It was Russia that secured the border with China, Russia that helped fight off the Japanese in 1939, Russia that had provided much of the investment, and then the best markets, and the troops that had guaranteed Mongolian security through the Cold War, and the aid, and the educational advantages. So presumably the solid houses of Altai, none of them older than about thirty years, were also down to the Russians? The suggestion hit a raw nerve, for Russian dominance did not equate to Mongolian sub-servience.

'You cannot say that *all* buildings were built by Russians and Russian money! It would be very great ignorance of Mongolians!'

And now the Mongolians were on their own, trying to make a go of a rock-bottom economy. Their old markets had gone, the infrastructure was virtually non-existent, and their experience was negligible. After 'transition', anyone who could get together some cash could buy a privatization voucher, go to the local privatization commission, and walk away with a hotel, a factory, farm machinery, things they knew nothing about. No wonder there was suffering. 'In 1992, it was *bad*,' Erdene said. 'You know, the Mongolian bank tried to play the game of capitalism, and lost $100 million! There was high inflation, and things disappeared. All factories closed. In cities, just to get bread – I stood in line for three to four hours, just for two pieces of bread!'

And now?

Away from Ulan Bator, Mongolia is still a herding economy, and a very effective one, effective enough to carry its people through the few harsh years after Communism collapsed. It was the countryside that saved them. In a nation of just over 2 million, with an intact tradition of mutual support, almost everyone in the town can find a relative in the countryside, and almost everyone did. In trucks, on horseback, in the underfinanced, undermaintained, fuel-strapped planes, churns of milk and sides of beef came to feed the city. Pasture again proved the country's real wealth.

Now, some things work again – witness the difference between the hotel last night, and this hotel, with its garish disco, its strobe lights and its frescoes. And the town had fuel. And when we went shopping next day, there was a fair range of goods, local and imported: wooden saddles, blocks of green tea, a Japanese kid's bike, slabs of Blue Omo soap, carpets for gers, Russian boots, and – the aim of our quest – two bottles of good-quality vodka as a gift for the head of the Gobi National Park – Askanov Vodka, billing itself in English as 'Europe's Elite,' made in Belgium, at $6.00 per bottle.

You would think, looking at Altai's buildings, that the place was short on history. Not a bit. This is an ancient land. Altai's museum has the evidence, though it would take years for an outsider to make sense of its unmapped archipelago of objects. Here there are axe-heads dating back 3,000 years, chain mail from the thirteenth century, Stone Age grinders, a bronze Buddha from the seventh or eighth century found at a mountain down in the Gobi, a slate covered with ash which could be scraped off to write a letter, obscure scripts – Sogdian, Uighur – from around the first millennium, Chinese money from the first century BC, all random finds hinting at the flow of peoples and cultures that preceded and overlapped the Mongols.

Meanwhile, Byamba had been solving a more immediate problem: how to find the way to our next staging post, Tsogt (a common name for places as well as people). The answer was to hand, in the form of a woman, Eeke, who wanted a lift with her child. With them on board, we headed for the mountains.

A beacon in the wasteland

The first range was a minor bulwark, the Khan Taishir range, barring the approach to the Altai proper. We ground up and over a high and windy pass. No mistaking the road here: progress was only possible because it had been graded and built up. Occasional gers were flanked by tethering lines for horses and dried dung, formed into crumbly logs for fuel and gathered into neat piles. There were no camels up here, but yaks instead, their shag-pile coats a necessary protection against cold even in high summer.

In the rough grass, marmots scooted for their holes as we drew level. Marmots are odd creatures. They watch curiously, then flee with a sort of undulating run, like furry doormats flapping in a draught. They make good eating, and their curiosity makes them easy to catch. People have reason to be wary of them, however. They – and their fleas – are among the several creatures that harbour the bacillus that causes plague, the Black Death. The Mongolian for bubonic plague is 'marmot-disease'. Every now and then, for reasons that are still obscure, the plague used to break out of its heartland, as it did in the fourteenth century, when one-third of Europe, 25 million people, died. Millions more died in lesser outbreaks before and since. The plague is killed off by cooking, but every now and then someone, a child perhaps, stumbles across a stricken marmot and the plague jumps from marmot to man. Action is rapid: warnings issued, the area quarantined, any victims treated. Deaths are rare. And since the marmot and flea soon die, the outbreak is self-limiting.

On the edge of the Gobi, the plague enforces a peculiar interaction between grassland and desert, mediated by marmots. They are on the whole grassland creatures that do not penetrate deserts. But if marmots get the plague, they commute into the desert to harvest the leaves of the gnarled and slow-growing saxaul trees, bushy growths that dot many parts of the desert. The leaves, it is said, contain an antidote to the plague. If so, perhaps it was thanks to the marmots of Mongolia, busily carting saxaul leaves from the desert to their mountain burrows, that the Black Death did not strike more often.

As we ran down into the desert basin between the two ranges, heading east, parallel to the saw-backed ridges of the Altai, I realized that all was not well with my stomach.

We were in the middle of a plain dotted with tough cushion-plants which make good camel fodder but which provided cover for nothing much bigger than a lizard, certainly not a squatting homo sapiens. The nearest ravines were in the ash-grey foothills off to our right, from which on occasion flood waters obviously poured, scouring the gentle slopes and spreading detritus into shallow fans and deltas. We were heading for a town called Biger, where we would turn south into the Altai. It was my intention to hang on until the mountains could provide a little privacy. But as yet Biger was not even a tremble on the horizon.

I began to view everything as a possible source of cover. Low mud walls, the remains of a lamasery destroyed in the purges of the 1930s and 40s, vanished in the dust of our wheels. We crossed outwash channels, deep enough to jolt my sphincter towards collapse, but not deep enough for my purposes. The flood waters must have been terrific, flowing down to a distant salt lake. The map showed Biger near a lake. I prayed that it was near *this* lake.

But Biger would offer nothing but a crowd to witness my distress. We passed two camels couched in the dust, grey and naked, their winter wool shed, baled up, and trucked out. They were the first sign of life in the last hour. Better to give in to the inevitable now, before we hit civilization.

'Erdene. I have a stomach problem.'

'Oh, my goodness.'

Byamba stamped on the brakes. I walked gingerly away over the stone-scattered, baked-mud surface, finding at last a declivity perhaps forty-five centimetres deep behind a little bush. This was the world's most unprivate privy. I could have admired the view for fifteen kilometres in all directions, along the roller-coaster flanks of the Altai, down to the salt lake and beyond to the rippling horizon, along to the distant gers and palisades of Biger. Two thousand metres above loomed a snow-capped pinnacle, the range's highest peak, Burkhan Buudai. But the feature that held my total attention was the thirty-centimetre-high tamarisk that screened me from the car until I was able to return, restored to health.

As we veered past Biger's concrete shacks and palisaded gers and climbed over the grey skirts of the Altai, my spirits rose at last. Soon we would be entering the region that was the proper subject of my research. We groaned up a rubble-strewn valley, past a collection of five gers, and emerged onto alpine meadows. Above, snow still lay in blinding sheets between lichen-flecked rock. We dropped to Tsogt, took Eeke to her ger, and then, in late afternoon, breasted the last of the Altai's descending ridges.

At this point we came in sight of the Sacred Mother mountain.

Standing in purple shadow thirty kilometres out into the desert, with one grey flank merging into cloud, its western slopes were touched by the setting sun. For several minutes I gazed, entranced by the revelation of another world. The interplay of grey, purple, blue and red; the surge of rock from the desert floor; the faint curves of the dust-devils; the rainbow that bloomed across the cloud – every element combined to create in me the feeling that this first view of the Gobi was a happy omen.

'John! We go.'

We were still 300 metres above the desert floor, with an unknown stretch of foothill, dune and plain to cross before reaching our goal for the night.

I shivered, and turned to the car.

2

A Camel, a Bear and a Baby Gazelle

The undulating flanks of the Altai seemed to be the preserve of nothing more than scattered bushes, until, as dusk approached, Erdene shouted and pointed. 'Gazelle!'

To our left, over grey and barren dust, two of the creatures bounded away at our cumbersome, noisy approach. I hardly had time to see more than their upturned tails and white rump patches. They were Persian gazelle (*Gazella subgutturosa*), or 'black-tailed' gazelle in Mongolian, members of one of the two main Gobi species. The other, the more thick-set grassland or goitred or 'white' gazelle (*Procapra gutturosa*), prefers the eastern Gobi and its neighbouring steppes.

Several more caught my eye, a hundred yards away to our right, leaping bushes, matching our speed. They were obviously frightened, but this was an odd way to flee. A few took off at a right angle. But none reversed course to run in the opposite direction, or cut in behind us. Four continued to run parallel to us, as if trying to outpace us.

'Watch!' Erdene called out. 'They will come in front of us! When they do, that is good luck.'

The going was firm, the race exhilarating. The gazelles, travelling at a good fifty kilometres per hour, seemed on the point of pulling clear, but then began to close in, as if drawn like comets to a star. They turned ever more sharply, until they seemed actually set on collision.

This behaviour did not evolve as a deliberate brush with death. On the contrary, it is a strategy shared with many other plains species to frustrate predators by drawing them on to top speed, then forcing a turn just at the moment they need maximum velocity for the kill. But there is a new predator now. With the coming of cars, the ploy has become suicidal, because it brings the animals into rifle range. Across much of Central Asia gazelle numbers have suffered a severe reduction over the last half-century.

Wherever you go in the Gobi, these are the commonest large wild animals, and they have a phenomenal turn of speed. In the 1920s, Roy Chapman Andrews claimed to have paced desert gazelles at 100 kilometres per hour. I wondered where in the Gobi you could drive a 1920 Dodge at 100 kilometres per hour, but there's no doubting his general point. 'We followed one desert gazelle, a fine buck, for ten miles,' wrote Andrews. 'He left us easily in the first three miles, and we could just keep his bobbing white rump patch in sight; then he settled down to a steady pace of thirty miles an hour, keeping about one hundred yards in front of the car. He continued at this speed for seven miles until we punctured a tire.'

The gazelles also displayed astonishing tenacity. Since the Americans shot hundreds of animals for food, for sport, and to collect museum specimens, Andrews also had opportunities to record some pretty grue-some details. 'With a broken foreleg, the animal can easily reach thirty-five miles an hour; a shattered hind leg slows it considerably, but it can still do fifteen miles an hour for some distance.'

By comparison, Byamba was hardly much of a challenge. The four gazelles flashed across in front of the car and took off across the gravelly dunes with a stiff-legged gait, as if on pogo-sticks, bouncing away over the scattered bushes, leaving little spurts of dust every time they landed. In the failing light, they were out of sight in seconds.

Rolling on over and round the incised foothills we came, towards dusk, upon grassy tufts grazed by a herd of sheep and goats and then, to my surprise, a stream, tumbling from the higher ground and turning the desert green. There were only a few square yards of emerald grass, but enough to reveal a truth about the Gobi. The soil itself is not necessarily barren. It is only made so by the lack of rain. With moisture, it blooms. Where the cushion of turf graded down towards desert, a herding family had created a plantation, a ranch, almost a garden: a little allotment of vegetables and a line of poplar trees, at that moment being used by two camels as a shield against the wind. At our approach they shied off across open gravel, dancing away at the end of spindly shadows cast by the setting sun, while we struck out into the plain.

We were following a track, and on occasion a line of telegraph poles. Both had to lead eventually to the only settlement within eighty kilometres, Bayan Tooroi, but the two did not always run together and there was no telling how far away the town was. Behind us were the dark masses of the Altai, and to our right the Sacred Mother, now a solid lump of shadow backed by the soft glow of twilight. Ahead, the saxauls and the gravel plain stretched to the unbroken horizon.

Darkness enclosed us. There was no more sign of the telegraph poles. Our world reduced to a scattering of stars, the wheel tracks, and the bushes, briefly lit by the pitching headlights. I was beginning to plan on a cold night out when we rejoined the marching poles and a single light glimmered in the darkness ahead.

Bayan Tooroi – 'Rich in Desert Poplars' – is an unlikely name for a Gobi town, even when you get to it. There are poplars, a line of them straggling along the northern boundary of the National Park, but they stand well clear of the community, which is not rich in anything much. Our headlights picked out no streets, merely single-storey buildings separated by a surface as barren and dusty as the surface of the moon. Byamba stopped to ask the way, and was directed towards the house of our contact, Avirmed, the head of the Gobi National Park. I was apprehensive, having had a warning back in Ulan Bator: 'He's a little Chingis Khan!' Whether this was a term of abuse or a compliment, our unheralded arrival would need sweetening. Hence the two bottles of vodka.

As it turned out, Avirmed was away in Ulan Bator. It was his wife, Khorloogarad, who welcomed us. Khorloo was not just the boss's wife; she had a natural, easy authority of her own and style to match, with gold-rimmed glasses, jet-black hair set in a clasp and a silk neck scarf. Urban elegance did not fit with this outback setting, but her welcome was that of a nomad. It was after 10.00 at night, and we arrived out of the desert unannounced, yet she plied us with rice and reboiled meat and hard curds, and a number of other ingredients that delighted Erdene.

'Dzambaa,' he said. 'It is my favourite.'

While children watched *The Little Mermaid* dubbed in Mongolian on the video, Erdene revealed to me the delights of dzambaa. This is the recipe: assemble a bowl, a spoon, a bag of barley flour, salty green tea, butter made from the cream of fermented cow's milk, and sugar. Now pour a little salty tea into the bowl, add rancid butter to taste, allowing it to dissolve. Ignore the smell. Add a spoonful of sugar. To this sweet-and-sour, salty, buttery tea, add a good helping of stoneground barley flour, allowing it to float on the tea. Insert a finger carefully through the flour, lift the bowl to the lips, tip gently, and suck out some of the tea, leaving the slurry of sweetened tea and butter. Mash the whole lot together with your fingers until it thickens into a doughball.

'Now to consume.'

I played for time. 'This is popular everywhere?'

'Mainly it is in the western provinces. Still they have not lost the habitude of consuming it.'

'Even here, in the Gobi?'

'Yes, because this province is part of the west.'

'But we're in the middle of a desert. Do they grow barley round here?'

Erdene nodded. 'In oases. We call it "traditional area of irrigated barley cropping". Perhaps a bag or two for each family. It is enough.'

I took a bite. My apprehensions vanished. It was delicious, a tang of sourness counteracted by the sugar, and all the better for a slug or two of vodka.

Restored, we followed Khorloo across a compound past a scattering of thorn bushes to another little tin-roofed house. This was the base of the American snow leopard researcher, Tom McCarthy, who had offered me the place as a refuge when we met in England earlier in the year. A hefty, four-eyed dog loomed up from the darkness, and proved to be a softie, corrupted by Tom's American ways. It pushed its way in with us, as my torch revealed everything we needed: two rooms, four beds, a table, three chairs. That was it. No bathroom, no water, no toilet, no electric light. Such things were not expected. By candle and torch, I hauled my sleeping bag from my pack, shook out the dust, and climbed in.

The following morning, having used Thermos water brought by Khorloo for coffee and washing, we prepared to head into the park itself.

The existence of a park in this remote region reflects something fundamental in Mongolian culture: their closeness to nature. In the West, urbanization overlies nature, reducing it from being a foundation for life to a mere adjunct. This is not so in nomadic cultures, not so in Mongolia. The Mongols were ecologists long before the word was invented. They had to be to ensure their own survival. If the pasture fails, death follows, death for cattle and then death for the herders. And here, pasture – like life itself – is on the edge, in ways very far from modern experience in the West. In March, when the pastures await the bloom of spring and the cattle are thin, late snows and frosts kill as surely as slaughterers' knives. Herders must have expert knowledge of animal behaviour, fodder growth, springs, rivers, lakes, soil fertility. From the pasture stems all wealth, starting with the 'five animals' – horse, cattle, camel, sheep, goats. (In the desert, camels replace horses as pack animals, and in the mountains yaks make a sixth.) The animals provide the meat, the milk, the multiplicity of dairy products – over 150 kinds – ger coverings and clothing, and the transport that allows the people to migrate back and forth between winter and summer pastures. As a result, rural Mongols do not *possess* land; they use it, moving on, moving back, in rhythms dictated by established practice combined with unexpected extremes, like deep snow in May or an extended drought.

This way of life has always bred a reverence for the natural world. It is there in the ancient name for God, Tenger, which also means 'sky' (as in European languages: 'heaven', *ciel*, *Himmel* all share meteorological and religious meanings). Chingis Khan claimed that his mandate to rule came from the Blue Sky, Khökh Tenger, by which he meant the supreme God. Tenger ruled a pantheon of minor deities, among them the spirits of place and feature and weather. The shamans and their rituals by which the spirit world was contacted and controlled have now virtually disappeared, but the belief is still there, expressed in the obos that mark the high places, in references to the spirits, in the names of mountains: most are 'holy' or 'sacred'. Every spring, mountain, grove and stream has its spirit.

Pantheism gives the Mongols a singular passion for their country. This sometimes emerges sounding like raw nationalism, sometimes mere romanticism, but at its best it is something deeper, a spiritual affinity with the environment. The attitude was formalized seven centuries ago, when Bogd Khan (Holy King) Mountain, bare rock jutting up through forested flanks just south of present-day Ulan Bator, was made sacrosanct, with hunting and logging banned. An eighteenth-century story about Bogd Khan illustrates the intensity of pantheistic beliefs. A certain official went up to celebrate the spring worship of the mountain, and was caught in a storm. He berated the mountain: 'I came here to worship you as a duty, not because I wanted to. What do you think you are up to?' Then he condemned the mountain to be whipped, to wear fetters, which were placed on its obo, and to a fine. There is a twist to the story: the official was Chinese, a Manchu billeted in what was then a colonial capital, and the fine he imposed involved seizing all the mountain's horses, for himself. Even Mongolia's gods, it seemed, were subject to Chinese depredation. Perhaps to prevent such a thing happening again, and certainly as a formal expression of reverence, this magnificent peak was declared a protected area in 1778, making it the world's first nature reserve.

It took another century for other nations to take similar steps, led by the United States. Yellowstone was established in 1872. Canada, South Africa, Australia and New Zealand set up parks in the 1890s. Sweden established Europe's first ones in 1909. Britain had no national parks until the 1950s. By the end of the 1980s, the USA had some 20,000 square kilometres reserved, while the Soviet Union had 44,000 square kilometres. At that time, when Communism collapsed, Mongolia had 56,000 square kilometres – some 5.6 million hectares – of park.

The 'transition' to capitalism inspired a renewed passion for national parks. Idealism and self-interest marched hand in hand. Poor countries that are rich in natural resources can do well by pushing conservation onto the international agenda. Free travel for impoverished officials, aid, education abroad, eco-tourism, research grants, international status, new trade links – all these were potential returns on Mongolia's greatest obvious asset, her wildernesses. At the 1992 UN Earth Summit in Rio, Mongolia proposed that *the whole country* be declared a special biosphere reserve. The suggestion caught the attention of the world's ecologists, with some even more astonishing statistical consequences.

With help from the United Nations Development Fund to the tune of $750 million a year, Mongolia added another 7 million hectares to its national parks, more than doubling its protected areas. Mongolia, which is about one-sixth the size of the US with less than one per cent of its population, has over one-third its area of protected land. Compared to Russia, the figures are even more extreme: one-fourteenth the size, but double the protected area. In parkland, per head of population, Mongolia is the richest country in the world.

Almost half of this is the Great Gobi National Park. Set up in 1975, it takes up a good chunk of Mongolia's southwest corner. It is huge, over 5 million hectares, almost half the size of England. Not only is it Mongolia's largest park: it's the largest in Asia and the second largest in the world, after Greenland. In fact, it is actually two-in-one, the two sections being most commonly referred to by initials. Gobi A, also known as the Southern Altai Gobi and Trans-Altai, is the larger of the two. This was the one I was about to broach. Gobi B, or the Dzungarian Gobi, lay further west by almost 300 kilometres at its closest. Bayan

Tooroi, headquarters for both sections, is just outside the northern border of Gobi A.

A wilderness of rarities

Starting about thirty kilometres from the Altai, Gobi A stretches south-wards, increasingly arid, increasingly desolate, for 200 kilometres to the Chinese border. The park stops there, at the 25-kilometre-wide strip of no-man's-land, but the wilderness recognizes no frontier and merges with the greater desert regions of western China – the Desert of Lop, the Takla Makan.

On first acquaintance, anyone from kinder regions might find Gobi A a grim place: a stark patchwork of hummocks, mountains and valleys, divided by stony desert which covers almost half the area. But such reactions are relative. All wildernesses – the Scottish Highlands, the Alps, the Sahara, the Amazon, Siberia, the Canadian Northwoods, Antarctica – had their early detractors and all are now appreciated on their own terms. It is the same with the southern Gobi. Studies, almost all of them postwar, all of them Soviet and Mongolian, have revealed the region's variety, fragility and importance. It was as the result of a mass of papers published jointly by the Soviet and Mongolian Academies of Science between 1950 and 1975 that the reserve was established, and a rash of further studies followed between 1975 and 1982. One day, perhaps, the area will have its poets, too.

The climate is as cold, as hot, as windy as the rest of the Gobi, and even drier. Skies are almost always blue and clear – on average, there are only five to ten cloudy days a year. The stony plains are burnt with a 'desert tan', caused by the reaction between exposed rock, rain and sun. Over ninety per cent of the ground cover is irredeemably bleak, of interest mainly to those few geologists who have mastered arcane disciplines that distinguish a super-arid hammada from a chestnut-brown humus. Rainfall could be ten times greater, and the place would *still* be arid. It's hardly surprising no one lives here.

The little water that does fall defines the park's character. Rainfall, combined with the minimal snowfall, averages sixty millimetres, with the wettest month July, producing on average twenty-two millimetres. The rains create temporary rivers and streams, though they are so transitory that very few people have ever seen one. A storm may fill a depression with a river eight or nine metres wide, but within twelve hours, there is nothing left of it except a few puddles. The rains wash topsoil into channels, winds gather soils and sands together, streams gouge out clefts quicker than wind and frost erode their sides. In these varied land-forms, water remains, some of it in granite bowls, some under the ground, emerging in springs, most of them in the high ground towards the centre. About forty were recorded when the park was set up, which meant one spring – in effect, one small pond or boggy patch – every 160 square kilometres in hilly areas, and one every 600 square kilometres on the plains.

Not much then, and less now, for over the last few decades the park, like the Gobi as a whole, has become more and more arid. As the result of a succession of droughts in the 1980s, the ground water is drying up. In 1993, a joint Russian–Mongolian expedition could identify only eleven oases. A few years ago, if stranded in Gobi A, you could have cheered yourself with the knowledge that there was a spring somewhere within twenty-five kilometres, assuming you chose the right direction. Now you would have to go an average of 100 kilometres.

Yet even this declining amount is enough for a range of plants. Around water sources – springs, pools, temporary streams – grasses form clumps and turf, while shrubs serve to bind the soil and create micro-climates for insects. These sparse communities consist of two dozen species of grass, which if you say them fast make the park sound like a water meadow: couch grass, wheat grass, sheep's fescue, spreading meadow grass, meadow oat grass, three types of lyme grass, rushes, sedges, and barley. Shrubs, too, come in a dozen different species, though they all look much alike to the novice. In some protected mountain valleys, there are even groves of scrub and trees, mainly poplars and tamarisks. All in all, according to two analyses published in the 1950s, there are twenty-one different types of ecosystem in Gobi A alone.

Plants and water together sustain animal life, sparsely scattered but of surprising variety. Exactly what animals, and their numbers, emerged only in 1980–2, when scientists driving and flying across 7,700 square kilometres of desert listed ninety-two bird species (though almost all are migratory), fourteen reptiles, mostly lizards, and forty-seven species of mammal. Most of the mammals are small rodents: voles, hamsters, mice, gerbils, jerboas – twelve species of those – and shrews. They are shy creatures, seldom seen.

Once, though, returning late from a trip one night, the car's head-lights brushed something dark pattering off behind a bush. Byamba stopped, reversed, realigned the car. Caught in the lights was a hedge-hog. It looked exactly like the ordinary garden variety back home, except that it had long upstanding ears. These evolved to help locate prey on nocturnal prowls, and possibly to radiate heat, but they also give the hedgehog's face an enchanting expression, of which I caught a glimpse just before it rolled itself into a pincushion. I had to have a picture of that face, no question. That meant taking it home. I pulled my sleeves down over my fingers as makeshift gloves, picked the spiky ball up gingerly, and put it in a hold-all. It weighed hardly anything, and remained utterly still. Back at McCarthy's place, I slipped it some dried curd and placed the hold-all gently by the open door. At dawn, I took my camera bag, and lifted the hold-all as if my featherweight captive was made in Meissen. There was no movement inside. I guessed he was either asleep, or terrified into catatonic immobility. I walked slowly to the gateway of the palisade surrounding the courtyard, placed the bag with infinite care on the gravel, and slotted a 70–210mm zoom lens into the camera. The light was perfect, with the rising sun throwing long shadows from two gers and scattered poplar trees. I foresaw a great shot, a full-frame portrait at about three feet, side-lit, against a backdrop of fuzzy gold. Moving very slowly, I unzipped the bag, tilted it over, lay down, camera focused, and waited. I nudged the bag with the zoom lens. Nothing happened. I looked inside, and stared, astonished. There was nothing there, except a few crumbs and some droppings. He had burrowed out through the hole left at the end of the unlocked zip. I glanced around, feeling horribly foolish. The only sign of life was one of the dogs, which began a deep-throated racket. I beat a hasty retreat, before anyone started to ask what I found so fascinating about an empty hold-all.

It is the larger mammals that attract most attention, and rightly so, for in these marginal conditions they are highly specialized, extremely rare and getting rarer.

One of the rarest is the wild Bactrian camel. They were first recorded in western China in the 1870s by the Russian explorer, Nikolai Przhevalski who, when presented by hunters with three skins and a skull, was certain they represented a subspecies ancestral to the modern domestic Bactrians. Back in St Petersburg, zoologists were not so sure. Perhaps the camels were the descendants of domestic animals that escaped into the wild centuries ago. Even now, no one is quite certain, as the plethora of Latin names reveal: *Camelus ferus Przewalskii*, *Camelus bactrianus*, *Camelus bactrianus ferus*, plain old *Camelus ferus*. Mongolians themselves see domestic and wild camels as distinct enough to call the two by different names.

To find out the numbers of these wary and far-ranging creatures has proved a tricky business. Research in what is now Gobi A started in 1927, and results of this and later surveys formed part of the justification for the park's establishment in the 1970s. The present consensus is that the wild camel once occupied a far larger area, but was reduced in the nineteenth century to small pockets, some in China, with one spanning the Chinese–Mongolian border. Even at the turn of the century, though, 'herds of scores or even hundreds of camels were common', according to the Russian explorer-biologist, and Przhevalski's protégé, Pyotr Kozlov. Later, all connection between these groups was severed by a new road running south of the Chinese border. Thereafter, the survivors in China wandered three interconnecting wastes – the Desert of Lop, the Takla Makan (itself seven times the size of Britain) and the Gashun Gobi – but the numbers were unknown. Surveys in Mongolia gave estimates of 300–900; more detailed work in 1980–2 narrowed the range to 500–800. The most recent estimate suggests about 400.

One man who focused on these graceful and wary creatures was the American zoologist and conservationist George Schaller. Schaller, Director for Science of the Wildlife Conservation Society, the research branch of the New York Zoological Society, is a legend for his work with threatened animals and for the dedication with which he pursues his chosen tasks. Over thirty years, he broke new ground with gorillas in Zaire, with predator and prey species in the Serengeti, with pandas in China, and with snow leopards and mountain sheep in the Himalayas. Driven by a need to know, and a terrible vision of what will be lost if rare creatures and delicate ecologies vanish, he goes his chosen way with a fierce austerity, inspiring others. One protégée was Diane Fosse, who dedicated herself to Zairean gorillas, and became the subject of the film *Gorillas in the Mist*. In the 1980s, Schaller turned to the Gobi, in particular the unique ecology of the Gobi A reserve.

By then, having spent so many years leading the fieldwork himself, he and the WCS devised a new strategy worldwide: to act as a rapid-response unit – to identify threatened species and threatened ecologies, get in ahead of civilization, make sure that the enclaves were secured, and then train local biologists to take over the projects.

Sound in theory, the practice proved problematical in Mongolia. Mongolians are as responsible as anyone else when they manage their herds, but for fifty years Communism eroded the will to undertake wider responsibilities. Always, there was someone else, above, to take decisions. In the old days, pre-1990, you didn't need to look after a machine if it wasn't yours. So what if it broke? So what if you couldn't do your job? Someone would order a replacement, and you got paid anyway. Meanwhile, why take initiative, why place yourself in the firing line? Not that personal responsibility – whether pure idealism or enlightened self-interest – was entirely absent; but its rarity undermined Schaller's efforts to set up long-term local research. Of course, there was a contract, in which some ministry agreed what was to be done. But the contract hid another agenda. Look (the frustrated fieldworker might have said), it says right here 'three months in the field'. Oh, sure, came the implied reply, of course it says that in the *contract*, but all our contracts always say things like that. You and I know that was for official consumption. You don't think that anyone is actually going to spend *three months* in the desert?

As a result of such attitudes, there were only a very few Mongolian field biologists who had the dedication to produce data that would live up to the standards of western journals, and none in Gobi A in the early 1990s prepared to match Schaller's stern demands. The need was there, the funding was in place, staff were available; but when Schaller left, so did they. Without his guiding genius and the example of his self-denying leadership, the wild camel project ended.

But one man at least had been infected by Schaller's passion. His name was Tsend, and he had been a Protection Officer for twenty-one years. Dressed in an ancient jacket, open-necked shirt and floppy hat, he came to us and asked for a lift out into the park to look for a wild camel.

As Byamba drove us away from Bayan Tooroi towards a ridge defining the northern edge of the park, Tsend became eloquent on the subject of wild camels. I doubted my ability to recognize a wild one from its domesticated kin. He assured me I would know one if I saw one. They were graceful creatures, with longer legs and a much easier gait than domestic camels. They hold their heads high to get a better view of their surroundings, because they are very nervous, of wolves, and of the other great predator, man. Gobi herdsmen don't like wild camels, especially the males. They swashbuckle in from the desert, infiltrate domestic herds, seduce the females, and sire crosses that are useless to the herders, who usually kill them.

Why, then, would a wild camel remain around this populated area? The previous year, Tsend said, park rangers had caught ten young ones, and raised them here. It was easy to catch them. 'If you see a baby camel, less than one month old, you drive at the mother, the mother runs away, and you stop, and the baby simply comes to you. Then you feed it with camel's milk until it's old enough to be released.'

Byamba had driven up a long gradient, an outwash of grey gravel leading from a rocky spine, the Edren Ridge, climbing until we overheated. After parking the hissing minibus with its face to the light breeze, Tsend led us on up the ridge, where he could get an overview of the surrounding landscape. We climbed over scree and sat, panting, looking down from brittle rock splintered into diamond shards by sun and frost. To one side lay ravines, ridges and peaks all black and burnished as if painted with tar. To the other, an immensity of gravelly yellow dunes, measle-spotted with scattered saxauls, rolled northwards to the snow-capped Altai, and westwards to the pale grey shanks of Sacred Mother mountain.

So what were my chances of seeing a wild camel? Were there any left in this part of the park?

Tsend looked around. Across the alluvial fans and saxaul-speckled plains, nothing moved, not a bird, not a goat, certainly not a wild camel.

'There used to be a lot of them here,' he said. 'Back in the 1960s, before drought drove them south.'

Thus the southern section of Gobi A has become the last redoubt of these shy and graceful creatures, in particular a mountain range known as Atas Bogd and Chingis Uul. One spot, Baruun and Dzuun Sharga – 'West and East Dun-Coloured' – has a small spring with rush-sedge marsh, patches of downy poplar and stands of saxaul and tamarisk. It is sheltered, and mild by comparison with what lies north and south, ideal as a winter resort.

Apart from the remoteness of the study area, wild camels are hard to study because they cover immense areas in search of food and drink. Unlike gazelles, they are not truly nomadic. They favour a base to which they return, but they need to exploit different plants at different times, and do so with maximum efficiency. So they form small groups, averaging seven or eight individuals, and travel fast, and far, distributing themselves using tracks that form interlinking networks of camel roads. One herd of eighteen, tracked in 1981, covered forty kilometres in four hours. In a year, they range many hundreds of kilometres. But still no one really knows what they eat, when, how far they travel. They await their definitive biographer.

But he or she will have to work fast. In China, even those wild camels that have retreated to the remotest regions are under threat from roads, hunters and mining operations. In Gobi A they are protected from human intervention, but every year drought saps their homeland a little more. One of these years not enough of them will remain to sustain a breeding population and they will vanish.

On 4 August 1943 two Russian scientists, Murzayev and Yunatov, were on camels in Gobi A's southeastern corner when they saw a dark brown figure 'running unhurriedly with its nose down, evidently searching for food'. Yunatov jumped off his camel, which groaned. The animal, which looked like a sort of European brown bear, turned, then ran off with 'amazing agility and speed'. This was the first scientific sighting of the Gobi's most extraordinary animal, the Gobi bear, a creature so rare, living in a habitat so little visited, that until the 1943 sighting the madzaali, as the locals called it, might just as well have been a myth.

The bear presented the scientific world with a mystery. Bears do not belong in deserts. They are creatures of mountains and forests. Since no bear would migrate across desert to settle in such a habitat, what on earth is it doing there? The only possible answer is that it is a subspecies of Himalayan bear left over from a time when the Gobi was a more fertile place. Officially, the Gobi bear has been considered a subspecies of the Eurasian brown bear, *Ursus arctos pruinosus*. But some dispute this. In Ulan Bator, Dulamtseren insisted to me that it was a separate species, *Ursus gobiensis*.

As aridity increased, the bear was forced to retreat until it became isolated. 'My parents told me that the bears used to be seen outside the park, in the surrounding desert,' Tsend said. Then, as drought spread, the bears were cut off in their mountain fastness, hermits surviving on the few springs and stands of plants that enlivened the encroaching desert. Research in 1980–2 estimated there could be no more than thirty of them left, but no one knew how they lived, whether they had a real chance of survival, or how best to protect them.

Again it was Schaller who sought to set research on a sound footing; and again the project faltered when no Mongolian arose to take on the burden Schaller offered.

You would think that with so few of them then, they would be gone by now. Perhaps they would be, were it not that after the park was set up, rangers began a feeding programme.

'They hibernate from October to March,' Tsend explained just before we headed back down to the car. 'The worst time is just before they go to sleep and when they wake up. If the vegetation is poor in October or in the spring, they cannot live. That's when we make sure they have fodder.'

This intrusion works both ways. It draws the bears towards a few oases, makes them easier to observe, ensures their survival. But times are harsh now for humans, and the park administration has cut back its work, with results that cannot be predicted. Possibly, they will find their own way to survive – in 1995 a Gobi bear was seen in the Gurvan Saikhan (Three Beauties), which means that at least one must have made a 240-kilometre journey across open desert. Perhaps this will open a migration route that will offer a greater chance of survival; or perhaps it was a last-ditch effort by a lone individual doomed to die.

In the Gobi bear project, Schaller's successor is Tom McCarthy, who hopes to solve these and other mysteries, as a sideline from snow leopard research, drawing on a battery of new techniques. Minute samples of hair and faeces will allow DNA research which will establish how many bears there are, and how they are related to each other and to their brown-bear ancestors.

With luck, and the right backing, the bear, like the wild camel, will survive. But it will be a close-run thing.

We were on our way back when Tsend pointed. Byamba stopped.

Wondering what had caught Tsend's eye, I followed him back along the track, then off to one side. He pointed again.

'*Khar sült*,' he said.

A snake? A wolf? I had no idea what to look for. Then, in the shade of a saxaul tree, I saw what he had seen – a young, black-tailed gazelle. At any second, I knew, it would see us and bound away. Astonished at our luck, and at the little creature's passivity, we approached. Tsend waved me forward, and I went ahead, trying for silence and invisibility, feeling foolish, for as I took another pace, it became clear that the animal could see me as clearly as I saw it. We stared at each other. I took another step. It remained silent and still, spindly legs folded under its fawn body, head high, ears pricked, staring at me with soft brown eyes into which I could read no expression. It seemed to feel no fear, nor did it seem ill. Why did it not move?

Erdene spoke from behind me. 'Tsend says it is too young to walk.'

'How old does he think it is?'

'One day old. It was born just here, probably.' We glanced around: no sign of mum. 'We are lucky. Tsend says that never in his life has he seen one this young.'

Later, I found out just how lucky I was. Roy Chapman Andrews, in his three great expeditions into the Gobi, never had such an experience. 'The fawns were very clever at hiding. They would lie flat upon the ground beside a sage bush only a few inches high, with their ears dropped and neck stretched out. Many times have I tried to creep up and throw a coat over one, but just before I was within reach it would dash away.'

He actually measured the performance of a ten-day-old fawn by chasing one in a car. 'For the first four miles it averaged 25 miles an hour, but soon tired after that and resorted to dodging to elude us; it ran a total of nine miles before we caught it. After the first three weeks a wolf could not equal the speed of a baby antelope. We did not find any wolves that could exceed 36 miles an hour even on the first dash, and the fawns could reach 40 miles an hour without half trying.'

So this brief time – a few hours at most – would be the most vulnerable period of its life. Unable to move, with its mother making forays for food, it was an easy prey for a desert fox, perhaps, or a wolf.

'Or birds,' Tsend added. 'If an eagle attacks, it will have no defence.'

That was why it had been parked here, protected by its camouflage, by the shade, and by its only form of self-defence: silence. In three days, it would walk easily, and after a week it would be running alongside its mother. Meanwhile, one species it had not yet learned to fear was man. We gathered round.

It was Tsend who touched it first, stroking it. Still no reaction. He picked it up, and it lay in his arms as placid as a pet. He handed it to me. There was no tremble in its lanky limbs, and even its quick snuffles sounded only mildly apprehensive, not panicky.

35

'I wonder, can he stand at all?' I don't know why I assumed it was a male. Perhaps because it summoned up childhood memories of Bambi.

Tsend took him from me, and placed him on his legs. He did not collapse, though it was a close call. He stood, knees bent, and quivered. I don't think it was fear that made him tremble, but the novelty of the experience. It was as if we had switched him on. In his brain, a billion synapses had been zapped into life and the heady flow of sensation made him hum like an electric toy.

I became concerned he would overload and collapse with convulsions. 'He better go back in the shade,' I said.

But he was learning fast. As Tsend reached to pick him up, another part of his brain came on line, releasing a flood of inherited information. Suddenly, he knew what fear was, and yelled. It was a surprising noise. You would have expected a high and babyish cry, but what came out was a bass bleat, as if from a decrepit sheep.

We all laughed with delight, like proud fathers chasing away a child's fears, while Tsend placed him gently back beneath his saxaul. We stood back a moment, waiting for him to settle.

'Maybe the mother will not like our smell,' Erdene wondered glumly. 'Maybe she will reject him.'

Tsend disagreed, because he had handled baby gazelles before. Besides, what happened next showed us we had released more than one new response.

The fawn got up, stood without a tremble, then placed a front foot forward, took one pace, then another. He walked – hesitantly, carefully, no hint of panic – round his saxaul then, more firmly now, left us, walking off across the sandy surface. He could hardly know his surroundings by direct experience, but he had a rich inheritance on which to draw. He headed straight towards another saxaul, perhaps thirty metres away, and then, as he discovered just how much control he had, he broke into a run, a foreshadowing of the taut spring that would, within days, allow him to outdistance fox or wolf. He found new shade, and lay down, a mere blur against the yellow and grey, as nearly invisible as when Tsend first spotted him.

3

The Domain of the Snow Leopard

The very words 'snow leopard' carry contradictory senses: mystic beauty, hidden danger, twenty daggers clad in velvet. These creatures are so rare and so exquisite, so wily and so destructive, that they long ago acquired near mythic status amongst the people of their mountainous lands. The poor who lived in the great crescent of mountains from the Himalayas, round through the Hindu Kush, Karakorums, Tien Shan and Mongolian Altai, feared and respected the massive paws, the silence, the wariness, the cloak of invisibility. Few saw the snow leopard; but everyone knew the signs of its presence – the scratch marks that defined its territory, the quarter-eaten sheep's carcass – and they killed it when they could, with snares and poison and sharpened stakes and, if one were cornered in a livestock pen, with stones and spears and guns. The rich paid well for the soft, light grey fur, gently marked with black rosettes, and in China they paid for the bones, ground up into medicine that promised to imbue an essence of power and skill and beauty. If the snow leopard had been reported in Europe in the Middle Ages, it would perhaps have become a symbol of an object to be yearned for, painted into medieval miniatures like the unicorn, or sought as a grail in epics of chivalry.

In the West, the creature's aura, more New Age than medieval, was created by the way snow leopards came to public consciousness. Because of the animal's rarity and the wariness, scientists knew virtually nothing of them. Prewar scientific references number half a dozen. The immediate postwar years produced little more than a few anatomical analyses. As for understanding the creatures – little of merit appeared until George Schaller researched them in the Himalayas in the early 1970s.

When Schaller started his research he had precious little to go on. Closely related to the lion, tiger, leopard and jaguar, the snow leopard's scientific name, *uncia*, derives from the Latin *Lynx*, which was the root for two terms. One retained the word unchanged. The other was distorted into dog-Latin as *luncia*, which Old French wrongly divided as 'l'once' (by an equivalent process that derived 'an orange' from the Arabic *naranj*. In effect, 'a norange' became 'an orange'). From 'l'once' came the English 'ounce', which by false etymology was confused with the weight and reLatinized as *uncia*. Now the term is outdated, for the snow leopard is part of a family, the Pantherinae, though the exact status of the snow leopard is still a matter of dispute. It is, at least, a separate species (*Panthera uncia*), but there is increasing support for the idea that it may be far enough removed from its relatives to constitute its own genus, *Uncia Uncia*.

These creatures are small as leopards go, measuring up to 120 centimetres at the shoulder and weighing around fifty kilogrammes for a large adult male. They are extraordinarily scattered animals, rarefied in their range as the air they breathe. In a crescent of Central Asian mountains, straddling a dozen countries, there are perhaps 4,000 of them, perhaps 7,000, for no one knows yet. That makes one snow leopard in an area the size of a county. They like high terrain, anything from 600 metres in southern Siberia to 5,800 metres in the Himalayas, without trees, rugged, with plenty of rocks and bushes for cover. They mostly prey on wild sheep and goats, though they will on occasion attack practically anything except humans. It is astonishing enough that these diffused creatures ever find each other to breed, more so considering their reclusive nature. Most of the time, they avoid each other.

At the same time as Schaller produced his reports, the snow leopard was brought to a wider public by the author, Peter Matthiessen, who in late 1973 accompanied Schaller on a ten-week trek into northern Nepal, to research blue sheep and their little-known predator. The journey became what he called 'a true pilgrimage, a journey of the heart', and his 1979 book, *The Snowleopard*, grew into a modern classic of wildlife description, of exploration, of self-exploration.

Matthiessen's book gave the snow leopard an aura of mysticism. At a moment when he was facing the possibility that he might never actually see one of these elusive cats, Matthiessen met an ancient lama who showed him the way forward, beyond disappointment. The lama, who had been living in isolation as a hermit for eight years, was crippled by arthritis. Matthiessen asked if he was happy.

'Indicating his twisted legs without a trace of self-pity or bitterness, as if they belonged to all of us, he casts his arms wide to the sky and the snow mountains, the high sun and the dancing sheep, and cries, "Of course I am happy here! It's wonderful! *Especially* when I have no choice!" '

For Matthiessen, a proponent of Zen Buddhism, the not-seeing became a part of a greater experience, immersion in the wilderness, and a part of his own spiritual journey.

'Have you seen the snow leopard?' Matthiessen asked of himself. 'No! Isn't that wonderful?'

Wonderful if you are a Zen Buddhist, but not if you are a practical zoologist, like Schaller, committed to researching and protecting snow leopards. Snow leopards have always been killed, both for their pelts and to protect domestic stock. Records suggest that throughout the century several dozen skins, as well as live specimens, were exported annually from each country in which the animal lives. Mongolia alone produced between twenty and eighty skins each year this century. The trade was declared illegal by international agreement in 1973, but for some years Mongolia stayed outside the agreement, because it said the snow leopard could be hunted without its becoming an endangered species. Now, in response to international pressure, Mongolia too has signed, and all snow leopard hunting is illegal.

But money talks. In 1993 one traveller flew in with three Spaniards who had a licence to hunt snow leopards, bought for a reported price of $25,000. Poachers hawk pelts around Ulan Bator, and the price is rising. Three years ago you could buy a pelt for up to $100. In Ulan Bator in 1996, a missionary told me he was offered skins for $500 in two separate incidents, by men who were hawking them by knocking on foreigners' doors. A smuggled snow leopard skin can fetch up to $9,000 in the US, and a whole coat can retail for $50,000.

To be protected, they need to be understood, and research elsewhere is no substitute. Mongolian snow leopards have a particular significance. They are on the fringe of their territory, and have to exploit a wider range of environments, from the mountainous borderlands of Mongolia and Russia, down through the Altai, and from the Gobi Altai across the desert to the Gurvan Saikhan.

Their precarious position gives them a special status. In both mountain and desert, they act as a 'diagnostic species', their numbers and behaviour reflecting the health of the environment as a whole, at a time when drought and population growth are combining to accelerate the pace of change. Since 'transition' undermined the urban economy, more and more people have returned to the countryside, where, with the parallel collapse of collective farms, herds have grown and been moved into marginal lands. In the mountains of the snow leopards, more domestic animals have moved into valleys that were once the exclusive preserve of the ibex. For snow leopards, this is easy meat, the only deterrent being the presence of humans.

When I was there, this trend was only just becoming apparent, the stuff of anecdote rather than statistics. It is McCarthy's aim to reverse that, researching how many leopards there are, how widely they range, where their strongholds are, where they breed, and what they eat. On his answers depends an understanding of the Gobi's future, and the policies that could help find a lasting balance between people, snow leopards and a delicate wilderness.

Of large, fierce dogs and larger, fiercer cats

I had been in snow leopard country already, up in the Altai. As we ground over the alpine uplands, I had asked Eeke, the woman upon whose occasional direction Byamba was depending, if she had ever seen a snow leopard. No, she hadn't, but her father had.

'I have a friend,' I continued, haltingly. 'An American, Tom McCarthy. Do you know him?' It wasn't unlikely, because McCarthy was famous locally as the protector of a predatory species that local herdsmen would happily see exterminated.

'Oh, yes. My father knows him. He helped Tom catch a snow leopard.' This apparently startling coincidence turned out to be rubbish. Somehow, she had conflated two bits of information – her father knew McCarthy; and her father had caught a snow leopard. But I didn't know that until later, and at the time I took her words as a sign of imminent good luck.

Descending with Eeke and her silent child from the pass over the Altai, we emerged onto a plain divided by a scrawl of melt-water. Below hills with dark rock cutting through their summits lay Tsogt, her father's hometown. We passed a fuel tank and its pump house, guided by Eeke's pointing finger, and pulled up beside a wooden stockade, above which the mushroom roof of a ger showed.

This, my first approach to a family living in a ger, confounded my expectations. Any traveller in the Mongolian countryside will tell you that you approach a ger borne up by the near-certainty of a sunny welcome, once the dogs are under control. But in towns all you see of gers are the tops of the domes poking over stockades. To outsiders, these stockades seem the equivalent of crossed arms and a blank stare. The high fences define the space allotted to families when they set up within the confines of a town, but they also keep stock in, dogs in, possessions in, and those with light fingers out. In towns, nomads are as much townies as any western suburbanite. You have to get beyond the Fort Apache defences to feel the warmth within.

There was a dog, a massive black hairy thing with a white spot on its heart. Eeke held it while we filed through the doorway of the stockade. Until this moment, I had assumed that dogs were pets. But there were too many of them, and they were too big, and too vicious.

'Erdene, why does everyone have to have a dog?'

'Protection.'

Still governed by western, urban attitudes, I assumed for a moment he meant protection from thieves and drunks. But Mongolians have always kept big, fierce dogs. The *Secret History of the Mongols*, the semi-historical, semi-mythical biography of Chingis Khan, records that as a boy Chingis was frightened of dogs, and that was in the late twelfth century. Protection from what?

'They are used to guard flocks at night,' Erdene explained. 'They must be as big as a wolf.'

'So they are all dangerous?' We were filing past an ancient truck, a motorbike in bits, a stack of bricks, blankets, piles of dried dung, a half-butchered goat carcass, and several curious children.

'Not all dogs are dangerous to people. You can never tell.'

'Are there many attacks?'

'Not often, because we take care. Everywhere we go we shout "Dog!"'

'And if there is an attack?'

'Oh, many injections, and usually the dog is destroyed.'

Arriving at the painted, wooden door of the ger, I felt the sense of warmth and hospitality I had read about. With their canvas cladding, felt linings, and lattice walls, gers are big enough for furniture, a stove, and several beds. Cool in summer, warm in winter, stable in a gale, a ger is a snug little world with many roles: a home, a haven, a shrine. Some possessions were reassuringly familiar – the TV, the mains electric lights, the stereo, the video. Other things made me hesitate: the cupboards and beds carefully positioned round the wall, the shrine-like display of photographs and china teapots, the half-dozen adults and teenagers on the bed and the floor – there was a formalism that put me on my best behaviour. What that behaviour should be, though, I had no idea.

Erdene prompted, inducting me into practices that ran from mere politeness to outright taboos. No need to knock, he said, or make any excuses. Just enter. It seems rather rude, until you get used to it. 'Be careful not to step on the threshold. Go cleanly over,' he instructed, relaying the remnant of an ancient prohibition. In one area of Inner Mongolia, they say that stepping on the threshold is like stepping on your host's neck, and once all across Mongolia it was a capital crime for a common person to touch the threshold of a noble. The reasons for the ban are obscure, and old ways have dissipated, but there's no arguing with their residual power.

Now go to the left, Erdene went on, around the stove. Men go to the left, women to the right. If there is no stove, you should never cross the space under the roof hole, which does more than provide ventilation and light. It and the space below, including the hearth area, has particular significance, a dim folk memory perhaps of a pre-Buddhist reverence for fire. What once was a sacred ritual is now often mere etiquette – people break the rules when necessary – but the old practices carry weight still.

I was seated on a low stool –

– 'And if you sit on the floor,' Erdene whispered, 'do not put your legs straight out in front of you' –

– almost opposite the door, just beside where the shrine would have been if there had been a shrine, and a silence fell. No one seems to mind long silences, to feel a need to fill them with inconsequential chatter.

The dog looked in the open door. Erdene noticed my nervous glance. 'Don't worry, it will not come in. In Mongolia, you will never see a dog inside, even in winter.'

'That seems harsh.'

'A dog is a dog. Once it's a dog, it should stay outside.' He grimaced at my softness. 'Once I was in Scotland, for a conference on animal husbandry. The professor was absent, because his dog was sick. Come on, really! I say, "Let the dog die, and let the professor come to work." '

'Do you mean no one cares about dogs?'

'They care, because good hunting dogs and camp-keeping dogs are important. We say, "A good dog is better than a bad person." But when they die, you get another.'

As he was speaking, a man in a well-worn deel stepped forward, went down on one knee, and offered me a little jade bottle. It was snuff, the offering and taking of which was a normal part of ger life. But I had no idea what to do.

'Now I will be your teacher,' Erdene said, 'and when I come to England you will be mine. You see how he offers? With his right hand, and the left touches the right elbow.' The palm-up gesture, a hint of support for the right arm, was so reduced I had not even noticed it.

Now, under approving gazes, I copied Erdene's actions as he performed this male ritual (women do not own snuff bottles, some of which are wonderfully decorated, and do not share in the exchange). The taking of snuff is a quick ballet of hands and fingers. You remove the cork, to which a tiny spoon is fixed, and use a thumb and forefinger to gather a pinch, sniff it up, then return the bottle, matching your host's hand-to-elbow gesture. Then it was my turn.

'Erdene, I have never taken snuff.'

'Not to worry. Pretend to take.'

That was all that was required. It's the ritual, not the snuff itself, that is the small change of social currency.

'Oh, John, this is the man who caught a snow leopard.'

Caught up in returning the snuff, I had not noticed the arrival of an elderly man, who wore a Homburg hat and a blue deel. He was sitting on a bed near me, staring at me. His name was Jantsan, and he was sixty-six. He was silent for a while, sipping salty tea, taking a few crumbs of curd, then, when I asked about his catch, he spoke softly.

'One day, gathering my animals over by the Geget river, about eighty kilometres from here, I came upon a partially eaten goat. I knew it was the work of a snow leopard, because this was a rocky area, and the jugular vein was cut. I knew that the snow leopard would be back. That's what they do, they eat a little, then return a day or two later. So I got a trap, a metal one, like the one over there that we use for wolves, and put it beside the dead goat, hiding it in the ground. The next morning we came, and saw it was captured by one foot. We caught it with two lassos' – herdsmen use lassos attached to long poles – 'held it at a safe distance and wound a rope round its legs. We thought we might be able to sell it. Then we lifted it into the back of the truck, and were on our way to Altai with it, when it escaped.'

The loss of a goat didn't seem too high a price to pay for the presence of such a beautiful creature. But he wasn't talking in terms of single kills.

'Twenty days ago, I lost six sheep in one night. The leopard killed them, and just ate a little of each. Six sheep! Even one goat is a lot.'

I was embarrassed by my ecocentricity. This was no pussy cat. 'Would you kill a snow leopard if you had the chance?'

'Oh, they're hard to find.' Like all herdsmen in snow leopard country, he knew the law, and answered carefully. 'Even the dogs don't notice when there's a snow leopard around. I've seen many, especially early in the morning, but they're so fast they're impossible to follow. Nothing can catch them.' He paused, and sipped his tea. 'This year, I've lost five cattle, and about thirty smaller animals! And two horses.'

If Erdene understood him right, these were dire figures. A snow leopard won't attack a horse in open country, but might if it finds one near rocks. It seldom manages to kill the horse, but the claws tear the flesh, often leaving scars that affect the operation of the bridle. The chances are that a horse attacked by a leopard, even if it recovers, will be useless.

He was in no doubt that the snow leopards should be reduced. But he was well aware of the problems. 'If you hunt it, you get punished. People used to use poison, sometimes. But poison is dangerous, you don't know what other animals will eat it. Anyway if the land protection officer hears . . .'

This was the conundrum faced by Schaller and McCarthy – the rights of a rare species versus the rights of the individual, with no solution in sight.

The lair of the mountain king

McCarthy's base was a two-hour journey from Bayan Tooroi. We set off there in a party, under the auspices of Khorloo, who appeared wearing a silk scarf, a trim mac and smart leather boots. With lipstick and a clasp holding back her black hair, she looked more set for an embassy dinner than hours of bouncing across sand and gravel. We were joined by her sister-in-law with her eight-year-old daughter, a thirteen-year-old boy in a gawdy T-shirt, and a ranger, Choinjin. Choinjin, who wore a green deel that came down over his leather boots and a crumpled cabbage-leaf hat sporting his badge of office as a protection officer, was the head ranger for Gobi A, and the oldest ranger. Austere, expert, and committed, he was one of the few who matched Schaller's exacting standards. With Erdene, myself, and Byamba driving, we were eight all together, off for a day's jaunt.

We drove across the soft plain, cutting north of Sacred Mother, heading for a valley that plunged into the Altai. The valley was blocked by a curtain of rock, which looked like a peculiar geographical formation, but turned out to be a dam, for what purpose I could not see, for there was no greenery in sight. Just beyond was a family living in what looked like an old and much modified railway carriage, carted there as accommodation for those building the dam and now taken over by locals as an occasional residence. Over ridges and foothills we drove, into a gorge floored with scree the size and colour of bark chips. We ground past a ger and a herd of goats, proof that even this unpromising place, where tough little bushes and blades of grass clung to thumbnails of earth, counted as pasture.

Pausing to lock the van into four-wheel drive, Byamba took us upwards, through a stream, then over and around boulders the size of tank traps. The cliffs closed in around us, making a tunnel leading from the higher peaks to the plain. The wind screamed down it, whipping dust from between the boulders and making the scattered camel thorns tremble. Ahead, above rocks, standing out against a dark cliff, was a flash of white, McCarthy's ger. Rock-bound, we shuddered to a halt, reversed, bucking and rolling, and sought another way, until Byamba turned the hissing minibus and let it draw breath in the gusting wind. We walked on to the ger.

This austere setting was literally one of rocks and hard places, but it was also one of beauty. A steep-sided bowl had been carved out over millennia by occasional flood waters, which had left a floor of gravel, scree and boulders and tough little bushes. A stream, which surged past a few yards from the tent, emerged around a cleft. The ger itself, backed by dry-stone walls used for storage, was locked, and battened under roof ropes weighted with rocks, holding down canvas that was heaving about in the gale as if about to give birth.

This was where Tom McCarthy spent anything up to six months at a time, trying to refine what was known about snow leopards. Six months is a long time to be out in the wilderness, with only one or two companions, whose language you do not speak. The life demands unusual qualities, tolerance of hardship, infinite patience, an ability to endure isolation. Tom McCarthy is an unusual man. He has a lean and hungry face, sculpted by months of rice, noodles, lots of meat and no vegetables or fruit. In a different age, he might have been a hermit.

'Don't you ever get depressed, Tom?' I asked him once.

'No. You really have to enjoy what you're doing. And I guess I just do. I really don't think about it much.'

There had been time enough to test his resilience. As with Schaller, the way of life and the man reflect each other. He did wildlife studies at the University of Idaho in the 1970s, moving to Alaska in the early 1980s to work on brown bears on the damp, forested islands off Alaska's southeast coast. Then, for several more years, he, his former wife and two sons lived in the wild, with brown bears, black bears, mountain goats, Sitka black-tailed deer. That led into a growing awareness, which now infuses the whole conservation movement, that it is not enough simply to focus on the species. Understanding, and thus conservation, involves whole ecosystems, in this case the Alaskan forests, then being depleted by loggers. The campaign that has built up over the years, in which McCarthy took part, was not wholly popular, because logging underpinned the local economy. But, ran the environmental argument, better that people lose their jobs now and the ecosystem be preserved, with its possibilities for other types of employment, than lose those jobs in ten years' time when all the trees are gone, leaving a wilderness without animals, without jobs, without people.

Alaska, though, did not offer enough. Where was the work, the excitement, the hardship leading? Twenty years more of the same until retirement? He needed a new challenge. It happened that a friend, the Alaska-based film maker and conservationist Joel Bennet, was due to film Schaller in Mongolia. McCarthy sent a letter along with Joel Bennet, asking about the possibility of work in Asia.

Schaller, with the experience of the Gobi bear and wild camel projects behind him, was already finding that his snow leopard project was in trouble. He liked the sound of McCarthy, who flew east in early 1992, with Bennet.

McCarthy's first experience of Schaller was unnerving. He was reading Matthiessen's book when he first flew into Beijing, where he was meeting Schaller for the first time. He had got to the part where someone wrote to Matthiessen about Schaller: 'I shall warn you, the last friend I had who went walking with George in Asia came back – or more properly *turned* back – when his boots were full of blood.' Schaller remembered, and had no sympathy. 'That chap was out of shape,' was all he said.

That set the tone for McCarthy's first experience of Schaller. 'Working with him in the field is amazing. You get up in the morning, then you go to the food ger – we had three gers set up the first year – and you sit down, and have your tea and breakfast, and then he'd stand up and walk out, and the first few times I'd think, "Well, he's going to go to the other ger, and get his equipment, and we'll chat a little, then we'll leave." No. He just got up, and left, and you'd see George's footprints, off up the mountain in the snow. That was it. If you didn't keep up, you didn't keep up, that's all there was to it. You just had to learn to stick with George.

'George doesn't look for anything in the way of amenities. With the three gers, there was one that was George's and mine, and one that belonged to Joel Bennet and his assistant. Joel had a nice fire going all the time, and everything was soft, with lots of padding on the floor, and a good deal of alcohol and snacks. You'd come into ours, and there was just a dirt floor, and no fire. George would say, "Why light a fire? We're going to bed in three hours." It was like – 20°C outside. He'd sit there and write until his hands froze, then he'd go to bed.

'When we headed out in the morning, rather than pack a lunch, he'd take a couple of bags of dry Chinese noodles. He'd say, "Why bother to cook them? They'll get soft in your stomach anyway." '

Schaller may not have much time for mystical talk, but there is an implied vision in his work. 'I think that for all his ideals he sees himself much like the early explorers in Asia. He likes the feeling of being the first one into an area, and to see things in their pure form, before they're touched. That's kind of his quest, his goal in the mountains. And to be there alone. If he didn't need a guide or a driver, I don't think he'd ever be with anybody. Heading out into the mountains from the ger – that's the way he would operate all the time.'

There is an old-fashioned scientific puritanism – again a religious metaphor comes easily – to Schaller's determination to get results fast. He seeks a holistic view, not one defined by technology. 'Although we were trying to radio collar a leopard, what George said to me is, "Your first year, don't go out and follow your snow leopards around with a radio collar. Go out and spend that year in snow leopard country, and see how much you can figure out." His aim was to get in, and try to understand enough to see where the problems are.'

The problems lie with that conundrum I had touched on with Jantsan – how to protect a creature that causes such destruction. It can be uphill work, as Priscilla Allen, McCarthy's wife and colleague, discovered. Allen, who had done Chinese at Leeds with an option in Mongolian, taught in Mongolia, and speaks the language well. On one occasion, she went to a remote ger on a motorbike to interview a herdsman, one of whose cows had been attacked, possibly by a snow leopard. He wasn't about to give any snow leopard the benefit of the doubt.

'How much is that thing around your neck?' he asked Allen, pointing to her radio telemetry gear.

'Oh, I don't know. Thousands.'

'You waste all that money on snow leopards! Why don't you stick a collar round my neck and measure how hard I have to work, producing food for snow leopards? Then you'd understand why I kill them any chance I have. You people –' he was outraged at the thought – 'you people, you catch snow leopards, *then you let them go!*'

At least that had the smack of truth about it. Often, McCarthy gets mere evasion. Even a good interpreter cannot overcome the unwillingness to talk about misfortune, particularly about death. As the proverb says, 'Mongols order their affairs according to their luck,' and death is the unluckiest subject of all, best avoided, even if you are only talking about animals.

McCarthy once asked a herdsman how many livestock had been lost to snow leopards in the last year or two.

'Oh,' came the reply, 'we *never* lose animals to snow leopards.'

'What about other natural causes?'

'Oh, our animals almost *never* die.'

A talk to the local vet revealed a different story. During the previous year, that same herdsman, like everyone else in his area, lost thirty per cent of his stock to parasitic diseases, and only he knew how many to snow leopards.

Yet sometimes, for no obvious reason, there is a natural readiness to accept the idea of conservation. In one area, known as the Valley of a Thousand Ibex, they tell a story.

'Once there was a man who went into the mountains and hunted for snow leopards. He saw one, tracked it, and wounded it. For three days, the snow leopard sat in a hidden place and howled. After three days it died. When the man reached home, he found that his son, who was studying to be a lama at a monastery, had been stricken ill three days before. For three days he had cried, and on the third day, just before his father returned, he died. That's why nobody in this area will kill a snow leopard.'

How to collar a big cat

One basic aim of the Schaller–McCarthy Snow Leopard Project is to find out how many cats there are. Since estimates for the whole country range from 700 to 1,700, there must be a few hundred in McCarthy's area, the Altai and Gobi Altai. Fortunately, there are more objective ways to research than by asking herdsmen. One way is to get out and look for evidence: scrapes by which the animals mark their territory, faeces, hairs. But the prime source of information comes from the creatures themselves, through radio collars.

To fit a radio collar, first catch your snow leopard. McCarthy uses cable snares, which tighten on the leg without pulling painfully taut. He puts the snare, with its pressure-pad trigger, onto a leopard trail, usually adjacent to one of their scrapes or spray sites. He places some large boulders on the side of the trail, to funnel the leopard towards the snare. He disguises the snare with dust and pebbles, then builds a little wall two or three steps ahead of the snare, forcing the leopard to jump, with luck making it take off right on the pad that activates the snare. And then he waits, a tediously long time. In three years of work, he has captured and tagged just five cats.

The first success, of course, had a special significance. 'We had a dozen snares out for a month before we captured a cat. To see that cat for the first time . . .' He paused, remembering the elation. 'When you first think of snow leopards, you think: "Oh, a white cat with black spots, out here in this grey, dusty desert, can't be difficult to see." But they match their surroundings so closely that even with the cat in the snare, even knowing where the snare was, it was difficult to see until I was just a few yards away.'

McCarthy injected the cat with an anaesthetic on the end of a three-metre telescopic aluminium pole. After ten minutes or so, it was comatose and could be handled safely, its body slack and velvet-soft.

'Just a gorgeous animal. The tail was as long as the rest of the body, and as big around as my forearm. Just incredible.'

Knocking an animal out like that is not a procedure any wildlife expert likes, because it imposes an immediate, short-term stress on the animal emotionally and physically, but it is the only known way to get the information needed to secure their long-term future. With all his snared leopards, McCarthy takes a tiny nick from an ear to act as a source for genetic research – eventually, by comparing DNA samples, it will be possible to define relationships between individuals and whole groups – and attaches a radio collar. After forty-five minutes, the drug wears off, everyone stands back, and the animal walks away, groggily at first, then with increasing assurance, until it blurs back into the mountains.

Initially, he used a line-of-sight VHF transmitter, but that meant either tracking the cats by plane, which he didn't have, or trying to keep tabs on them by car and on foot by following these creatures – wily, almost invisible, with the agility of a cheetah – across 300 square kilometres of mountain, between 600 and 3,350 metres. No one could do more than keep in intermittent contact. In 1996 McCarthy acquired satellite-linked radios that are small enough to place on collars. In March he radio collared his first snow leopard, which can be tracked to within three kilometres with the position relayed to him daily by e-mail, wherever he happens to be.

Only once has McCarthy got close to an unsedated snow leopard. A cat slipped its snare, and he and his Mongolian assistant, Monsukh, tracked it to a cave. McCarthy crawled ten metres to the back of the cave, ending up on his stomach, shortening his jabstick to about a metre just to be able to handle it in that confined space, and set about testing an old adage, namely that a snow leopard will not under any circumstances attack a human. The cat was cornered; there was no way out except past McCarthy; and all it did was growl and hiss, with no indication that it would attack, even when he reached forward, and jabbed it.

Already it is clear that Mongolian snow leopards are a breed apart. In Nepal each animal can get enough of its prey – blue sheep – in a mere seventy square kilometres. In Mongolia, where there are fewer animals more thinly spread, a single snow leopard may range across seven times that area.

And some of this is desert, for Mongolian snow leopards live not only in the high Altai, but also in the archipelago of outcrops that scatter eastwards as the mountains give way to Gobi. If you trace the contour lines that would allow a commuting snow leopard to keep more than 600 metres above the desert floor, there are significant gaps between these islands of rock. To get from one fastness to another means crossing the open desert, up to fifty-five kilometres of it, which is not something these cats do anywhere else. Yet today they are over halfway across the Gobi, having crossed gravel plains with only scrub and shallow ravines for cover, and no water at all.

Weeks later, 640 kilometres to the east, near the far end of the Three Beauties range, the driver swung away from the trail, and drove round the shoulder of a mountain to a ger to see friends, drink tea, and gossip. The friends were away in the high mountains, but the children and several of their schoolfriends were there, on their summer holidays, looking after new foals, which were tied to a tethering line a few yards up from the ger. Above us, a herd of adult horses picked over the coarse soil, grazing on the tussocky grass. It was a beautiful afternoon, with the sun hanging low over the hills and turning the dust kicked up by the horses to a golden haze.

'Do you have snow leopards here?' I asked one of the boys on an impulse.

For a reply, the boy pointed to a foal. It was limping badly and had a scar on its shoulder. A month previously, not long after its birth, it had been attacked by a snow leopard only a few kilometres from that spot, in the ravine known as the Vulture's Gorge. The mother had kicked the snow leopard, which fled, leaving the foal with its flank torn open to the bone and a second wound on its back leg. The herders treated it with a compress made of a local plant, a sort of mint with a little blue flower that grew in large clumps up the mountainside. I saved some to identify, but by the time we had bounced our way back to camp it was bedraggled and unrecognizable. I am left with a memory of what it was like when I picked it – it smelt like lemon balm, and its name in Mongol was 'khunchir'.*

'So the snow leopards are growing in numbers here?'

---

* Various references identify this as a form of Astragalus, a genus of pea that contains some 1,600 species. There are 102 different *khunchirs*, I'm sorry to say, so I cannot help with a more detailed identification.

'Oh, there are many.'

'And do the herdsmen kill them?'

'If they kill, they must pay much money.'

'So what can people do?'

'Shoot them . . .' He hesitated. 'But not many.'

Here again was the core dilemma, herdsmen and their flocks on one side, snow leopards and conservationists on the other – and this time in an area way to the east of what was once considered the domain of the snow leopard.

While the others finished fixing ropes, I borrowed Choinjin's binoculars and set off to climb the nearby ridge, hoping for a better view of the surrounding cliffs. The thirteen-year-old joined me. As we scrambled up the loose scree, blinking away dust and turning away from the gusts of wind, I asked his name. It was Tseenorov, Norov for short. Then he added in English: 'What's yours?' He was learning English in school, which was something new, improving it in conversations with McCarthy. Until a year or two previously, he would have been taught Russian as his first foreign language. Now, there were enough teachers to start on something that will, within a few years, mark a radical cultural change.

I laboured up to join Norov on the ridge, and at once feared for my safety. Below, I had been protected from the wind. Up here, it leapt over the crest and grabbed at my camera case like a thief. My jacket flapped insanely. Though almost blinded by flying hair, I could see that the ridge I was on was the spur of an S-bend. Forty-five metres below me was the stream, which had cut through shattered and distorted strata to make a sheer canyon that snaked away into the heart of the mountains.

I squatted down, letting the gusts boom above me, and scanned the gorge. On the opposite wall, and in the peaks above, McCarthy placed his snares. That's where snow leopards stalked at dusk and dawn, because their main prey, ibex, cling to the ridges, and that's where they holed up during the day. Somewhere above me in the complex of frost-shattered cliffs, there would be scrapes, and a rich spray of urine; and possibly, within a few hundred metres, but concealed from my questing binoculars, a snow leopard.

Did I see a snow leopard? No! Isn't that wonderful? Absolutely not! I do not have Matthiessen's Zen acceptance. I regret the scant time spent searching. I regret my ignorance of the wilderness. I regret not being able to wake before dawn and climb a rock, and watch a ridge for signs of stealthy life. I regret not feeling the slack softness of a comatose leopard, not seeing the creature find its poise again, and dissolve like mist among the rocks. Not-seeing, I cannot claim to have felt at one with what I saw. Only in the seeing will I begin to understand.

Later, I asked Choinjin if they ever came down.

'Yes, because this time of year, when they have young, they sometimes hide the kittens under bushes. If they leave them exposed up there, and go off hunting, a vulture could take the kitten.'

I mentioned my conversation with the herder in Tsogt. Yes, Choinjin said, he knew what the herders believed – that there were more attacks now because the numbers were growing, and that the numbers were growing because the snow leopards were protected. He didn't know if the numbers really were growing, though. Maybe it was just that there were more domestic animals now, grazing marginal pastures, attracting the snow leopards. Whatever the explanation, 'They say that when the first snows come, you see snow leopard footprints everywhere.'

Perhaps in the end the conflict between herders and snow leopards is not the most significant one. McCarthy suggests that the kills are not frequent enough to inspire outright warfare. OK, he argues, if there's a kill, someone might set a trap, and if a snow leopard presents itself, and the herder has a rifle to hand, that's a recipe for a dead cat, and maybe a few hundred dollars in his pocket. But no one is going to go *hunting* snow leopards. Even when you know exactly where one is, you don't see it. You could waste weeks and not find one. He himself has been doing this work for three years, and he's never even seen a snow leopard in the wild, except the five he has captured.

The planned killing of snow leopards – whether by herdsmen or hunters – is not the real threat. The real threat is a more subtle one, to whole ecosystems, brought about by human pressure and natural change.

Logic suggests that there should be three main influences at work: the effects of protection, the effects of drought, the effects of population pressure. They should all interrelate to increase herd size, open up more marginal lands, impose increasingly on snow leopard territory, and change the balance between predator, wild prey, and domestic prey. These changes may in the short run encourage the snow leopard; in the long run they may erode the ecology of mountain and desert, and threaten both the animal population and the livelihood of the people spreading into it. To save both the environments and the economies, there may be no better way than to devise a general management plan based on the ecosystem's top predator and its key species, the snow leopard.

The agenda of such a plan becomes visible if you match the arguments to the snow leopard's domain, working metaphorically from the bottom up, from the valley of practicality to the pure high ground of idealism.

Consider first the severely practical: why should herders tolerate snow leopards? What's in it for them? The answer needs to be a common-sense one, because Mongolian herders cannot afford to accept altruistic arguments about the inherent value of a rare species, cannot be expected to bear the cost of international idealism. They need compensation for losses, incentives not to kill a creature that kills their stock. Who pays? The burden may fall back on those with higher motives – wildlife conservationists, necessarily international ones, like the International Snowleopard Trust in Seattle, Washington. The idea of funding conservation by rewarding locals for their tolerance and for improving their herding practices – for instance, by guarding and corralling them better – is already being tested in Mongolia. It may be that in exchange for flour, rice and children's clothes and other practical help, nomads might accept new herding practices and tolerate some depredation by snow leopards (though what happens if snow leopards ever become a plague is a question no one has yet addressed).

Above this region of practicality lie the zones occupied by administrators and officials. For them, the snow leopard can be made to serve a purpose, a higher purpose than making under-the-counter cash by selling hunting licences. The snow leopard seizes the heart in a way that beetles, for instance, do not. With its lifestyle understood and its status secured, it could be an enduring asset, drawing in ecotourists and hard currency.

Now move on up into the foothills of science, where zoologists cite facts about food chains and unified ecosystems. Protect the snow leopard, they argue, and by default you protect much more – the Altai and the western Gobi as a whole. This in turn could spin off benefits for the cause of conservation nationally and internationally. The snow leopard could be as potent a symbol for conservation as the panda and the elephant.

Finally there is a rarefied zone, the peaks of idealism, where the spirits of the great and good dwell in their purest form, the Schallers and McCarthys stripped of their severe scientific natures. Here, in the domain of philosophy and aesthetics, the snow leopard can be seen as an essence, an epitome, the end point of specialist evolution, an embodiment of beauty, an inspiration to the human spirit. By this argument, the death of any species diminishes humanity. In saving the snow leopard, we save something of ourselves.

The snow leopard itself spans these arguments as it spans the levels of its range. It is the mist that drifts between desert valley and snow-capped mountain, a proof, briefly visible, that the two domains are connected. If that connection is broken, if the mist dissipates, if the snow leopard vanishes, the Gobi, the Altai, Mongolia, and the world will be the poorer.

4

A Sacred Mountain

All the area we had driven over south of the Altai mountains was the realm of the Sacred Mother. She presided for fifty kilometres in all directions, east to the shattered hills of the Edren Ridge, north to the foothills of the Altai, west and south over speckled gravel. From a distance, she towered out of mirages like an island. She was a grey bulk under cloud and a beacon under clear skies, her flanks glowing orange in morning and evening light, her shadows modulating with the moving sun. She was as alluring and mysterious as the relic of a vanished civilization.

All I knew of the mountain was that it had been declared a 'natural monument' in 1992. To find out anything more, I would have to visit her, and asked for company. The journey looked easy enough. Compared to the distance we had come already, another fifty kilometres wasn't much, and compared to the Gobi's other protected areas, the Sacred Mother's 216 square kilometres was only a pinprick. I planned to drive round her – a mere fifty-eight kilometres, by my reckoning – climb her, anatomize her.

These were high hopes, born of ignorance and arrogance. The Sacred Mother would prove somewhat Kafkaesque, a castle that seemed accessible from afar, but which shifted ground and became something else the closer one got. If I had known more about mountains and the name, I would have been more wary. 'Khairkhan' has a sense of 'sacred', in that it is a title that expresses reverence, but it is also a word used when you wish to avoid using the real name, because presiding deities become angry if addressed directly. 'Khairkhan' is a Mongolian equivalent of Your Holiness. Next time I shall approach her with a good deal more respect.

The same party as before, we drove for an hour, always with two or three dust-devils spinning upwards in the distance like attendant spirits.

Saxauls dotted the desert from the southern horizon to the snow-clad wall of the Altai mountains. Gazelles, lone individuals or small groups, scooted away in little explosions of dust. We rode off firm ground into soft dust, and began to slew between bushes. The Sacred Mother blocked the way ahead, looming like a Gobi version of Ayers Rock.

'Do you go there much?' I asked Choinjin.

'Not much. We just like to look at it.'

'Does anyone live there?'

No, he replied. Once, a lama lived there, all alone in a cave, but there is nothing to support human life. Only Buddhists ever went there. Years ago, Choinjin said, he was part of a procession to place a plaque on the crowning obo, but under Communism there were not many visitors. This year, though, there was a big ceremony, when people came from Inner Mongolia and held a service at the obo.

It was becoming difficult to see which summit he was talking about, because as we approached, the Sacred Mother seemed to be less of a unity, more of a family. Instead of one pure line sweeping up in a succession of steps to a single peak, there were several lines, several mountains, each with its own flanks. That thought planted another image in my mind. The smoothness, the sweeps of grey, overlapping and intertwining: the Sacred Mother had produced a brontosaurian brood, all crowding around her, backs, shoulders, legs, and great domed heads nestling against her for protection.

I wondered how this peculiar outcrop had arisen, how it fitted with the ranges over which we had come a few days previously. Answers came later, and then only in the most general terms, because this is pristine territory for geologists. Andrews opened it up, but in the 1920s, when the Gobi was a blank, work involved merely listing finds and trying to place them in chronological order. The findings read like a jumble of technicalities. After that, for decades, the only geology done here was by Russians and Mongolians, and much of that was directed towards finding oil and minerals. In the words of a 1996 paper on the Altai mountains by Brian Windley of Leicester University, one of the few geologists to work in the area: 'The basic question of why a 4,000-metre-high mountain range exists today in the centre of Asia has hardly been addressed by field-based geologists.' If there is hardly anything about the Altai, there is nothing at all as yet on the Sacred Mother mountain.

But there are pointers. Firstly, those shards of evidence gathered by

Andrews now have their unifying principle. This is the theory of plate tectonics – or continental drift – which explains the shape and lie of all land masses, marshalling a rabble of facts into a coherent narrative (actually, Andrews does have an indexed reference to 'continental shift and instabilities', but these were early days. 'Interesting theories,' he wrote. 'We have no definite conclusions.') Secondly, geologists are now criss-crossing the Gobi as never before, hungry for prizes both commercial and academic. No single expedition will match the heavy-weight assaults mounted by Andrews in the 1920s, but there's no need. With better transport, communications and tools, much smaller projects can hope to make equally significant progress. From the mists of the distant and immediate past, a scenario is emerging.

Go back in your mind's eye millions of years, before today's desert formed; tens of millions of years, before the mountain ranges came into existence; over 100 million years, before the dinosaurs that left their bones in the Gobi even evolved. Now double that time-scale, and double it again. There is no neat starting point, because the earth's surface has reformed itself many times in the last 500 million years, but this is as good as any. Back then, when the continents formed a very different pattern, Eurasia and North America were in pieces, island continents well apart from a vast land mass that linked South America, Africa, India, Antarctica and Australia. But the forces that carried the continental rafts back and forth across the face of the earth, the currents of molten rock welling up from the earth's interior ovens – all this was the same then as now. As Europe became welded to North America, volcanic rock pushed up along the edges of the continents and into subsurface cracks, creating ranges stretching from Finland, across Scotland, and down the eastern seaboard of America.

Seeing the Sacred Mother from a distance, there is a burst of recognition. She is not unique. Those rounded shoulders, so different from the steep and angled alpine slopes of young mountains, recall Glencoe, or the stubby peaks of New England. Like them, the Sacred Mother is granite. The rock of the Sacred Mother was not originally a mountain, but an intrusion of magma that squeezed up from a basement of rock into an overlying stratum, warping it, forcing it apart and upwards. As the magma cooled it turned to granite, and lay like a pearl in an oyster awaiting the changes that would reveal it.

Over the next 300 million years, continents formed and reformed, plants colonized the land, animal life followed. The area that is now the Gobi, once perhaps part of a free-floating continental island, became fixed to Siberia, China and Central Asia. The dinosaurs evolved, diversified, and died.

Sixty million years ago, just after the dinosaurs vanished from the earth, a great sea washed the southern shores of the eastern part of Eurasia. It was over 2,000 kilometres from the present-day Gobi, but there were no mountains to cut the area off from the soothing effects of the sea. It was savannah land, its climate milder than today's, its soils rich. Already, though, forces were gathering that would recreate this part of the world, for the land that would form today's India was approaching, millimetre by millimetre, surfing northwards from its original base – Africa – on a subterranean plume of molten rock.

For a God's-eye view of what happened next, imagine the following 40 million years compressed into minutes. In a twinkling – it is after all a mere one per cent of the earth's age – India collided with eastern Eurasia, crumpling its coastline and continental interior into new mountains, the Himalayas, the Pamirs, the Hindu Kush, the Tien Shan. Ripples from that cataclysm rolled northwards, and sideways, east and west, from the isolated deserts of Uzbekistan to the Tibetan uplands that form the sources of the Yellow River, the Yangtse, the Mekong.

The Gobi – several hundred kilometres from the Tien Shan, 1,000 from the Tibetan plateau, 1,600 from the Himalayas themselves – is part of the outer crumple-zone. That is why the Altai mountains exist, why they are young, why they range from northwest to southeast, facing the direction of the force that created them. In two great waves – the Altai proper and the Gobi Altai are actually separate ranges – they tumble down from their western heights into the Gobi, dividing desert from desert, diving into the earth, and re-emerging in a final flourish as the Gurvan Saikhan, the Three Beauties, in the southern Gobi. It is this inclination – high in the west, low in the east – that makes the Gobi what it is today.

It is, of course, a little more complicated than this. The push from the southwest is not only head-on. It has a lateral component as well. Two fault lines, one along the eastern nose of the Altai, the other running right through Gobi A, cut the Gobi into three sections. To the north of each fault, the land is pushing westwards; to the south the thrust is eastwards. The distortions this creates build ridges with a flattened S-shape, almost invisible to non-specialists, but quite distinctive to those who know what to look for.

All this slow-motion activity sets up stresses that eventually find release. This is not an ever-shifting land on the continental fringes, like California, but it is earthquake country. The effects are there in the fracture zones that run along the base of the mountains, sometimes visible as a contour. Visible or not, they dominate the ecology and economy of the Gobi because it is along these lines that subterranean water – and there's a lot of it – is squeezed to the surface. The springs mark the fault lines, like weak spots in a water tank.

Most of the time, the stresses induced by India's steady drift northwards are released slowly, because this area is not on the edge of a continental plate. But every now and then the pent-up forces explode. In December 1957 an earthquake shook all the southern Gobi. It measured at least 7.9, and perhaps up to 8.3, on the Richter scale, equivalent to the largest known earthquake along California's San Andreas fault in 1857, and exceeding the Tokyo earthquake of 1923 which killed 143,000 people. The Gobi quake would have been a catastrophic event almost anywhere else in the world. Here, though, there were no cities to fall, no roads to crumble. The quake ruptured the desert for 250 kilometres along the northern flank of the Ikh Bogd range, starting about fifty-five kilometres south of the route we had taken from Ulan Bator. When Russian geologists hurried to the area, they found that two segments of the earth's crust had slid past each other for up to ten metres and in places raised scarps three to six metres high.

After India crashed into Asia 50 million years ago, the forming Himalayas cut off airflow from the south, and turned Central Asia in upon itself. Deprived of monsoon winds and rainfall, the savannahs turned to deserts. In spring, air rising from the high, dry heartlands drew air in from the north and west. Prevailing winds scooped up dust that worked at the new mountains, blew dust on dust into the desert, and drove it east and south, into China. The process continues to this day. Occasionally, dust storms sweep from the Gobi right across to Beijing. With time, over the course of 20 million years, hundreds of metres of soil blew away eastwards. The finer grains were winnowed out, being dumped as a smooth loess, which formed deep sandstones in central China, in places sixty metres thick. Further east, the soft dust laid down rich soils which became some of China's richest lands. In effect, China owes its agricultural wealth to the Gobi winds. When Chingis Khan invaded China, he was unwittingly seizing land that had once been Mongolian.

All of this leads back to the Sacred Mother. For aeons, she had remained protected and enclosed. Only in geologically recent times, when the winds blew and the soft rock eroded away, did the underlying dome emerge, revealing the Sacred Mother as she is today.

'Does *anything* live there?' The barren rock, sliding up in slate-grey sweeps, did not look promising.

'Oh, yes,' Choinjin nodded. 'There are two oases. Goats. Wolves. Lynxes. Snow leopards.'

It seemed unlikely that snow leopards would find enough here to sustain them. Choinjin had not actually seen one, but he was certain. 'I have seen footprints. I have seen a camel half-eaten.' And there are occasional tracks, and McCarthy's son Keegan actually radio-tracked a large male across the desert to the mountain.

We were not far from the wall of rock – a few kilometres – when we were halted by a surreal sight. Saxaul-studded desert opened out, revealing a standpipe belching water. It was one of a line of standpipes, a hundred metres or so apart, most of which stood rooted in gravel. This one, though, fed a pond, beside which grew sparkling grasses, forming a few yards of Irish brilliance. We were on the edge of a cultivated area, supplied by water from the Altai, which reared up a few miles to the north. Here, they grow watermelons and tomatoes. This was once a natural oasis, the product of water flowing up from below through fault lines along the edge of the Gobi Altai, then running down into the gently sloping desert. Some years ago, a decision had been made to encourage this process – hence the dam I had seen when we drove up to McCarthy's mountain base. The water ran through a buried culvert, then burst out of its standpipes. Some way ahead, I could see a ger, a field – this was the barley Erdene had been talking about – and a fence to keep out marauding camels. It was the first fence I had seen in the Gobi.

Byamba slowed, swung into the oven wind, halted by the pond and then set to work with a rag washing down his vehicle as if it were a sweaty racehorse.

Erdene looked on, and shook his head. 'We say, "He is watching the pace of the rotten back." '

'What?'

'He is washing his rotting Buck's Fizz.'

'Erdene, please, what are you talking about?'

'You know what a buck is? A male goat? You know that a male goat when it is sexually active is a very revolting thing? When it is rutting, it gets –' He made a gesture of disgust, at the gross nature of a randy billy goat's face.

'Oh, *rutting*.'

The others were splashing themselves with water from this unexpected lake, and Byamba was busy with the windscreen.

'When people wash it off,' Erdene continued patiently, 'it comes again. Do you understand?'

I still looked blank.

'John, if you wash the face of a rutting buck, you are doing a useless thing. The filth comes again. What Byamba is doing, it is useless. As soon as he has finished, the dust will come again. When anyone does anything useless, we say "he is washing the face of the rutting buck."'

'O-o-oh, I see. Thank you.'

There was a brief pause until he asked: 'What do you say?'

'We sometimes say, "thrashing a dead horse".'

'What is thrashing?'

'Beating.'

'You beat your dead horses?'

'No. There is no point. That's the point.'

'Ah. That is very good. Byamba is thrashing a dead horse. I will remember.'

The rutting buck now had a temporarily clean face, and we were off again, skirting a fallow field that had, the previous year, grown oats, then on, beyond the last fence, into soft sand. It was all rather tentative, as if the farmers didn't really believe in what they were doing. The fields were sandy, and some of the standpipes were dry, standing forlorn in barren ground. I wondered at the contrast between yellow and green, at the difficulty of making the desert bloom, and wondered too if nomads in gers, ready to move with their flocks at a few hours' notice, could ever sustain the commitment to be farmers.

There was a track, weaving through the tamarisk, but it was little used and the sand was deep. We ground along in four-wheel drive until we overheated again. We paused on a rise, with a fine view over the sea of dark green to Sacred Mother's wall of grey. We seemed to be constantly skirting her, never approaching.

We shared soft drinks and sweets. Someone pushed in a tape, and the rapid yodelling of a bass singer and a two-stringed fiddle mixed with the shush of wind-blown sand on tamarisk leaves. Something extremely big and dangerous flew into the car, and buzzed round. I grabbed one of my books, and prepared to swat it.

'No, no.' Erdene raised a hand. 'You must not kill anything near the mountain. Not to move any stones, either.'

I guided the monster through the open door, wondering if we would ever reach the Sacred Mother.

'Do not worry. This music is lucky. It is a long song.'

'How long?'

'Not of importance. That is the type of song. We have something called "long song" and something called "short song". This long song is very famous. It is called "Lucky Rich". It says like: with luck, everything good will come to you. What would you call it, this song, in English?'

Byamba climbed in and pulled out a cigarette. The conversation was due to continue for a while yet.

' "Blue Skies Smiling on Me?" ' I thought it sounded very Mongolian.

'It is a famous American short song.'

'Perhaps something more poetic.'

After several suggestions, Erdene accepted 'By Fortune Blessed', as if the words were themselves a talisman. Ploughing on, ever nearer the surging wall of rock, we climbed onto firm ground, round boulders, and realized we were after all lucky rich. A notice confronted us, proclaiming, in English as well as Mongolian: 'Please respect this sacred place. Eej Khairkhan National Monument.' And then more blue skies, more fortune, blessed us, in the form of a decaying shack, itself in the totally un-Mongolian form of an A-frame, without walls, all one wooden roof corrugated by rain, wind and snow. Clearly it was a base of some sort, though there was no explanation for its presence.

Scrambling towards enlightenment

Ahead was a path, through immense chunks of rock that had been prised from the heights above by rain and frost. It was an odd discovery, for the path, of coarse gravel, was as clear and smooth as a suburban driveway, weaving between the boulders.

'Is it made by people?'

'No!' Choinjin set off, and we all followed, the thirteen-year-old exploring rocks like a puppy, the mother carrying her child. Khorloo abandoned her coat, revealing a smart silk shirt.

As we crunched along the gravel path I saw not a single animal, not even an insect, but in spots of sandy soil to either side there were hoof marks. There was no telling how old the prints were, but sometimes goats and camels browsed here. In crevices, dwarf roses sprouted. Bending now and then to avoid briars, we passed small piles of rock, miniature obos marking a trail, like shrines along a pilgrims' way. Above, fallen boulders merged with rock carved by rain and wind into weird shapes: heads and ears, melt holes, bore holes, open mouths. Byamba had disappeared on his own up into the heights, and behind us the women dawdled and chattered. With Choinjin leading on, Erdene and I entertained ourselves by spotting rock creatures – a mouse, a dog, a tortoise, the head of a stegosaurus, a crowd of dinosaurs, smaller versions of the Sacred Mother's image from afar.

Erdene became concerned about Byamba. 'Perhaps he has been captured by an *almas*.' The *almas*, the Mongolian equivalent of the yeti, is sometimes referred to as the Wild Man of the Gobi, although reports of its existence emerge from the western highlands, not the Gobi at all. He vanished in pursuit, and I followed Choinjin as he climbed over and around boulders.

All at once, ahead, set deep under an overhang, was what seemed the dwelling of a mountain elf. Its floor was rock, its roof was rock, three sides were rock, but the front wall was of mud-brick, with three windows and a door no more than a metre and a half high. It faced east from beneath its beetling crag. It was, of course, the lama's cave, and beside it was a tree, dense and convoluted. Once, perhaps, it had offered shady space and the promise of enlightenment.

Buddhism, or rather the lamaist Yellow Sect of Buddhism, established itself as the dominant religion in Mongolia after 1550. It did not spread as the result of missionary zeal, but by the invitation of a powerful khan, Altan, who sought to sideline rivals by establishing an official state religion from 'the land of snows', Tibet. It was he, in fact, who conferred upon Tibet's pope-king the title 'Dalai', Mongolian for 'ocean', to symbolize the range of his spiritual influence. Thereafter, the effects of lamaism were comparable to Christianity in medieval Europe, only more so, becoming a state within a state. In the capital, Urga, as Ulan Bator was formerly known, the only buildings were temples, until the Russians built a consulate there in the late nineteenth century. At best, monasteries were centres of learning and theology – almost all translated from Tibetan – providing education, recording information, gathering libraries, dispensing Tibetan medicine. At worst, they sucked the population and the economy dry, drawing from it whatever was left by acquisitive Manchu officials, usurious Chinese money lenders, and extravagant princes. Throughout the nineteenth century, lamaism became less and less a blessing, increasingly a curse, because in the appalling conditions into which Mongolia had fallen, the church offered the only (though diminishing) hope of material protection and advancement. One-third of the male population were lamas, trained from childhood in anywhere between 900 and 1,700 lamaseries (estimates vary radically), a few of them lavish, many nothing more than two or three small houses. The whole system was parasitic. In these dark and superstitious times most lamas lived outside lamaseries, supporting themselves by performing rituals, expelling demons, pacifying the souls of the dead, telling fortunes. Spirituality and pastoral care ebbed, while the church's rulers absorbed whatever wealth they could to finance expensive pilgrimages to Lhasa or sustain drunken, syphilitic lives.

In these grim circumstances, those who sought true spirituality, those who reacted against the abuses and those unable to make a living, simply retreated far from the clashing cymbals, ringing bells, groaning Tibetan chants and demon masks of the monasteries. Returning to an ancient Buddhist tradition, they became hermits, in mountains that were sacred long before Buddhism. One of them lived here, seeking solace in celibacy and renunciation, and surviving – on what? The occasional offerings of the faithful?

I climbed onto the rock platform that formed a sort of verandah, past a side cave in which some empty soft-drink bottles had been discarded, stooped almost onto my knees, and entered. Inside was a single room, a cave that sloped back into gloom to a natural cupboard, and a rock shelf. The roof was blackened, by smoke perhaps, or paint. In any event, the place was not abandoned.

For a second, I thought I saw a figure. As my eyes became accustomed to the darkness, I saw there was no one there, no ancient lama sitting cross-legged in the gloom. But he remained imprinted on my inward eye, his face as gnarled as mountains, burnt dark as desert-varnish on rocks. Sometimes, staring out over the Dorset hills as I write this book,

I imagine who this old familiar might have been and what he might have said.

'Come. I have been waiting for you.'

'For me?'

'Must I remind you of what you already know?'

I am baffled. 'What do you mean? How is it that you speak English?'

His gaze clears. 'I am sorry. For a moment I thought you were one of them, returned.' He pauses, and then speaks of the past.

He has been there for over seventy years, since the time he first sought wisdom and a release from the bonds of desire and the material world. He was raised in a Buddhist temple, now long since destroyed, and at the age of fourteen went on a pilgrimage to Tibet, then on from Tibet to Nepal, wandering the Tibetan monasteries of the Himalayas. There, he met Englishmen mapping remote peaks. Hired as a porter, he learnt the language with all the facility of his youth, and then served on an expedition to conquer the greatest peak of all, Chomolungma.

'Everest,' I breathe. 'You were with . . .'

'Mr Mallory, Mr Irvine, yes. I saw them leave, that last day, so near the top. I watched them through the magic lens of Captain Noel. And when I knew they had found what they sought, life as it really is, I returned to follow my own route to the happiness they found.'

'You have found it – the secret of happiness?'

'Oh, yes.'

'You could tell me.' I foresee a book of great wisdom, the fruits of six decades of meditation, reduced to a tenfold path by the Lama of the Sacred Mother.

'Ah,' he shakes his head, with the trace of a smile. 'It is a secret that cannot be given or told. It is a secret that must be sought by you alone. And yet not sought, if it is to be found.'

'Sought yet not sought? How and where must I seek and not seek?'

'Within, and without. Within yourself, without desire. Looking, you cannot find. To find, you must give up the search.'

The vision lasts only a moment, fortunately, for I never had any wish to be called to a life dedicated to seeking, yet not seeking enlightenment through paradox and self-denial. Give up the search? Certainly not. I have a journey to complete, a wife and four-year-old daughter, a deadline. I have no time for visions.

Still, the cave really had not been abandoned. The shelf was a table and an altar, for on it were little pyramids made of cloth and a ram's horn; but also a medicine bottle, pens and a school exercise book.

It was an odd collection. All of it had to be recent for, as Choinjin said, the lama who had lived here had vanished in the 1930s. Those were terrible years, when Mongolia fell under the sway of its own Stalin-figure, Choibalsang, who in effect wiped out the established church. New taxes, new laws, new jobs as herders, craftsmen and soldiers, an enforced change from Tibetan to Mongol – all undermined the church, which was then finished off by outright violence. In 1937–8, lamaseries were destroyed, their property seized, lamas executed. By 1940 only 251 lamas survived, paraded as tokens that the regime respected religious freedom and the rights of the individual.

But the site endured, and the knowledge of what it was; and people kept coming. Through the years of oppression, Choinjin said, lamas continued to make their pilgrimages here, in secret. Now, others come, impelled by a variety of motives. Candle grease suggested genuine piety, as did the little medicine bottle. But the pens and the exercise book and the soft-drink bottles: these were left by children here on a school outing and teenagers out for a lark in a spooky old cave, laughing away whispers from the past.

Perhaps, though, the children and the teenagers went on beyond the cave, to see more, something that Choinjin was determined I should experience.

'The Nine Pots,' he said, and led me on upwards. We followed small obos up a natural staircase of smooth boulders, onto open sheets of rock. Here, on these exposed slopes, the outer layer had been baked and frozen into a wafer-thin tortoiseshell that crackled underfoot. Little chips slipped and spattered over the rocks below. Why, at that rate, in a few million years, these rocks would all be gravel scattered over the desert. A wooden ladder – a sign that this was a regular pilgrimage for some – led up a small precipice, and down beyond into a cleft, a hidden fold in Sacred Mother's skirts.

The cleft opened into a second larger one, which ran across our path down a steep slope. Here water had once fallen with such power that it had carved out a series of pans, like a Japanese water garden. These were the Nine Pots, each one a few feet lower than the last, each with an eroded lip to guide the flow. A mere trickle linked them now, ending in a small pond. Where this overflowed, a patch of mud supported grasses and a bent old tree. From its lower branches fluttered a score of blue ribbons, the same sort of cloth strips that adorn large obos. This was a shrine, one that had been honoured for far longer than any Buddhist presence.

The water flowed from some invisible source beyond the highest spot, but the sides of the cleft were too steep to climb. If I wanted to see more, I would have to take another route. I heard a call. Choinjin was ahead of me, beckoning from halfway up the other side. I followed, climbing easily over the mountain's rough hide.

We paused, on a ridge, and looked down onto the Nine Pots and the stream that flowed into them. It ran across a little valley, from the surrounding cliffs, though from what source I could not imagine – a hidden lake of rain water, perhaps, or some fault up which water rose. The valley itself, filled with good, well-watered earth, was a secret garden, thick with grass and tussocky turf and bushes. This half-acre would have been rich enough in barley and beans to keep a lama. From thirty metres up, the grass looked as trim as a lawn. Perhaps it was grazed – by gazelle? Horses? I could see no sign of animal life. If there was a way up, they would surely find it, for there could be no greater contrast between this jewel in its rocky clasp and the surrounding desiccation.

I turned to see what lay outside. Across from the ridge where Choinjin and I stood was a summit – the highest, for it was topped by a pyramid of piled rocks – while below us was the shattered wasteland of fallen boulders through which we had walked earlier. Beyond that, the gravel plain, speckled with saxauls. Marked by cloud shadows purple as bruises, the plain spread north for twenty or twenty-five kilometres until it came up against the Altai, which, like the wall of a rift valley, rolled eastwards until its snowy peaks faded into mist, or dust, or the coming twilight.

I saw now why Choinjin had led me up here. This was the Sacred Mother's real glory. We stood for a while, looking out. There was not a breath of wind, and nothing to break the silence. Besides the others, unheard and invisible somewhere amongst the rocks below, there was no one else on this mountain, and only a scattering of people within a day's drive. We were in rare isolation, set apart from the earth and halfway to the blue sky. I wondered whether the lama had after all been so wedded to self-denial. This was surely a better place to seek, and not-seek, enlightenment.

Choinjin, too, was looking out over the plain. I touched his shoulder briefly, awkwardly.

'It's beautiful,' I said. 'Very beautiful.'

He raised a hand to his cheek.

'Very beautiful,' he repeated softly, and kept his face turned away.

5

The Return of the Native

I n April 1879 the Russian explorer Nikolai Przhevalski set out from
Zaysan, on the border of what is now a political patchwork divided
between Kazakhstan, northern China and Mongolia. He was on his
way across a northern tongue of Gobi-like terrain flanked by the Altai
mountains in pursuit of a dream: to become the first European to write
a scholarly account of Tibet's capital, Lhasa.

That achievement would cap a brilliant career. He was already Russia's
greatest explorer, having crossed the eastern Gobi twice, working his
way into the Tibetan highlands, penetrating areas of Central Asia as
dark for Europeans as central Africa. In doing so, he wove himself into
the modern history of the Gobi.

He didn't get results by charm. He was puritanical, demanding, scathing. But he had qualities useful in an explorer. He did not drink, he
avoided women, he led from the front, and he was never depressed by
the rigours of climate, food or travel. He was good with money. In his
early days, he financed himself by winning at cards – his brother officers
called him the 'golden pheasant' – and later, with admirers in high
places, was able to rely on official backing. He was a prodigious recorder
of information: by the time he died in 1888 he had collected 1,700
species of plant, and dozens of animals – the wild camel was one – had
been named after him.

He was driven by many ambitions – to achieve, to know, to discover –
but perhaps the deepest passion was his imperial zeal, a chauvinism
too extreme for many of his fellow Russians. Even as a young officer,
all severe looks and waxed moustaches, he developed a character that
seems now to be the very epitome of xenophobic hauteur. Beijing was
a place of 'unimaginable foulness', and 'the Chinaman here is a Jew
plus a Muscovite pickpocket, both squared'. As certain in his superiority
as any missionary, officer or imperial administrator, he sought to

civilize – to civilize not only the barbaric regions he opened, but also his own effete and decaying culture, rejuvenating it with the zest of achievement, knowledge and discovery. Central Asia was his New Frontier, Russia's Manifest Destiny; and Lhasa was his El Dorado.

Success, of course, demanded that rivals be excluded. He was quite consciously a part of what Kipling would later call the Great Game, the rivalry between two expanding empires, the Russian and the British, in particular British-ruled India. In pursuit of glory and imperial expansion, Russophobes and Anglophobes – explorers, geographers, missionaries, spies in odd disguises, bands of soldiers and the occasional diplomat – probed and parried from the Black Sea to China, with the little-known mountains and deserts of Central Asia, from Persia through Turkmenistan and Afghanistan to Tibet, all up for grabs. This was why Przhevalski dreamt of Lhasa. Tibet was to fall to Russia, not Britain. As he wrote in a memorandum to the Russian Geographical Society and the War Ministry in August 1878, 'Scientific explorations will mask the political aims of the expedition.'

So it was that in the spring of the following year, he was on his way eastwards into China and Mongolia, when Kirghiz hunters brought him the skin of a strange horse-like animal. He guessed at once that it was a type of wild horse often rumoured to exist, but never seen by a European. It had the stocky body, short legs and large head of a Mongolian pony, but it had no forelock, a mane that stood erect like a donkey's, deep-set eyes, short ears and massive teeth. He said it was a sort of 'tarpan', the European wild horse that was already near extinction (the last one died in 1918, though since then breeding between domestic and tarpan crosses has resulted in something like a reconstituted tarpan).

It was an inspired guess. He had discovered what was in effect a Mongolian tarpan, making it one of three or four (expert opinion is divided) wild strains of horse that survived the ice age. From one of these – the species or subspecies that migrated into the Middle East and north Africa – domestic horses emerged some 5,000 years ago. By the late nineteenth century, other strains were extinct, near extinction or officially unrecorded. His discovery therefore was greeted back in St Petersburg as a great find, and the horse was named after him: Przhevalski's horse, or more formally *Equus przewalskii*. Some nit-pickers now argue that this is a species name, and that technically it should be *Equus przewalskii ferus*. (There are many ways to transliterate his name, with all combinations of prz/prez, z/zh, w/v, y/i, or even ij at the end. To confuse things further, he was actually Polish, but at that time Poland was part of the Russian empire.)

The Kirghiz, Kazakhs and in particular the Mongols would have been astonished by the European reaction. The horse, once widespread in Central Asia, had been driven into ever-more remote regions by the spread of people, but it was still well known to the locals. In Kirghiz, it was 'kurtag', in Mongol 'takhi' (that's the usual transliteration; in fact, the final 'i' is a mere breath, a soft-sign in Cyrillic, for which English has no equivalent). They knew its character, too – tough enough to wring a living from these raw mountains and desert steppes, grouping in small herds dominated by a male, with wariness and wiliness bred in the bone. Wariness above all, because humans did not like them. They were totally intractable, they ran off with domesticated females, they produced offspring as wild as they were themselves, they were good for nothing but eating. For millennia, the only relationship between the wild horse and humans had been hostile.

Przhevalski saw the consequences for himself. After following the narrow fertile strip of the Ulungur river to its source in the foothills of the Altai in the far southwest corner of Mongolia, he found himself in the heartland of the surviving takhi. Here he saw two groups of mares, each led by a stallion. 'One of them let us creep to within a marksman's distance, but the animals caught my companion's scent at not less than 1,000 yards, and withdrew,' tails arched, sometimes stopping in a bickering bunch to check on the opposition, then vanishing at a trot. Unable to shoot or catch one, Przhevalski pressed on south into China. (He never did reach Lhasa, but before his death in 1888, his journeys helped feed the astonishing paranoia among the British that ended in the 1903 invasion of Tibet led by Francis Younghusband.)

Przhevalski thus never knew that the horses named after him existed in fair numbers in the mountains he crossed as he headed south into China. Indeed, their far eastern end were, and are, named after the animals: Takhin Shar Nuruu, the Yellow Range of the Przhevalski Horse. Only eleven years after his death were the first ones caught – seven foals, captured on an expedition financed by Friedrich Falz-Fein, the owner of the first private wildlife park on his estate in Askania Nova, in the Ukraine. A further expedition in 1901 captured another fifty-two foals, which were sold on to half a dozen zoos and parks in Europe and the US. This operation was double edged. It intensified the decline in the wild, for to seize a foal the mother was shot, but it granted Przhevalski's horse a new lease of life in captivity.

Though still a precarious one. Only in a few places – New York, Cincinnati, Woburn, Halle, Askania Nova itself – did the foals breed, for their genetic base was too restricted for a healthy species. After the war only thirty-one survived, bearing the genes of just thirteen individuals. Despite the risk of inbreeding, new foals were born, survived and sold. A stud book keeping track of all zoo-bred Przhevalskis was opened in Prague in 1960. Now, around the world in dozens of zoos and private parks, there are some 1,500 of the creatures born over thirteen generations, enough to save the species.

In the wild, the decline continued. Isolated by geography, restricted by human pressure, the takhi were now persecuted anew, by the harsh climate, by people. The Mongolian zoologist Dulamtseren, now sixty-four, was born in the area Przhevalski crossed, and he remembered seeing one when he was a six-year-old in the 1930s. 'My parents told me that in the spring and autumn, the takhi were in the lowlands, and in the summer went up into the mountains.' But by then they were rare indeed, and near their end. In the 1940s, Kazakhs were allowed to settle in the area, and shot them for food. The growing military presence as Mongolia sealed its borders, first against the Japanese then against the Chinese, forced them into ever more restricted and infertile areas. In the Yellow Mountains of the Takhi, the last redoubt of Przhevalski's horse in the wild, a solitary male was spotted in 1968 and two adults, too distant to see the sex, in April 1969. Since then, nothing but rumour.

Yet with luck I might be able to see them back in their homeland. Months before, when researching this trip, I learnt that some of those zoo-bred survivors had been brought back. It was the start of a great experiment to return the species to the wild, to save the raw genetic material from which domestic horses had been bred. Over in Gobi B, the second, smaller, remoter part of the Gobi National Park, there was a takhi reservation: Takhin Tal, the Plain of Przhevalski's Horse.

Back in Bayan Tooroi, Khorloo had come out with some startling information. She mentioned casually that some new horses were due to be flown in soon, that day, the next day.

'What? Erdene, can she discover when? We could see them. I could talk to the people bringing them in.'

But there was no easy way to find out, except by going there. Takhin Tal, the furthest west I could hope to go with Erdene and Byamba, had always been my goal. Now there was real urgency. The sooner we left the better.

It looked as if we should head directly west through high mountains. But we took Choinjin's advice, deciding to veer south towards the Chinese border, then north through the Yellow Mountains of the Takhi. It was longer that way, but the mountains were lower, and we would be able to pick up fuel at the town of Altai (another one: there are several with the same name). Besides, on my map there was a nice brown line supposedly marking a road all the way to Takhin Tal. We had 400 kilometres of desert travel ahead of us. It would take all day, if we were lucky. If not, we would camp en route.

We headed back past Sacred Mother, past the brief splash of greenery at her base. We drove south, through soft, saxaul-strewn sand, then climbed fast across flat, smooth gravel speckled by cushion-like thorn bushes tight as curled-up hedgehogs. The way ahead was blocked by a range, the Aj Bogd. Skirting it, we crossed badlands of gravel and small stones, easy going, but hostile to herdsmen and wildlife alike. For mile after mile, there was no sign of human existence, other than the tracks we were following. In hours, as we turned with the sun towards the west in the lee of the Aj Bogd, the only living things I saw were three gazelles and one hawk.

Then, in the distance, two men appeared on horseback, and three camels grazing in the distance, and something else: a beer bottle beside the track. We were on a truck route to the Chinese border. I thought: this is pristine wilderness. People really shouldn't do that. When Erdene prepared to sling out an empty water bottle, I stopped him.

'What harm?'

'Erdene, look.' To one side, there was another glint of glass on the greys and browns of the desert. We saw not a single vehicle on this section of the wilderness, but enough thirsty drivers passed this way to mark their progress with refuse. We counted the bottles. There were about half a dozen every mile.

Into Erdene's blank expression I read a mild judgement. A bottle, every few hundred metres? So what? I shut up, and considered. In the West, a discarded bottle means carelessness, thoughtlessness, pollution, irresponsibility, the mixing-up of recreation land with rubbish land, the threat of cut feet and forest fires. But here ... What harm indeed was done by the presence of a few bottles in a slab of desert the size of a country? The glass could have been there for years already, and there could be a hundred times as many bottles without anyone or anything being changed or damaged. I wondered if I was suffering from environmental hypochondria. Perhaps these bottles were only rubbish because I saw them as such. Perhaps I should revise my ideas, and see the glass as a mineral among minerals, not the beginning of the end for a pristine wilderness. I didn't know what to feel. Guilty of being a western-style litter lout, embarrassed by my guilt, I secretly hoarded our bottles, and disposed of them back in Ulan Bator, in a dustbin, where rubbish is unquestionably rubbish and I didn't have to think about it any more.

By now it was almost dark, and it was obvious we would have to sleep out. I was beginning to look around for likely campsites, hoping for a picturesque outcrop with an apron of gravel in front of it, when we cut down through the foothills of the Aj Bogd, and saw a flag, a building, a barrier, a uniformed guard.

We were at a military post.

Erdene offered my passport, while I sat mute. The guard vanished towards the building, a shadow in the dusk. An officer appeared. Children gathered. One looked inside the minibus and said, in English, 'Good morning.' Byamba offered cigarettes to the soldiers while they discussed our case.

'We are supposed to have permission from the Ministry of Defence in UB,' said Erdene.

'But how could we know that?'

'We could not. But it is a military area.'

'They didn't even tell us in Bayan Tooroi.'

'I have no passport,' Erdene said. 'I think I will have to go to prison for a few days.'

'Are you serious?'

'Oh, very serious. You see lights over there?' He pointed across the band of darkness to the south, where a car headlight wove hesitantly at some indefinable distance. 'That is China. Very dangerous.'

There was a crescent moon, and above the darkness of China, a line of clouds lit red by the sun, now well below the horizon. The clouds struck me as a remarkable feature, lying low in a pure sky of darkening blue. I wondered for a moment about some distant industrial city, then realized they were not clouds at all.

'Erdene, look: mountains.' It was a startling and beautiful sight, those snows floating above their darkened bases, marking the far reaches of the Chinese Gobi, or Dzungaria. They were the eastern end of the Tien Shan. A glance at the map when I got back home showed they were 250 kilometres away.

We were, of course, merely an administrative problem, not a political one. We could pay. Forms would be filled out. Erdene would not have to go to prison. But it was late, and all the work would be better done in the morning. By chance this would be possible, because the military base was also a hostel. The officer, the guard and two wives, one bearing a baby with wild hair, led us into our quarters: a single room with four bedsteads on a platform around the edge, and roughly painted frescoes.

The frescoes showed what I took to be a camel engaged in crushing a bush and a dog attacking a large black bird in snow, while a horseman looked on. Later, I discovered from Erdene I had completely mis-understood. The camel was rutting, and was marking the bush with its scent. The large black bird was attacking, not being attacked – it was a hunting eagle seizing a small fox, and the horseman was the eagle's Kazakh owner. In this isolated frontier region, someone had taken care to make sure strangers were reminded of home, whether they came from desert or mountain.

Now came supper: salty milky tea, Parmesan-like curd, stewed mutton and rice, and a vast saucepan of fresh yoghurt. We each had one bowl, which was licked clean after each course. There was even running water. It ran into a basin from a little tank hanging on the wall, which contained about two pints of water. For the Gobi, this was plentiful, enough to clean teeth. There could be no thought of tackling socks and underpants, which had been maturing nicely ever since we left UB.

We went out to look after our horses, picking our way gingerly over a newly dug trench – drains, perhaps, or a defence against a billion Chinese – and stood in silence beneath a bowl of diamonds set in velvet. I had never seen a night of such purity, with not a wisp of smoke or distant neon glow to dull it. With skies like that, the Mongols would have been great astronomers, if they had ever had fixed abodes. As it was, with the practicality of sailors, they saw significance in little more than Polaris, 'the Golden Stake' for the circling stars.

Perhaps, though, there was more. When I told Erdene the various names of Polaris's nearby constellation – the Plough, the Big Dipper, the Little Bear, Ursa Minor – Erdene stared up. 'We call it the Seven Gods,' he said, using the word that also means Buddha. The Seven Gods, the Seven Buddhas: a hint that those who worshipped the Blue

Sky also recognized divinity of a kind in its glittering counterpart.

The luck of the wild ass

The next morning, leaving that sparkling view of the Tien Shan behind, we dropped into a well-watered town, Altai, for fuel and military permissions to get us through any other road blocks. In this substantial and much-dispersed place, the main administrative office was beside a football ground where squaddies jogged round, in the style of the US military, boots thumping. Here, since we had no idea of the best route, Erdene asked advice, a conversation that flushed out a teenager who wanted a lift to Takhin Tal. He said he knew the way well, which was good news. Then on, veering south, skimming the border, past a line of trucks piled with bales of camel hair waiting to cross into China, and westwards, and at last north, across open desert towards mountains.

But this was wrong. We shouldn't have been heading towards mountains yet, we should have been running parallel with them. We were still not far enough to the west. Our young guide was looking worried. We were on a track, following tyre marks, but they were definitely leading us in the wrong direction. We had missed a turn somewhere behind us. Or maybe the turn was still ahead.

We pressed on, always north, always closer to the wrong mountains, ever more anxious, until Byamba became impatient, and veered off westwards. Now we had no tracks to guide us. As we swerved between camel thorns, and bumped up and down outwash gullies, I became just the tiniest bit anxious.

We overheated. Byamba pulled to a halt, facing into the oven breeze. We got out and stared round. Not a track anywhere. No one had ever been here, and there was no one, no animal, no *thing* – except the mountains, stones and heat-hazed saxauls – in sight.

'Erdene,' I said. 'Do people ever *die* out here?'

'Only in winter. No need to be nervous. We know the direction we should go. There is a road somewhere.'

'But what if the car won't start?'

'We have water.'

'But we can't stay here for ever. I don't much like the idea of walking for help.'

'No, no. The man knows that somewhere there is a main road.' He spoke as if we were near a motorway. 'One day, a car will come.'

'One day!'

'Today, tomorrow.'

'But would they see us?'

'Probably not.' He paused, allowing me just enough time to imagine our whitened skeletons face down beside the minibus. 'But we would see them. They make dust. Then we know where the road is. Then we walk to the road.'

He was right, of course. Anyway, the car cooled, and started, and we drove on, and ten minutes later hit the track we should have been on in the first place. This was not after all a place that people die in, at least not in high summer.

By early afternoon we were on a track in the right range, the Yellow Mountains of the Takhi, climbing a pass between bare rocks, past an oasis with long grass shielded by a tamarisk, and up through a cleft of barren rock, right on the southern fringe of Gobi B. We were in the domain of wild sheep, mountain goats, a few snow leopards.

Suddenly Byamba pointed and shouted: 'There! There!'

A horse-like animal scrambled nimbly down the side of the ravine on our right, galloped in front of us, and then away ahead in a cloud of dust. My mind, of course, had been filled with Przhevalski horses: those that awaited us ahead, the fact that this was the last place they had been seen in the wild, the rumours of their continued existence. I had never seen one in the flesh, even in a zoo, but there was only one conclusion, to which I leapt instantly.

'Stop!'

I grabbed my camera, slammed open the door and sprinted after the beast, pausing to take pictures, astonished that fate should confer upon me the privilege of being the one to bring back proof that the takhi was not, after all, quite extinct in the wild.

I watched, still crazed with excitement, as the animal trotted behind a ridge, reappeared briefly, then disappeared for good.

Erdene came up, panting.

'You took a picture?'

'Oh yes. Wasn't it wonderful?'

'Oh, yes, very lucky.'

'Lucky! It was a miracle! I mean – a takhi!'

'No, no, not takhi. It was a wild ass, a khulan. Did you not hear me shout?'

The excitement drained from me. I felt foolish, and confused. What did he mean – lucky?

'Our friend, he said if anyone see wild ass here, it is a sign of luckiness. There is no water up here, not much wildlife. Khulans up here are *very* rare. It is the first time for me as well. I have never seen khulan before.'

But that was not the only reason we were lucky. During horseraces, the dust of the best horses, the five-year-olds, is very lucky. People run through their dust after they pass. It means a year's good luck. 'Khulan – it is the same as a five-year-old horse,' Erdene finished. 'Byamba is delighted. We drove right through the khulan's dust! A year's good luck for us all!'

After a long climb up to a height of 2,400 metres, we emerged onto a tableland of soft green, then dropped steadily, running parallel to one snow-covered ridge – Alag Khairkhan, the 'Sacred Colourful Range' – and aiming towards another which had that odd rosy tinge I had seen a number of times along the way, an indication of something metallic in the rocks made rusty by exposure. Before we reached the mountains, at the end of a broad and gentle descent, lay a collection of simple brick houses and gers, where we dropped our would-be guide.

Now for the takhi themselves. Not far beyond, on the bank of a river, women were making mud bricks, slapping river-bottom clay into wooden squares and turning them out to dry. Byamba slowed to ask the way.

'Erdene, ask them when the horses get here.' With luck like ours, I thought as Erdene strolled over to the women, perhaps the plane would arrive, by pure chance, just at the same time as us.

Erdene returned. 'The plane came yesterday, they say.'

'Where are the horses?'

'They say to follow the river. The river will lead right to them.'

That river, the life-giving Bij: 300 metres further on, where the track crossed, turf grew as soft and green as an English water meadow. We parked, and for the first time in three days there was water enough to wash. While Erdene and Byamba decorously bathed hands and feet, I stripped naked, crouched to hide from the women upstream, picked my way hunchbacked into the centre of the river, and with little cries of shock and delight lay down full length on the stony bed in the gloriously cold, mountain-fed shallows, letting the icy water bubble away the sweat and dust and grime.

Minutes later, we arrived in Takhin Tal. We swung over a smooth plain, all gravel, with hardly a blade of grass, lined on three sides by mountains, as if we were on the stage of a vast amphitheatre. Or, if you like, the world's largest airport, for the first odd thing about Takhin Tal was a set of approach lights for the cargo planes that brought in the takhis. I stared out over the plain, and could see no sign of any Przhevalski horses. The only life lay right ahead: half a dozen gers, and four horses tethered. The gers were not for herders, for they were all in a line, backed by a protective fence, and each had a wind-powered generator whirring on a pole.

Byamba pulled up by the first. Behind the fence, two men in jeans and T-shirts were loading what seemed to be railway sleepers onto a truck. Children emerged, then a woman, who held back the dog while we filed into the ger for tea and explanations.

The tent belonged to one of the men, Galbadrakh, who acted as driver. An older man, Chinbat, was an environmental officer, and a younger man with glasses, Tsogtsaikhan, was a postgraduate in mammal biology who was preparing a thesis on the takhi. It was Galbadrakh's wife who handed us tea and a bowl of sweet, soft curds squeezed out into the shape of noodles.

Staring round at the gaudy cupboards, the shrine-like collection of portraits, the dado over one of the beds designed to display the Chinese twelve-year cycle of years, eating the rice and the stew, making much of the suckings and slurpings in which everyone indulged, I wondered impatiently: where were the Przhevalski horses?

Not to worry – it was Galbadrakh who was in charge of arrangements – they were close by, in enclosures, very happy. We could see them tomorrow. Today, it was getting late. After we checked our gers – there were two kept specially for visitors – perhaps it would be good to see the wild asses, the khulans? There were many khulans, he said, often up on the nearby slopes this time of day, returning from an oasis in the hills.

Wild asses, the ancestors of the domestic ass, were not what I had come for. But as soon as we were on our way, my spirits rose. The three men came with us, accompanied by Galbadrakh's wife and the two children, nine in all, the locals crowded in the back with me. With the briefest, most tantalizing glimpse of the takhi enclosure – high fences, coarse desert-steppe pasture, distant light-brown figures – we drove away over hard rising ground, lightly dusted with green, towards the westerly line of hills. At once, it was clear this was a rich land, a land for animals, not people, for gazelles by the dozen scooted across in front of us, and there was not a ger in sight.

Chinbat pointed. 'Khulan!'

Half a mile ahead, further up the long incline, was a herd, ambling south. I couldn't see individuals. The setting sun, beyond the hills ahead, haloed the soft cloud of dust around them. Then, as Byamba accelerated towards them, they drifted into focus.

Once upon a time, up into the late 1800s, these animals, grazers which thrived in grasslands and yet could also survive deserts and low mountains, were widespread in the Middle East and Central Asia, leaving only the higher reaches of the Himalayan massif to their rougher-coated relative, the kiang. Steadily losing ground to spreading humanity – in particular to hunters with long-range rifles – khulan are now extinct throughout most of their former range, with small pockets amounting to a few thousand remaining in Iran, India, Afghanistan, Nepal and Turkmenistan.

In Mongolia, though, they survived well enough, living over almost all the Gobi, numbering tens of thousands in the 1940s. Then, for decades, they suffered a sharp decline, mainly because they were hunted. One of the hunters was Roy Chapman Andrews, who was thrilled to have a go at them on behalf of the museum. 'I fired again at 300 yards. He winced, ran a few steps and rolled over, legs waving wildly in the air. We all yelled as he went down. It had been a great race and a new animal had been added to my long list of Asiatic game.'

But industrious hunting by visiting Americans hardly rivalled the impact made by locals. In 1974, a hunter who lived in Bayan Tooroi boasted to Soviet scientists that he used to shoot 300 wild asses a year in what would shortly become Gobi A. Though now legally protected, the khulan are still at risk from hunters. In 1996 newspapers reported that an army captain, after having been contracted by a food company to provide camel meat (anybody can apparently buy anything from anyone under privatization), had found himself unable to fulfil his promises and made a deal with herders to shoot khulan instead. The herders were arrested, but the captain escaped into China.

Once protected, the khulan were, it seemed, hardy enough to endure the combination of aridity and harsh winters in remoter areas, grazing on grasses and wild onions through the summers, eating snow when water sources are frozen, and browsing on shrubs when grasses are covered by snow. Though much about their behaviour remains obscure, they are socially very flexible, sometimes ranging in small groups of two or three – and apparently on their own on occasion, if our experience was anything to go by – sometimes forming bands and herds. Such flexibility allows them to adapt well to changing rainfall, temperatures and plant growth. Now, they are doing well, though how well is still unknown. Recent estimates for the population countrywide range from 6,000 to 15,000.

Ahead of us there were scores, perhaps over a hundred khulan. There was no time to count how many, because at our noisy approach they took off, cutting across our path at a right angle, casting up a denser pall of dust. Byamba altered course, and began to move in on them, approaching diagonally to intercept them. For some reason, they didn't sheer off, but held their course.

These animals have astonishing speed and endurance. Andrews once pursued a wild ass for forty-six kilometres, the first twenty-five being covered at an average of forty-eight kilometres per hour. He stated categorically that '40 miles an hour for a short dash is the greatest speed any of the Mongolian wild asses can reach.'

'I wonder how fast they can go,' I muttered to Erdene. It wasn't a request, certainly no decision to challenge Andrews, merely a question that maybe one of the rangers could answer. Erdene, up in the front beside Byamba, translated.

It was Byamba who seized the moment. As he explained later, he had never seen khulan before, and was keen to find out what they could do. Without saying a word, he moved the bus in closer, accelerating to match their speed, so within a few seconds we were running parallel with them, as if we were one of the herd, part of the beating hooves and the hard, smooth surface and the dust.

'Can you see our speed?' I shouted, above the rattle of the doors, the roar of the engine and the shouts of delight from children and adults.

'Sixty!' called Erdene, reading off the speedometer in kilometres per hour. 'Perhaps you get a picture.'

In the growing excitement, I had forgotten about my camera. I opened the bag, fought the bounces, changed to a wide-angle lens, hoping something would stay in focus, and pressed up to the open window.

'Sixty-five!' Erdene called. We were still losing ground, but Byamba was urging the UAZ on.

'Seventy!'

The khulans looked as if they could gallop like this for a while yet. They would pull away from us if we ran off the hard ground onto softer or rougher going.

'Seventy-one . . . seventy-two!' Erdene yelled.

Now we were gaining on them, inching ahead of the leaders, getting a clear view past the dust of the slope beyond them. A perfect shot, except that the camera was bashing my eye, and in my viewfinder the image of the herd kept leaping out of frame.

'No good! Too bumpy!' I yelled, again with no idea of action in mind.

Erdene seized the moment. We were out in front of the herd now, but the race was almost done, for ahead the hard, gentle slope ended in an outwash plain where, at this speed, ravines would batter the bus about like a shuttlecock.

'We stop, OK?'

Byamba meant well, as always. Intent on giving me a stable platform and a clear view, he locked the brakes and hauled on the wheel. We slewed sideways, providing what would have been a perfect view of the oncoming herd, except that all seven of us in the back slid along the seats, crushing each other in two heaps against the side, burying my camera in arms and legs.

Through the window, I saw the world turn to dust again, and with a rush of hooves and shadowy shapes the herd was past. Even before the delighted shrieks of laughter died and Byamba switched off the engine and silence fell, the khulans were gone, with no more than a drifting cloud to mark their progress along the mountainside.

We had eased ahead of them at 72 k.p.h, which meant they must have been making 70 k.p.h, give or take. That's 43 m.p.h., Mr Andrews, not 40: forty-*three*. Not bad going for a herd of donkeys.

It was not pure luck that we had come across this herd.

After seeing them off, we turned, heading back across the same gentle slope, then up and over to see the oasis from which the khulan had come. The ground became soft between clumps of grass, then suddenly sandy. Byamba spun the wheels briefly to test the extent of this pit, and then switched off. The engine needed cooling anyway. Everyone got out, to wander around, smoke, and 'look at horses'. The wheels were in up to the axles. Byamba knelt by the front wheels to lock into four-wheel drive – it was an odd feature of the design that this could only be done by hand, externally.

I joined Erdene and the environmental officer, Chinbat, and asked about the khulans. They seemed to be doing well, for a species once in sharp decline.

He agreed. 'Earlier this year, I made a round trip and counted 3,000 of them' – a figure that made the highest official estimate of 15,000 nationwide seem conservative. '3,000 in an area 40 kilometres across! You will see.'

'I hope so,' I said to Erdene, with a glance at the bus. 'Looks like we're in the shit.'

'Always the shit. So many phrases with the shit.'

'Yes, now you come to mention it. It is a common way to express anger, or trouble, or mess. We could say: the shit has hit the fan.'

He ruminated on the phrase. 'This is a paper fan?'

'No, an electric one.'

'It is going round, the fan?'

'Yes.'

'Ah, I see.' He nodded. 'Big trouble, big mess. Is this the same shit as the shit of the bull? Is this bullshit?'

'No, just any old shit.'

'How does the shit get to the fan?'

'I don't know. Perhaps somebody throws it.'

'Mm. For exactitude you should say: the fan has hit the shit.'*

We stared at the bus, exhaust-deep in sand.

'Well, are we?' I asked, looking round at the far, snowy mountains, the miles of scattered grass clumps, the sand, the gravel.

'Are we what?'

'In the shit.'

'Oh, not to worry. The car is good.'

So it proved. Byamba started the engine, accelerated, engaged, and the bus scooted backwards onto harder ground. We were back on course, over gently rolling hills.

Far off, where a plain rolled up into exposed rock, I could see puffs of smoke, spotlit by the slanting sun. It was as if there was an artillery

---

* The origin of this expression has since been the subject of research. Emeritus Professor Charles Bawden, formerly Reader in Mongolian at the School of Oriental and African Studies, revealing an unsuspected familiarity with urban mythology, recalls the story of a New Yorker caught short in an office block and finding relief in a ventilation shaft. 'On descending, comforted, he finds total chaos, and is confronted by the office manager (or landlord, for versions vary) with the enquiry: "Where were you, buddy, when the shit hit the fan?"'

A family portrait, framed by wilderness.

Above A herdsman's ger in the Gobi-Altai.
Below The Altai from the north, under the first snow of winter.

Above A herd of camels on the move, shedding winter wool.
Below Tom McCarthy with sedated snowleopard.

Above A herdsman. Tsogt, Altai mountains, 1996.
Below Ruins of a desert monastery.

Top Dinosaur eggs at Bayan Zag (the Flaming Cliffs), 1923.
Bottom Roy Chapman Andrews in the desert, 1928.

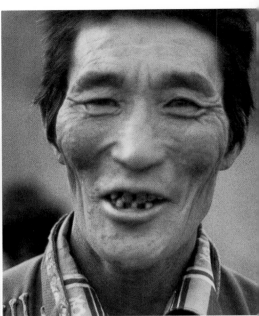

Above left The Wolf Man, Badamtsetsen.

Above right Baatar, herdsman
in the Three Beauties.

Right Natsagdorj, No. 5 on the Mongolian
Railways payroll.

Below 1950s trans-Gobi train,
on display by Ulaanbaatar station.

Above The Lama's Cave,
Eej Khairkhan.

Left & below
Wrestlers in training, near Bulgan.

Above Sami, the oil company chef, from Lebanon, via the North Sea to the eastern Gobi.

Right Tsend with a baby black-tailed gazelle in Gobi 'A'.

Below John Man in a chill wind from the Altai foothills.

duel in progress. In fact, it was herds of khulan on the move, too far off for individual animals to be seen. As we drove, the cloud spread until the rosy peak seemed entirely separated from its shadowy base by the dust. Within an hour, I must have seen, or almost seen, a good percentage of Chinbat's total. By comparison with the emptiness of the eastern Gobi and the desiccation of Gobi A, this part of Gobi B was a full and rich place.

And, for the Gobi, well watered. As dusk drained the colour from the landscape, we arrived at the oasis, another of those desert emeralds, a bubbling stream in the lee of a crag, a meadow, a slice of Alpine lushness. It was even dotted with yellow flowers that looked just like buttercups. Here, sheep might safely graze, if there had been any herders around. As it was, khulan and gazelle had the place to themselves.

As we headed back to camp in the gathering gloom, I thought what a treat this place would be for anyone wanting to experience a living wilderness, if only they could get there.

'Do they get many visitors here?'

Erdene passed on Chinbat's reply. 'Besides the people who flew in with Przhevalski horses yesterday and the people involved with the park, not many.'

'How many visitors from outside, from abroad, this year?'

'He says you are the first.'

I was beginning to see how lucky I was. And I still had not seen the park's greatest treasure.

Face to face with the wild horses

Dawn: I awoke in my ger, and stepped outside. It was a soft morning, with the sun rising behind high clouds. Seized by the clarity and the silence, I stood and listened. Not a breath of wind, not a sound of any sort from the gravel plain before me or the distant mountain walls or the line of hills where the khulans had galloped. No machine whirred, no horse snorted, no voice came from the nearby gers, no bird called. It was another moment like that on the pinnacle of the Sacred Mother mountain, that odd feeling both of isolation – on the edge of thousands of square kilometres of empty land – and of support. This was one of the emptiest places on earth, but without networks of other people – Erdene, Byamba, Mongolists and wildlife experts, geologists and historians, my family, my publishers – this isolation would have been impossible in the first place, and if possible then unbearable. What made those infinite spaces beautiful rather than terrifying was the knowledge that I was not really alone, merely a tourist in a lonely land, and far from suffering. Freed of all distraction, I held my breath, and listened for my own heartbeat, for the blood pumping through my veins. I sensed nothing. There was no wind to move clouds, or dust, or bushes. No sound, no movement, no scent, no warmth yet in the sun, no cold remaining in the air. The only sensation was through the eyes: the desert, the mountains, the hills.

A bird twittered. The mood broke, and I turned to action. I had to pee and shave, using water from the Thermos provided by the Galbadrakhs the previous night. Erdene appeared from the next-door ger. A dog barked, a voice called. We were off to see the takhis.

Over breakfast, Chinbat was keen to talk, to make me feel, as he did, the importance of the takhis. He began by recalling the Mongolians' tradition of national parks, from the first one in the eighteenth century to the establishment of the Gobi National Park when the Cold War was still at its height. We allowed the takhi to disappear, he said, so we have an obligation to get it back, to restore what we lost. It is a symbol of something the Mongolians need to remember, that economy and ecology are one.

I said I hoped I could get close to the animals. That would be hard, the postgraduate, Tsogt, said. They were wild at heart, untamable, with a natural instinct for self-protection that made them aggressive. True, when they first arrived they were used to people, and might even eat from your hand if they knew you. But the main difference from domestic horses – besides the physical differences like the erect mane and the uniform sandy colouration – was the wildness. That was their protection, that was what had to be conserved if they were to survive. So it was the rule that people had as little to do with them as possible. In the course of a few months they learnt to be wild again. I simply wouldn't be able to get close.

Again, we all piled into the bus and drove off over the plain. Despite my feeling of isolation in an infinite wilderness, we were not, after all, far from our goal, which lay down a gentle slope, where the river Bij followed a gravel embankment. Here were five wire-fence enclosures, 136 hectares in all, holding thirty horses.

Approaching between two fences, the horses were hard to see, pale sand against pale sand, and besides, they were skittish. In the first enclosure a female and a foal trotted away from the fence well before we got near. But our goal was the other area, for that was where the new arrivals had been penned.

A few metres inside the fence, two and a half metres of criss-cross wire fitted to sturdy wooden uprights, were six Swissair horseboxes standing open. And beyond, fifty metres away over the clumps of rank long grass and gravel patches, were the horses themselves, a stallion and five females trotting restlessly back and forth, back and forth.

'That is what new arrivals always do,' said Tsogt. 'Moving around all the time.'

'Exploring?'

'Yes. They've just come from a zoo, so this is all new to them. Imagine, two days ago in Zurich.'

I needed to get close, but it was obvious that if I merely circled the fence they would pull away at my approach, leaving me a long walk, simply to have the same thing happen again.

'So if they're zoo-bred, perhaps they're not so wild after all,' I said. 'Perhaps we can approach them.'

Tsogt shook his head. 'No, no, they must become wild.'

'I understand. But I think it might be good to have close-up pictures. For the sake of Mongolia.' As Erdene translated, I could see Tsogt relenting. 'Tell him I could go alone,' I added.

That seemed to do it. Tsogt reached out and began to unwind a tangle of wire locking the gates. 'If they are nervous, you will leave?'

'At once.'

'OK.'

He pulled the gate open for me, and I went in.

The story of how all the takhis came to be here is something of a soap opera, a saga of dreams and jealousies, petty disputes and serious science, and not a little egomania. The cast is international and varied, including zoo people in Prague, Cologne and Marwell (near Winchester, England), and three private foundations in Switzerland, Germany and Holland.

It is hard now to say who first had the idea of returning Przhevalski horses to the wild. I would put my money on a Swiss architect, Werner Stamm. For him, architecture was a way to earn a living. 'I don't tell people I am an architect,' he used to say, 'because our generation of architects spoiled the world with horrible buildings.' His real passions were quite different. As an ex-cavalry officer, Stamm loved dressage and as the inheritor of his father's farm near Basel, he loved the natural world. Horses and nature – those were his twin obsessions, so much so that when he became an international judge in dressage he made a point of going to the zoo wherever he was called upon to judge. In 1968 he was in Prague, where he saw his first Przhevalski horses. It was love at first sight.

This story was told to me back in Ulan Bator by Stamm's widow, Dorothee. Imagine a sturdily built, round-faced lady in her seventies, speaking in accented English, in love with her husband's memory, her husband's cause and the animals to which she too had dedicated her life. At crucial moments, her eyes would fill with tears. I found her utterly endearing.

The first Przhevalskis, a stallion and two mares, arrived at the Stamms' farm in 1971, from Rotterdam Zoo, followed by two other purchases from Munich and Prague. And right from the beginning Werner Stamm was adamant. 'My husband always said that in the far, far away future they will go back to their motherland. So for that reason, he said, we must domesticate them as little as possible. Nobody was allowed to touch a horse, nobody was allowed to feed a horse by hand.'

This was pure altruism, a passion, not for profit. Though Werner Stamm bought many horses himself, he never sold any, always offering them on permanent loan, so that the new 'owners' could not sell them on at a profit either. The house was a private one in the middle of farmland, so it could not be used as a zoo. 'It was sacrosanct as farmland, you see, which was why they were allowed to build stables. Besides, if you have the public, you have to have car parks, toilets, a shop. No, no, it was just for the Przhevalskis.'

Werner Stamm died in 1984, leaving Dorothee to administer his estate, and his dreams, which she would fulfil only eight years after his death.

Meanwhile, the subject of the horse and its reintroduction had taken off. Though zoo-bred animals ensured the survival of the species, it became clear through the 1970s that zoos could not provide a complete answer. The problem of the narrow gene base could be partly solved by an exchange of horses between zoos; but zoos were not breeding stations and could not absorb increasing numbers. Better that nature should be allowed to take its course, with extended breeding and the strengthening, winnowing effects of wild living. There was only one answer: reintroduction.

This concept opened up new sets of problems, of politics, of ecology, of sociology, each with their potential for misunderstanding and rivalry.

The first practical steps were taken by a German businessman, Christian Oswald, who imported and exported game. His speciality was deer; in fact, he opened a museum in Munich dedicated to nothing but deer. Like many who exploit nature, he also had a sense of responsibility towards nature. What is taken, he felt, should be returned. With deer, he found no easy way to achieve this aim. Przhevalski horses, though, were another matter. In the 1970s he visited Mongolia, established relations with the Communist government, talked of a reintroduction programme; and encountered suspicion, prevarication, bureaucracy, resistance.

Undaunted, he turned to China, which proved receptive. In 1985 five Przhevalskis from Munich Zoo were flown to an enclosure in Xinjiang, to Jimsar, some 290 kilometres southwest of Takhin Tal. It was a start, but no more, for the Chinese kept their horses behind a wall and did not intend to release them back into the wild for years, if ever.

In a parallel development, a Dutch couple, Inge and Jan Boumann, had set up their own foundation for reintroduction, building up a herd of some seventy horses through the 1980s.

Oswald's experiment in China, combined with the growing interest, had an unexpected effect. The Mongolians, needled by China's response, suddenly showed an intense interest in Przhevalski horses and in collaboration, with Oswald, with the Boumanns, with those zoos interested in the subject of reintroduction.

At this point, tensions surfaced. For who was to decide which horses should go, and how many? Until then, information was paramount, and there had been good collaboration between zoos and private foundations. Now, though, the stakes were higher. If horses were to be reintroduced, they had to be top-quality horses, and who better to decide on the quality of a Przhevalski horse than the most experienced breeder, which happened to be Cologne Zoo? From here, the headquarters of the EEP – the Europäische Erhaltungszucht Programm (the European Conservation and Breeding Programme) – the decree went out. Stud books were examined, every characteristic analysed. Przhevalski horses should be between this and that in height. Black hairs were banned. Super-fair hair was banned. And since those who would actually be *paying* to send horses – the private foundations – had a full range of colours and sizes to hand, the result was inevitable: a break between the zoos on one hand and the private foundations on the other.

'It was so silly,' says Dorothee Stamm, 'because everyone agrees there were a lot of colours in the wild. My husband always said that nature should make the selection.'

Another bone of contention was the EEP's decision to limit breeding. 'The zoos are full, so they say all those with Przhevalski horses must not breed for several years. They come to us and say, "You are not allowed to breed any more." And we said, "We are a breeding station! We are not a zoo! Our animals have no value as show animals!" What should we do? Give up our work? Nobody knows by what right they tell us such things.'

Another thing: where should the horses be released? In this dispute, with its very practical implications, it was the private foundations that were in dispute; nothing acrimonious, but a certain rivalry. Some, principally the Boumanns, argued that Przhevalskis were originally steppe animals, and should be taken back to grassland. Others – including Oswald himself – pointed out that the takhis were last seen in the far southwest, in the harsh lands of the mountains named after them, and that self-evidently they should be replaced in the area they last colonized. Ah, countered the steppe-landers, but they were in the desert only because they were forced out of the steppes. Once, they were living all over Asia. They only became desert animals because they were driven there, not to live but to die. Why return them to the place where they died? Why not return them to the place where they lived?

The result, just before and just after the Communists were ousted, was two agreements, for *two* Przhevalski horse reserves, one for the Dutch on steppe-land not far from Ulan Bator, signed with the non-governmental body MACNE (Mongolian Association for Conservation of Nature and the Environment); the other for Christian Oswald in Gobi B. The first horses came into both reserves in 1992.

Dorothee Stamm learnt of the pent-up antagonisms when she attended a conference at Marwell Zoo in 1993. 'There they talked a lot of bad things about Mr Christian Oswald. Within the EEP, they said, "No one is allowed to give animals to Christian Oswald, because it's bad what he is doing." I thought they must be a bit jealous because he has all the connections and the money, and they didn't, and I think it

Above The Lama's Cave,
Eej Khairkhan.

Left & below
Wrestlers in training, near Bulgan.

Above Sami, the oil company chef, from Lebanon, via the North Sea to the eastern Gobi.

Right Tsend with a baby black-tailed gazelle in Gobi 'A'.

Below John Man in a chill wind from the Altai foothills.

was they who wanted to be the first ones to release Przhevalskis into the wild. So I wrote to Mr Oswald, and he came to see me, and we said, "Goodbye EEP!" I agreed to give him some of my horses.'

With this second batch, transported courtesy of Swissair, she flew with Christian Oswald's nephew Franz from Basel to Beijing, and on to Ulan Bator, and finally Takhin Tal, arriving the day before I did to a huge and moving reception. Almost all the locals were out at the runway, dressed in deels. A dozen people lifted each horsebox out of the plane and onto the truck, to be carried down to their enclosure. 'It was so moving. I thought: what a shame my husband could not see this. When the horses came out, they did not seem to be nervous at all. They walked round, sniffed, and started to eat. The Mongolians said, "They are kissing their homeland." '

That summer of 1996, there were fifty-eight takhis in Hustain Nuruu and thirty in Takhin Tal. Both were on the verge of re-establishing wild communities. Indeed, the experiment had already been tried in the Gobi, when six horses were released, only to be brought back in again for the winter. And the foal I saw when we drove to the enclosures was the first offspring to be born to a mare who had herself been born here. It had become a breeding community.

I stepped slowly across the coarse grass and gravel. The horses, crossing the centre at a restless trot about 100 metres away, stopped, gathered in a huddle, and stared. Despite what I had been told, the stallion seemed reticent. It was a female who moved first, walking towards me, leading the others. I could see that they were not, after all, all the same colour, any more than different types of sand are. One, the stallion, was a darker tan, and the others had subtle shadings in their soft greys and light browns. One had the delicious tones of the crust on newly baked white bread. I paced forward, cautiously, feeling as if I were a witness to something rare and precious.

Of course, I could hope to get close only because these were still zoo animals, hemmed in by wire. That was one reason I felt moved. A dozen of their generations ago – only two or three in human terms – the ancestors of these creatures had stood there, against these same snow-capped mountains, and in view perhaps of gers like those just visible up the long and easy slope. Those ancestral horses would have been very edgy, out here in the open, for any ger would have spelled danger, and the presence of an outsider, a European, would have meant captivity or death. Now here were the descendants, back for keeps, in safety, thanks to the involvement of Europeans. Europeans had played a role in the creatures' decline; now, in restitution, they had played a role in the horses' salvation.

Suddenly, when I was about forty metres away, the six took fright, and trotted away, across to the wire, then along it, and back, swishing through the long grass, before coming to rest again. Again, I approached, until I could see their white muzzles and mohican manes, hear their shuffling hooves. The same female paced forward. They let me get to within about fifteen metres, and we stood in silent confrontation.

Listening to the soft breath, noticing how the pastel brown shaded into darker hair on the legs, looking at the mud splashes on the underbelly of one of the females, I became hypnotized by their attention. I realized then that we, the horses and I, were all on the brink of irreversible change. They were destined for wildness, and this was, quite possibly, the closest an outsider would come to them from now on. The next foreign visitor would find them wary and distant. If I ever came here again, they would keep well away; they might even be out there, with the khulan, and would take care never to be close enough or still enough to meet my gaze so directly for so long, before shearing away with thudding hooves.

As I write now, it is months later. Those horses will be facing their first winter, standing out in icy winds that sear their pasture, freeze their water, cut into their thickening coats. There may be a death, or two. But from this Spartan regime, the survivors will emerge stronger than they would be in any zoo.

Both reserves are mere beginnings, and both are test tubes in which no one has any idea what will happen. This is a genuine experiment in biology, the outcome of which will take decades to emerge. Over that period, the horses will be part of an ecological mix involving developments in the country as a whole. As the population grows – current estimates predict a doubling to 4 million over the next few decades – so pressure on the countryside will increase.

The 60,000 hectares of the Hustain Nuruu reserve can hold some 300–400 horses, but it is surrounded by grazing land; and Przhevalski horses, remember, were not popular with herders eager to protect their grazing, protect their mares and maybe short of food. The horses must always be protected, against herders, against wolves, or they will perish as they did before. And if they survive, how wild, in the end, will they really be?

In Takhin Tal, where the horses will have more space, they will have less protection. Wolves could become a menace. The water may dwindle, and with it the food supply. It is possible that this experiment, too, will end as the horses ended: in another extinction.

At present no one believes this. The inspiration is right there, in the thriving wild asses. The khulans are a model, perhaps, for the takhis. They have similar needs, similar problems, and they have come back from decline. Having seen the drifting clouds of dust kicked up by khulan, I could daydream, for which I had ample time over the next three days.

We set off back to Ulan Bator by another route, cutting through the mountains to the east, through towering grey foothills rounded and stubby as elephants' feet, along a trail that shrank into a rocky pass that was also a river. Then, in the mountains, we were lost. In a high valley, we stopped at a ger, where the biggest Mongol I have ever seen, all 6'4" of him dressed in black, offered tea, and then turned out to be slurringly and aggressively drunk. When he asked for a lift to the next town, I knew it was time to go. When a companion tottered in and collapsed in a maudlin heap at my feet, Erdene agreed. We left, suddenly, too fast for our staggering host to follow.

'They had been cutting children's hair,' Erdene explained. 'They do that when the child reaches three or four, and invite people, and drink. Do not think it is just the Mongols who drink. Russians and Chinese, too, are famous drinkers.'

Two hours later, we were still lost. The track divided, one way leading along the rolling crests, another dropping into a valley. Up or down?

'You decide.'

'OK. We will take the low road,' I said, for far below I could see a plain, and knew we would have to be on the plain eventually to skirt the end of the mountains.

I should have known what to expect. My advice fell like snow on a hot stove. Byamba drove off on the high road.

Later, when Byamba had found his way down to the desert on his own terms, we were still lost. Again the road divided. Again I was asked to decide.

'This one is more used.'

'OK. We take it.'

'But' – I glanced at the sun, the mountains, the map – 'it goes the wrong way.'

'Maybe it goes around.'

So we took it anyway and, feeling our way like mariners, we hove into our next port of call, Tseel. I was beginning to feel as if I really had a role to play on this trip. All I had to do was offer advice, and then we would do the opposite, and get where we wanted to go. Thus at last we came full circle, back to Tsogt, where I had met the man who caught a snow leopard, and after a brutally cold night in the mountains, on to Ulan Bator.

My daydream, as we wound and bounced across desert and mountain and steppe, was this. In twenty years' time, I return, for old times' sake, along the original route through the Yellow Range of the Takhis. This time when an animal bursts from the rocks, it is a takhi, and as we speed through its dust, I find luck at once, for up on the open high ground is a cloud against a hill, and I hear the sound of distant hooves.

Where once the wild horses galloped, they gallop again, this time safe from the threat of extinction.

6

The Three Beauties

Once upon a time there was a rich man with three beautiful daughters. The three daughters fell in love with three poor men. Their father forbade them from marrying, and the three daughters were so unhappy they ran away into the desert. They are there to this day: the Three Beauties of the southern Gobi.

Back in Ulan Bator, I saw an advertisement in the capital's English-language newspaper, the *Mongol Messenger*, singing the praises of the Three Beauties, which you could visit if you stayed at a desert tourist camp. It hadn't occurred to me that the Gobi would attract tour groups. I wanted to know more.

A little research revealed that there had been, before 'transition', no less than five tourist camps in the southern Gobi, which could accommodate a total of 500 people at once – up to 8,000 people a year. Some camps had closed, but not the one advertised, which was the grand-daddy of them all, having been running since the early 1960s. Though privatized in 1993, it had always been run by Juulchin, the official tourist agency, the Mongolian equivalent of Intourist, and with a similar reputation for high-priced bureaucratic bumbling. According to the advertisement, Juulchin still ran it.

But the man who answered the phone, in good English, did not divulge his business, and he was not a bureaucrat. 'Can you come?' he asked insistently, when I introduced myself. 'We can meet today, this afternoon, tomorrow?'

'But is that Juulchin?'

'Perhaps,' he said. 'You come here, we discuss everything. Our office is in the Building of Wrestling.'

If only to solve the mystery, I fixed a time, and he gave me a street and a number. It seemed easy. But finding your way in Ulan Bator is rather like navigating in the desert. You can't get lost exactly, because the spaces are large, landmarks obvious and buildings few. But maps are scarce, and out of date or just plain wrong, and drivers ignorant. This was because there had been a boom in foreigners, and a dearth of taxis, creating a gap in the market into which members of the public had leapt. To get a 'taxi' you simply stood with your arm up and someone would stop. Instant tradition dictated the amount charged. It was a system that worked only for major hotels, embassies and public buildings. Mere citizens do not have a Mongolian equivalent of The Knowledge that infuses London cab drivers. Mongolian would-be cab drivers are deeply versed in The Ignorance. Unless you can describe the route to be taken *as you take it*, you have to resort to desert tactics: stop and ask. In this case, even asking did not help. I gave up, and phoned again, to receive even more detailed instructions, discovering that the place I wanted was only a few minutes' walk from my starting point.

The Building of Wrestling was a seedy monument to socialist architecture, with no sign of any wrestlers. I climbed four barren flights, and found a more promising world of new wooden doors and clean glass. This was not the office of Juulchin, but of a company calling itself Ajnai, a term for a truly exceptional horse. In an office geared for capitalism – large desk, multiple phones, computer, fax – presided a sleek-haired and overweight man in his mid-thirties. His name was Sukhe, and he was one of those brash post-Communist newcomers busy galloping away with Mongolia's state industries, in this case Juulchin. Having acquired a controlling interest in bits of Juulchin, Sukhe now dreamt of capitalizing on Juulchin's turgid operations, adding something new and zesty of his own. He was Juulchin or Ajnai, as market appeal dictated. On this adaptable foundation, he planned to open his slices of Mongolia, and the Gobi in particular, to tourists *en masse*. His dreams made him an enthusiast, and keenly internationalist, shot through with a nervy insecurity.

'John, you must tell me. How is my English? Is my pronunciation good? Perhaps it could be better.'

'No, it's very good.'

'Really?'

Yes, really. He was no academic, but for someone who had not been to England or America, he spoke astonishingly well.

'That is because I had a very good teacher, a very beautiful teacher, from Manchester. I know Hockney.'

This was a startling revelation. He had not so far shown much appreciation of art.

'*Or roit?* This is Hockney. *Or roit?* It is good, my Hockney?'

Oh, *Cockney*. Well, yes, not bad, like the rest of his pronunciation, though like many Mongolians he had a small problem with his f's and p's.

'Oh, John, I am too pat. I have a faunch.'

'Paunch, Sukhe.'

'Yes. I have a paunch. Thank you.'

'But don't worry. A few trips to the Gobi will help.'

'Yes. I make trips, I make video of everything we do. In the old days, there was one itinerary. We plan five.' He went into a patter, selling me his dreams. 'Many people will come, maybe some even from Africa. You know, sir, I have seen many people from America and Europe, but never I have seen an African person. Many people, all the year round. Many people from Malaysia. One beautiful Malaysian lady, she told me that because in Malaysia they do not have winter, Malaysian people have never seen snow. John, we have snow! It is cheaper to fly to Mongolia than to Switzerland, so we show them snow! Many Japanese will come. The Japanese, they see many sunrises over the ocean, but never over the desert. They will get up at 5.00 a.m. with camera and video and tape recorder, and they will make their records. They will see the sun light up the mountain, like in a theatre. This they have never seen before.'

I smiled encouragingly, and sipped my coffee.

'And many other things. You know that in the south Gobi there lived dinosaurs, in the place called – ' he concentrated ' – Flaming Cliffs. You know, sir, the film *Jurassic Fark*? Where the dinosaurs are found, that is where we shall make a dinosaurs creatures fark. No: park, park. This is right? You must tell me. For this I make video. You will help with my video?'

'Sukhe, I'm not –'

'Oh, John, sir, you are great English writer. You will stay in my tent. I will take you to Flaming Cliffs. Japanese will see Englishman speaking English at Flaming Cliffs, and they will all wish to see my dinosaur fark.'

That was what I was afraid of. But put yourself in my position. An hour before, I had not the faintest idea how I would get to the Flaming Cliffs. Now, suddenly, I was offered the fulfilment of a life-long ambition. All I had to do was play the token Englishman and say a few words on a measly promo that no one would ever see, at least no one I knew.

Reader, I shook his hand.

The Flaming Cliffs would be only one episode in a journey through the whole area of the Three Beauties, the most easterly of the rocky archipelagos that juts up through the 'dry sea' of the Gobi. This knotty oval of peaks, canyons, high pastures, sand and gravel is part of a unique area that had been declared a national park only the previous year. By coincidence, when I was in Ulan Bator the Ministry of Nature and the Environment was holding a seminar for those most closely involved in this wilderness at a crucial moment in its development. They were there to begin work on a 'management plan' for the park.

Of the score of people around the conference table, I knew only one, the slim, aging biologist Dulamtseren, who had told me about his homeland, the Gobi National Park. Others included a suave ministry man, two or three managerial types in suits and ties, a western wildlife researcher, a grey-haired, goatee-bearded German working with a German aid agency, a couple of female assistants, and several rangers with faces as contoured as the Three Beauties itself. It was one of these who rose first.

Sangidansranjav, Sangi for short, was the park director. He looked the essence of practicality. His burnished face and his brown working deel spoke of a life of wandering, driving, observing. Now he was facing a new challenge for which he was ill-equipped, the challenge posed by a new loan-word, 'management'. He repeated it, as if it were an unfamiliar species. He had never come across it before in the south Gobi, until three years ago, and now this immigrant term was all around him, cross-breeding with other familiar concepts: control, command, implementation, directive, authority, coordination – he had counted more than thirty terms that overlapped 'management'.

Yet he conceded acceptance, because 'management' promised to protect the Three Beauties and back research into what it contained. Only the previous year, he said, had they worked out its exact size (21,716 square kilometres, which means that the Three Beauties on its own ranks well within the top ten in the world). Only now we are beginning to list and understand its plants, its animals, its rocks, its herding families, its beauty spots.

A ministry man – the vice-minister Shiirevdamba – took up the point, defining 'management' with incisive gestures, as if to carve freefloating hope into manageable bits. Mongolia had all the laws necessary for the protection of nature. Now it was time for action. There would be short-term and long-term goals, groups, teams, advisory bodies, all working to produce the management plan. Above all, he finished, no more words! 'We want to act within two years, but two years is too short if all we do is talk!'

It was down to the biologists to flesh out the high hopes. The brunt was borne by the western wildlife researcher, Richard Reading, a Yale-educated ecologist with the rumpled hair and harried look of the young Dustin Hoffman. In love with big, remote regions, Reading had worked on wildcats in Mexico and bandicoots in Australia, and had recently spent many months surveying the Three Beauties. He talked well, and fast, as if in a hurry to infuse others with his zeal.

Through an interpreter, he grabbed attention by making a scathing remark about the outline of the Three Beauties, pointing to an odd bite taken out of its western section, giving it the shape of a fish. Originally, the park had been officially proposed with parallel north and south boundaries. Then came rumours of gold, and a sudden change of heart from on high. The government removed that chunk, creating the park's fish-tail shape, because they might want to open it up for gold-mining. That action cast in doubt the political commitment to ecology, and showed the need to ensure the park's inviolability, fast. Otherwise, what would happen if some future administration suspected the presence of silver, or manganese, or copper?

Reading had a slide show that compressed months of travel and interviews into minutes, and thousands of criss-crossed hectares into a few square metres of light, squeezing nectar from this seemingly barren region. He spoke of fossil-rich badlands where dinosaur bones lay on the surface and high dunes – the Singing Sands – which emitted a strange ethereal hum when the wind was right. He showed mountains up to 3,000 metres, saxaul forests, salt-lake depressions and gorges. He flashed through sample shots of the 600 species of plants, 3,000 people, 150,000 livestock, 52 species of mammal, 240 species of bird (both resident and migrant). In the remoter mountains, snow leopard and wolves hunted mountain sheep. There had even been that report of a Gobi bear – a party of schoolchildren had actually seen it – which could mean that others had also migrated across open desert from Gobi A.

He ended with a picture of a little boy of six, with a beautiful, broad, burnished face. 'This is the main reason we're here,' he said. 'So that what we see today is still there for his children.'

I needed practical help, and found it in a coffee break from the elderly German with the goatee beard, who introduced himself as the head of a German aid agency, GTZ (Gesellschaft für Technische Zusammenarbeit, the Society for Technical Cooperation). His English was not good, but my German, left over from university and a journalistic posting in Bonn, was still serviceable.

'Just call me Siggy,' he said, handing me his card. 'Everyone does.'

A glance at the card explained why. His surname looked as if he had taken it from the pages of *Astounding Science Fiction* in the 1950s. The card read 'Siegfried Tluczykont'. No wonder he asked terrestrials to call him Siggy.

Siggy was sixtyish, with startling blue eyes and a deeply lined face, but in him was the fire of a man half his age, fuelled by decades of experience in distant places. He was born in Silesia, in the German-speaking borderland which became part of Poland in 1945. He went to university in Poland, learning Russian at the same time, and moved to West Germany to extend his studies, then spent thirty years abroad as an aid worker, mostly in remote and arid regions of French West Africa. He spoke German, Polish, Russian, French, some English, but as yet no Mongolian, for like many others, he found he could achieve more, faster, through good interpreters, rather than taking time to learn the language badly. When 'transition' came – Germans speak of *die Wende*, the turning-point – and government agencies looked towards the ex-Soviet empire, he could offer a unique combination of skills: his love of deserts; his Russian, of course; and his German, for by a quirk of history the Mongolians have a traditional relationship with German language and the culture.

In the 1920s, when newly independent Mongolia sought its first links abroad, the Communist government, with Moscow's temporary approval, began to trade with Germany. It also sent forty schoolchildren to Berlin to be educated. Since there were at the time only some 1,500 children in middle and secondary schools in all Mongolia, this had long-lasting consequences. Though purges took their toll of these privileged children between the wars, some eventually rose to high position. As German speakers, they preserved the cultural and economic link, with Soviet blessing, when East Germany emerged as a Communist power after 1945. Until the recent rise in English, German was second only to Russian as a foreign language.

It was this link that brought Siggy to Mongolia. His peripatetic life might have made him rootless. Far from it: Siggy's experience had made him a citizen of the world, with a passion for democracy and education. Three decades in the field had given him an aversion to socialism, central planning, anything that smacked of authoritarianism. 'You cannot tell people what to do. You can only help them to do what they want to do.' He spoke quietly, intensely, as if imparting a great secret. 'Your task is to help them see what is possible, by talking, asking, demanding reactions and ideas. It has to come from them, you see, *von unten nach oben*, from below to above. What do *they*, the people, want? All you can do is suggest. Then if *they* agree, you can act.' I had seen a good deal of intensity and commitment in Mongolia, but this was of a different order. Siggy struck me as a man of shining goodness.

The messages to him 'from below' were: help us protect our wilderness, help us use our water in the best way. He had advised on the establishment of the park, and on a cooperative venture based on an oasis near Dalanzadgad, the capital of South Gobi 'aimag'. I had to see both operations, he said, *had* to. He would show me himself, except he had to be in China for a conference. In his absence, I should use his apartment in Dalanzadgad, and work in his office, and rely on the help of his German-speaking assistant, Chimgee.

Dalanzadgad was an easy, twice-weekly plane ride away. I booked on a scheduled flight, and arrived at Ulan Bator's airport with an hour to spare. The section where my cab stopped was being reconstructed. Inside, I found bare walls and heaps of bricks, with no sign of other travellers. I had time enough to get to the check-in area. Beyond piles of cement, a glass booth contained the vague form of a uniformed guard, to whom I picked my way.

'Dalanzadgad?'

He nodded, picked up a mobile phone, punched numbers, spoke, listened, and heard something that snapped him to his feet. 'Come!' he said, and led me fast around half-finished breeze-block walls to the runway, then on past sheets of newly laid cement to an empty bus. He pulled himself into the driver's seat, opened the automatic doors for me, then slalomed around piles of hardcore, drawing up sharply by a plane, an old Antonov with its two propellers already turning. Convinced he had saved my day, I shouted thanks, taking the steps two at a time. With a cursory glance at my ticket, an attendant pointed me to the only empty seat. The door slammed, the growling props bit the air, and we were off.

I stared round, panting to regain my breath. The plane was packed with middle-aged Japanese tourists. I was on the wrong flight.

After a few moments of panic – where was I going? How would I get back? – I caught the eye of the only Mongolian, a man with a droopy moustache. He was guiding this group to the south Gobi. I relaxed. I would reach Dalanzadgad an hour early.

I stared down, watching our shadow on the grassland shrink as the plane climbed. Signs of human presence – the white pimples of gers, a field planted in strips to minimize wind erosion, the muddy circles of cattle enclosures – were emblems on a grey-green ground, and car tracks stood out as sharp as scratch marks on new paint. Then, in minutes, the landscape turned monochrome. From rising ground, dry gullies merged, spilling into dust and gravel. Hills flattened into wrinkles, wrinkles smoothed out into a palette of browns, greys and tans. Even when the steppe gave way to desert, there was an occasional ger at the centre of hairline tracks. In the Gobi, here as in the west, the barest land was pasture for someone.

It did not look like a countryside to attract tourists, but as the Mongolian guide said, leaning across the aisle to pass me his card, 'The Japanese people, they like desert, big space. Why? They work hard, all the time around them is peoples, peoples, building, building, building. Only in big space they relax.'

An hour and a half later, standing on a gravel runway that merged with desert to the horizon, the Japanese in their jeans and white floppy hats and money belts snapped each other against the silent Antonov, the plain, the white painted airport building, and the town's lumpish buildings. Happily they filed through a wrought-iron compound, settled into ramshackle buses parked with a litter of jeeps, minibuses and motorbikes, and rolled off in clouds of dust to relax in big space.

Behind the blunt buildings and wooden-fenced gers, saw-toothed mountains, sharp in the crystal morning light, sealed off the horizon about ten miles away. Here, the forces that had thrown up the Altai far to the west ran out. They were the most easterly of the Gobi's mountains, and the last of the Three Beauties.

*   *   *

As the last of the Japanese tourist buses bounced away over the desert, Chimgee arrived with jeep and driver, along with a score of others drawn by the roar of the next flight, the one I should have been on. She was in her thirties, with big glasses, a neat pile of black hair and a crisp white blouse. Under her prim and efficient guidance, Dalanzadgad briefly became home.

Open gravel linked the airport and the town, with its 15,000 inhabitants. Driving the few hundred metres to Siggy's office, and on to his apartment, the town made no sense to me. Apartment blocks stood randomly scattered over the desert, loosely linked by a web of electricity poles and car tracks, but with no streets. Beyond, against the line of mountains, ger compounds ran to the city limits. A single road of pitted concrete led downtown, to a museum, a canal with a line of wispy tamarisk trees, and three hotels that were hardly more than shells. Only one was open. This was where I ate. If you went into the kitchen and accosted the two members of staff directly, you could order rice, mutton and pickled cucumber, with Tiger beer on the side. Near the hotel stood a concrete camel which was peering over its shoulder in a half-squat, as if suffering from a painful stomach upset. Beyond lay a vast and windy space of dust and gravel at the centre of which stood a monument to Mongol–Soviet friendship.

Another flaking concrete obelisk commemorated the local revolutionary heroine, a teenager named Bor who came to a sticky end in 1932. She perished, according to old dogma, crying, 'Long live the Party, the Government and the League of Revolutionary Youth!' Like much else in Mongolia's big-brother past, the truth of what happened has long since been buried beneath sediments of pseudo-history and folklore. She may have died fighting bandits raiding across the border; or committed suicide by throwing herself off a high crag. Or was she killed by the all-purpose enemy, the lamas? Perhaps the uncertainty was deliberate, a way of conferring an aura of sanctity, ensuring that Bor remained forever untarnished by the mundane, to sustain her role as a symbol of Youth struggling for a better world.

In Dalanzadgad, Youth needs all the inspiration it can get. In the face of immense distances, non-existent roads, lack of water, erratic power supplies, and scarce materials, it is a cause for wonder that a town should exist here at all; and no wonder that life in it is a challenge, especially for outsiders.

Siggy's apartment had everything I could wish for: a bedroom, bedding, bathroom, furniture, kitchen with a stove, even a fridge. The inside was fine. It was what had to come in from outside – electricity, water – that led to problems. There was no hot water, but there was a pint-sized heater with a needle-thin pipe that could be directed to deliver a trickle of hot water, either into the basin or into the bath.

This raised the delightful prospect of a hot bath. I should have been warned – no one else had ever done this before, for there was no plug. The ascetic Siggy was obviously content with the cold shower. I created a plug with a rubber washer beneath a glass weighed down by a stone, and set the heater dribbling. After a minute, it had just about covered the floor of the bath. Thinking I could speed things up by heating extra water on the stove, I filled two large pots, placed them on the hotplates, and switched on. Somewhere, something clicked, and the lights went out. Now I had no lights, no stove, no hot water, and did not dare guess at the damage I might have done.

I wandered out into the gathering gloom. Two barefoot teenagers were playing football on the gravel. 'The lights,' I said. 'Gone.' The boys were from the next apartment. Together we looked for a control panel. There was one out in the hallway. Inside, there had to be a trip-switch. But it was locked.

There was only one source of help: Chimgee. I went back outside, looking round for inspiration. Except for the two boys, the whole place looked deserted, as if everyone went in as night fell. I had to find one woman among 15,000, in a town without streets and blocks without numbers.

I walked over to the office. It was locked. On my lonely way back past a compound of gers, my path crossed that of a twelve-year-old girl carrying a Thermos of hot water. She was almost swamped by an oversized dress that gave her the charm of a caricature waif.

I launched into what had by now become a familiar series of intro-ductory phrases, then struggled on. 'Chimgee, of the German company, you know her ger?'

'Chimgee?'

'Yes, of the German company, over there. You know her?'

'Yes.'

'Where is she?'

'Over there,' she said, and pointed. In the gloom, I could not tell which of several apartment blocks she meant. She took pity, indicated for me to wait, deposited her Thermos inside the compound of her ger, and led me back over the gravel. We stopped at Siggy's block.

'Chimgee lives here,' she declared.

'No, no. This, here, Siggy the German's ger. I know. He is my very friendship.'

Luckily, this made sense to her. She called one of the footballers, an eight-year-old boy. Yes, he knew Chimgee, knew where she lived, and would take me. We set off towards a group of apartment blocks, past barking dogs, and entered an unnumbered door in an unnumbered block. He led me up dingy concrete stairs to the third floor, and knocked on a door.

To my relief, Chimgee was in. I explained about the lights.

'Oh, you must have put the stove and the heater on together,' she said. 'It happens.'

We made our way back to Siggy's. On the wall in his apartment hung a key, which opened the locked fuse box. My torch revealed an array of trip-switches. Chimgee clicked one. Siggy's lights flicked on.

Into the Vulture's Gorge

Through Chimgee, I acquired a Russian jeep, a driver, and permission to enter the park. But I lacked an interpreter. Chimgee was not about to subject her clothing to days of desert travel and sleeping rough. A phone call revealed a short-term solution: a Russian teacher who had 'taught himself' English. He could act as my guide for a day, time enough to see a local beauty spot that lay a mere two hours away – the Vulture's Gorge, famous for preserving winter ice right through the summer.

When the Russian teacher, Tsogt, appeared, he turned out to be a sad little figure, nearing retirement, not old, but seemingly worn out. More worrying to me, he had never actually heard English, which meant that he spoke little and understood less, of little more use than my Russian and Mongolian. He didn't like to acknowledge his inadequacy. We were locked away from each other by a combination of linguistic incompetence and pride. As we headed west, over a plain rutted by a network of tracks, conversation occurred in minute packets, linguistic quanta, which shed little light on anything.

'Have you lived here long?' I shouted over the noise of the shaking jeep.

'Long?'

'Yes.'

There was a long pause, then: 'Fifty-six kilometres.'

'What?'

'To Vulture Gorge, fifty-six kilometres.'

'No ... I mean, how long have you lived here?'

'E-e-eh?'

'Many years – here? You have lived?' My own English was becoming infected by his.

'Lived?' he said, baffled.

'Yes! Much? Years?'

'Years!' His face cleared. 'Oh, many, many. I have fifty-four years.'

Climbing from the plain into the mountains, where gravel gave way to rounded hills and a patina of green, we drew up by a couple of portable cabins, decorated with a childishly painted snow leopard and two dinosaurs in combat. To one side lay a massive tree trunk twice as thick as a telegraph pole. Close to, it turned out to be a fossil, a relic of the time when dinosaurs roamed here over 65 million years ago, but rough and grainy as if it had fallen the year before. A sign in English declared: 'Welcome to Gobi natural museum.' One cabin was a shop. The other contained a faded collection of stuffed animals – vultures, marmots, a snow leopard, a fox, a wolf, an ibex. I was the only outsider around; but a visitors' book revealed that this was a well-trodden route, by Gobi standards. In the previous week, there had been several dozen foreign visitors, including an Australian, a Californian, several Russians, a German and a Chinese from Hong Kong.

Further on, through a shaky gateway of scaffolding poles, the road ended, blocked by a line of boulders. Beyond, the track continued, but it was overgrown. Quite recently this dead end had been made to form a car park, and spare the gorge the impact of tourist vehicles.

'Walk,' said Tsogt.

A pretty walk it made, over tussocky grass and by a river, into a steep-sided gorge. It might have been a Highland glen, except for the ground squirrels that darted away into burrows at our approach. High above us, the wind blustered and boomed among ridge crests spotlit by the afternoon sun, but deep in the shadowy cleft we felt only gentle gusts. The strong, sweet scent of junipers drifted down from bushes that dotted the lower slopes.

Deeper and deeper the river cut into the rock, winding into the mountains, while the sides closed in around us. This was odd – the river flowed downhill between peaks that climbed ever higher, which meant that the source of the river was actually lower than the range through which it ran. It looked as if the river had originally flowed uphill, and then cut down through solid rock.

This is no paradox. Only a short time ago in geological terms, a mere 20 million years, the mountains were not here, like the whole vast uplifted mass to the south, from the Tien Shan, through Tibet to the Himalayas and their neighbouring ranges. But the water tables beneath were there, laid down by much more ancient processes. And when the mountains began to lift, and the fault lines cracked open, the water squeezed up from below sought the easiest routes downhill. Now imagine titanic forces raising the ground, millimetre by millimetre, millennium by millennium, steadily but never fast enough to outpace the erosive power of the river or divert it. In Nepal, the great gorge of the Kali Gandaki, which cuts clear through the Himalayas, arose in this way. It had happened here, on a small scale. Like the Kali Gandaki, this little river had never been confronted with a rocky barrier. It had been there before the barrier ever arose. In a sense, the peaks above were more fluid than the river, for they had been pushed up around it.

After half an hour or so, when the valley was some twenty metres wide, I saw ahead what seemed like a light grey banner stretched across the gorge. It was ice, a low wall, dirty with mud and gravel, with a cavern cut into its base where the river vanished. As I paused, Tsogt clambered on top and walked gingerly onwards, along the top of what I now guessed was a small glacier some three or four metres deep, filling the gorge, not just from side to side, but for some unknown distance downstream as well.

Once on top, I saw it was not a glacier at all. The surface of the ice was pocked with potholes, at the bottom of which the river ran through caves and tunnels. Further on the water ran out over an ice-shelf, then down another hole through a maze of tunnels, grottoes and canyons. As my track shoes crunched over melting ice, I wondered what the chances were of breaking through to the river below. The place was alive with noises – the gusting wind, the gurgle of the river, the drip of melting ice. I stared into the deep blue shadow of a cave, and felt its chilled breath. The wind picked up drops, and scattered them over my face.

Ahead, Tsogt was pointing upwards. Above me was a marker, showing the thickness of ice built up during the winter. Ten metres of ice! This bulk, combined with the overshadowing peaks, ensured such a slow melt that most years – like this one – some ice lasted right through the summer. With the peaks above trembling in heat haze, the valley was a cool haven.

It seemed to me that there was more to this place than a tourist attraction. Pretty enough, certainly, and a pleasant walk, but mainly because it was so unexpected: intimacy amidst vast spaces, ice in a desert, greenery amidst desolation, brilliant white against grim grey. More than this, though, it posed a problem: how did the ice arise? No one I asked later had a convincing explanation, and I have found none anywhere else. At a point where the river and its sparkling overburden of ice swung away down the valley, it had gouged a bay in the side walls, and a grassy slope led upwards. I climbed through junipers in an attempt to gain an overview of this geological puzzle.

I sat panting on a knoll, looking downstream where Tsogt was picking his way around on the ice. Despite the gorge's name, there were no vultures, only a few quick little birds, darting about like swifts. Among the pungent juniper bushes were smaller, green plants with hard green berries. They looked like wild gooseberry, if there is such a thing. I picked some, and indulged in thought-experiments.

I imagined the gorge empty, the river running from a spring above, the winter coming on, the first frosts nipping at tiny backwaters among the boulders, the first snows dusting the peaks above. Somewhere along this mile of gorge, midday sun dislodges a high snowpocket, and a small avalanche of rock and snow tumbles into the river, damming it long enough for ice to form. Water runs over the top, freezes, thickens steadily, extends the dam up and back, until at last it blocks the whole gorge and the river freezes solid for the winter.

Still there were holes in this scenario. Would there really be enough water or enough time to build up this berg, this static glacier? And how, come the spring, did the water flow *beneath* the ice sheet? Why wouldn't it simply run over the top of the sheet, carving its way down, creating a canyon? Sometime, an ambitious and hardy geomorphologist will choose to spend an autumn here to watch the ice freeze, and a spring, too, to watch it melt.

Below me, Tsogt waved and pointed to his watch. My berries were too hard and tart to eat. I tossed them away and started to clamber down.

Back in Dalanzadgad, Chimgee had better news. She had heard of a girl who was studying German in Ulan Bator University, and was home for the summer vacation. German would suit me a lot better than my Mongolian or Tsogt's English.

Her name was Ariunaa. She proved to be a gangling, jeans-clad 21-year-old with slightly stained teeth and a taste for headscarves. She had only been learning German for two years and she was very quiet, looking down a good deal, lapsing into silence – not exactly the type, I thought as we sipped coffee in Siggy's kitchen, to have around if the going was tough. But she was already a tribute to Mongolia's language teaching, and she said she could be ready to go in minutes. A quick mind and an instant decision suggested there was strength behind the soft voice and averted gaze.

Well stocked with fresh meat, pasta, biscuits and water, Ariunaa and I were picked up by the driver arranged by Chimgee, Batöldzii, and set off along the northern edge of the Three Beauties, heading west. For an hour, this was familiar territory, the route I had taken to the Vulture Gorge. Then we sailed on over billowing gravel, the Three Beauties to our left, and a huge horizon to our right. Yet the wilderness here was well used. We were on a track freshly reformed by other vehicles, and marked by telegraph poles marching ahead until they vanished in quivering mirages. The ruts were made by the buses carrying Japanese tourists to their desert camp, and by the jeeps of the camp employees. Then the camp itself materialized ahead, flickering images hardening into solid gers, ranked with military precision behind a square metal fence. Compared to the unpeopled places of the far west, this was suburbia. We surged past and the gers dimmed in our dust.

Far ahead now lay the Bogd, the Holy Mountains. We would be keeping them on our right, then we would cut clear through the far end of the Three Beauties. The exact route, though, was muddled by a criss-cross of tracks. On a hill ahead, two tents stood. We drove towards them, to ask the best way and, with luck, have tea.

But this was no ordinary camp. One tent was a ger, the other a tattered canvas cube, a small marquee. As we drove up, a careworn, overweight woman in an utterly inappropriate tight black dress was sitting on the ground roasting something large and bloody on an open fire. Two men emerged from the square tent. They were dressed in shorts, and nothing else, except that one was wearing a traditional hat, pointed and curved in the shape of an onion dome. I was apprehensive. You don't see many bare torsos in Mongolia.

Almost at once, the appearance of a third man provided reassurance. His dress – a stylized jacket that was nothing but sleeves, tight decorated shorts and heavy leather boots – showed he was a wrestler. As we moved towards him, I noticed some homemade bar-bells on the ground. This was a training camp and these were local lads, feeding, toughening, psyching themselves up for Naadam, 'The Games', Mongolia's National Day. With this country-wide festival in mid-July, Mongolians reassert their identity. It was a special year, the 790th anniversary of the founding of the nation by Chingis Khan.

At Naadam festivals, athletes of every age engage in the three 'skills', archery, wrestling and horseracing, also known as the 'three manly sports'. Once, they were indeed all 'manly', but not so today. In Chingis Khan's day, the Mongols were the best mounted archers in the world; nowadays, archery is a tame sport in which men and women fire thick-nosed arrows at little wicker baskets. Racing is a marathon in which horses are ridden over twenty-five or thirty kilometres by children, both boys and girls, of between eight and twelve. Only in wrestling do young men come into their own, training from boyhood in stylized moves and rituals.

When we arrived, the half-dozen men were resting in the little marquee after a bout of training. They were bulky creatures, muscles hidden beneath fat pectorals and paunches, there being no weight categories in wrestling. Like all young men in training, they exuded an air of machismo, but there was nothing loud in their self-esteem. I asked if they could show me how they trained. They smiled and shook their heads – it would mean getting all dressed up again.

'This man was my teacher,' Ariunaa said deferentially, nodding at the oldest, a man in his late twenties named Bayanmonkh – 'Rich-Eternal'. The coincidence led on to a further quiet exchange that explained the mystery of the camp's presence in this particular forsaken spot. Bayan's father, who had been one of the local 'Falcons', a semi-finalist in the wrestling championships, had once herded round here and trained on this spot, so he had invited the area's top wrestlers to do the same.

The talk changed the mood. A teenager, who would act as a second in the championships, handed round bowls of tea, rice and mutton. Spontaneously, Bayanmonkh and one of the other men decided to show me a mock bout. They slipped into their gear, and beckoned me to watch as they squared up against the empty horizon.

Facing each other, opponents begin with a ritual 'eagle dance', a stiff, slow-motion flapping with the arms combined with a cockerel strut. Once locked together like judo experts, the two cling to each other's jackets, heads against each other's shoulders, leaning into each other, waiting for the right moment to snatch or heave. The aim is to force one's opponent to touch the ground with any part of the body other than the sole or palm. Usually, this involves throwing him. No one gets hurt. The loser then walks under the victor's raised arm in a mark of respect, while the victor does another eagle dance.

To outsiders, the time spent jockeying for advantage – there is no time limit, and in top-level bouts this prologue can last half an hour – is about as fascinating as watching rocks grow, while the actual fight is over in a blink. Few outsiders understand the appeal. The bullfighter jacket, the jockstrap pants and the stilted dancing make the whole process seem faintly ridiculous. To Mongolians, however, wrestling is a part of their character, their very identity, with three main categories of champion – Falcon, Elephant, Lion – and even grander titles for victors who win year after year. Every summer local bouts feed into national championships, and the champion of champions emerges on National Day in Ulan Bator. The bulky young men in this tent would soon be wrestling in Dalanzadgad, and the best of them would hope to be selected to wrestle in Ulan Bator in years to come.

The two had been grappling stolidly for a couple of minutes when with a laugh and yell, Bayanmonkh heaved his opponent into the air, and dropped him on the ground. I was not much enlightened. This was too good-natured to give a real sense of tension.

'Is he good?' I asked.

'Very good,' said Ariunaa. 'He is the "Lion" of this region.'

The local champion! I was privileged to have seen him in action, and wished him luck. It was a long way to Ulan Bator's stadium from this desert hilltop with its torn tent and sand-filled bar-bells, but Bayan had a precedent, another Bayanmonkh, who had won the Naadam title nine times, being granted a more prestigious title on each occasion. Perhaps this Bayan, like his namesake, would end up as the Eye-Pleasing Nationally Famous Mighty and Invincible Champion.

Towards dusk, we were moving fast over grey gravel, through the shadow of a red-tinted cloud-bank fringing the west beyond the mass of the Bogd mountains. To our left the Three Beauties were in sunlight, spotlit beneath a sky of eggshell blue. We were heading for a pass through the mountains, and there were no towns along our route. Around us, the desert was empty. I began to make plans for a night under the stars. I had Siggy's sleeping bag with me, and wanted to sleep out. Batöldzii and Ariunaa would, I supposed, sleep in the car. I wondered whether the prospect of being alone with two men would concern Ariunaa. I thought not: her soft voice and tightly wrapped headscarf were not signs of shyness, but of a discreet self-confidence.

In the mid-distance, across the darkening waste, a ger appeared. There was a brief conferral in front.

'The driver says it is late,' Ariunaa reported. 'Do you want to spend the night there?'

It was a bleak spot, very different from my fantasy of some snug rock shelter with a view of the rising sun. 'It would be nice if we could get to the mountains,' I said. Batöldzii nodded, and we passed the ger without slowing.

But we were not heading into the mountains yet. The sun vanished behind the cloud-bank, which now spread over the Bogd, forming a dark cape from which a smear of rain fell. The Three Beauties was a gloomy mass, and I was beginning to fear I had condemned us to a night in the desert, perhaps a wet one, when another ger appeared. How about here, asked Ariunaa. Yes, I said, if Batöldzii agreed.

He didn't; as the ger disappeared, he said he had suddenly remembered that somewhere ahead a friend of his had a camp.

'How far ahead?'

Batöldzii pointed towards a line of hills at an indefinable distance.

It was 10 o'clock, when in the fading light I happened to see white dots off to one side a mile away. We swung towards them, pulling up by three gers. This was the camp of a well-off family, for outside stood a motorbike, several horses, a tractor, and trailer in which stood two churns. This was not Batöldzii's friend, of whom we heard nothing more, but since it was almost dark, this was to be our base for the night.

A young woman, a solid, ruddy-cheeked girl, emerged to hold back the dogs, while we entered the first ger. Inside, we found a man and his wife, a grandmother smoking a pipe, and two children. After the brief greetings, I handed over a leg of mutton bought in Dalanzadgad. It was welcome, for the drought had delayed both the new grass and the possibility of fresh meat. Then, after falling into conversation with one of the women, Ariunaa murmured, 'I know her. We travelled from UB together.'

'*What?*'

'On the plane, when I was returning from university.'

Two such coincidences seemed, on second thoughts, rather more than chance. After all, the population of the south Gobi was not large. The odds must favour some sort of personal link wherever you went, ensuring that an expanse that seemed huge and pitiless could, with the appearance of a ger, suddenly be made warm and intimate.

As we ate rice and boiled fresh mutton, I found myself an object of curiosity for the nineteen-year-old who had held the dogs on our arrival. She was rather attractive, with brown eyes and heavy eyelids, more European than Mongolian. I glimpsed her staring at me hard and long, until I met her look and her glare melted into a brilliant smile. Her name was Uranchimeg.

'She has big eyes,' said Ariunaa, when I commented on her attention. 'That is very rare in Mongolians.'

'Why is she looking at me?'

'Usually, girls of that age in the country are married by now.'

This opened a frightening thought. She had to be very desperate indeed to consider a middle-aged Englishman who spoke hardly any Mongolian. I wondered where I was sleeping, and where she intended to be at the time.

As it happened, after eating well on the mutton, boiled up on the stove, Ariunaa, Batöldzii and I were left in the ger, together with the granny and the two children. The three Mongolians shared a bed, and we, the guests, settled into blankets on the floor, entirely unmolested.

I was awoken by the urgent sound of goats nestling up to the canvas and nibbling at the string used to tie the door open. The old lady was up first. She got out of bed, her deel loose, entirely unselfconscious about her naked and emaciated breasts, and headed outside, presumably for a pee. When she returned, looking less dishevelled, she sat on the floor, and brewed up a pipe, no more than a tiny bowl on the end of a thin stick. I decided to take my turn, and discreetly pulled on my jeans. 'Get the dogs!' the old lady yelled with surprising force as I made for the door.

Outside, the sun was rising in a cloudless sky. The gravel at my feet and the distant dusting of grass were all touched with gold, and my shadow, joining other shadows from the tents, the horses, the vehicles, stretched for a hundred metres. I was in the jeep, pouring cold water from a bottle into a mug to shave with, when Ariunaa came over with a toothbrush and held out her own mug. 'What do you do about washing?' she asked.

It was easy for me when travelling, I said. Usually, I had water with me. Even if I didn't wash for a day or two, I had a chance to use a stream.

'It is a big problem for Mongolians,' she said. 'Always we have to carry it, and we never have enough.'

For centuries, foreigners complained that Mongolians were an unclean people. When Chingis's warriors overran Central Asia in the thirteenth century, Arab historians wrote that the only warning of their mercurial approach was their smell. In the fourteenth century, a wandering monk, William of Rubruck, noted that Mongol women did not wash much. Throughout history, they have been a notoriously noisome people, and in some areas, until quite recently, people used to say that certain clothing should be worn out from use and not from washing. You would think, reading historical accounts, that the Mongols were simply filthy by nature. In fact, in a land where water is scarce – frozen for six months of the year – this was a question of necessity, not choice.

The mother appeared, and seeing us sharing a mug of water, pointed to the trailer. On it were two twenty-litre cans. She mimed splashing water on her face. We were free to wash and refill our bottles. You won't get much of a chance to shower in the Gobi, but at least containers are bigger and stronger now, transport better, and water more available.

Presented with tea, rice and last night's mutton by Uranchimeg, I ate breakfast in silence under the intense gaze of her big, brown eyes. She was still staring as we drove off across the gravel plain towards the Three Beauties.

The Singing Sands

In foothills cut by centuries of rain and wind into a cascade of sharp triangles, gazelle scooted in front of the jeep. These were the second species, the goitred gazelle, *Procapra gutturosa*, 'white dzeer' in Mongolian, sometimes transliterated as 'djairan'. More solid, with shorter legs than the Persian gazelle I had seen in the Gobi National Park, the creature is named after its oddly enlarged larynx, the purpose of which has still never been explained.

To our right, the mountains ran away into lowlands and desert, but ahead a dry river-bed marked by ash-grey gravel led upwards. Where the river-bed merged into soft alpine slopes, half a dozen mountain sheep scattered into a side valley. These sheep, known as argali, are becoming rare – there are only an estimated 3,000 of them in the Three Beauties – for reasons that are still obscure. Perhaps they make easy prey for snow leopards and wolves, now on the increase; or hunters eager for their swirling horns have taken a toll; or they are just being squeezed out in competition with domestic herds. Their status poses a challenge to wildlife administrators trying to understand the forces at work here and how best to control them.

High up, where grass gave way to crags, four ibex – mountain goats – fled away out of our path and up the steep sides of the valley. These agile creatures seem to be doing well – Reading estimates that there are some 13,000 of them. They moved fast and confidently, squirrelling up thirty metres of rock in seconds, their brown coats making them almost invisible. They rose in a stately silhouette against the sky before vanishing over the crest.

An obo of a most untraditional kind – bits of old metal and tyres – marked the top of the pass, and we stopped to brew water for coffee. Before us lay a glorious outlook. A long descent tumbled over a stupendous patchwork of ridges, dried rivers, and dark grey foothills, leading down to a plain. Beyond, some fifty kilometres away, lay two further ranges, the Sevrey and Zoolongin mountains, while off to the right, a sharp line of yellow led away beyond the end of the Three Beauties, vanishing towards the horizon. This was our destination: a line of dunes, the Singing Sands, where (according to Chimgee) there would be a ranger.

Out in the plain I could see specks of buildings, glinting white. I had read about this place. It was a camp for tourists who came to see the dunes, and hear them sing. As the jeep headed fast and smooth over the descending slope, I wondered if a busload of Japanese had beaten me to it, turning a pristine expanse of sand and gravel into a beach-club.

Rolling closer over a track softened by time and wind, I saw that it was in fact a ghost camp, a memorial to optimism blasted away by wind and dust. A wire fence guarded nothing but a few scattered huts and a concrete ger, labelled 'Bar' in faded paint. Cement circles on the gravel marked the spot where campers' gers had once stood. The only occupants of this mournful spot were animals. A hare danced away as we drove into the vacant compound, and when I got out I saw the ground was dotted with droppings.

'Before the camp, there were people growing vegetables here,' Batöldzii said.

Nothing now could have seemed more hopeless, for there was no sign that water ever ran through this bare, smooth apron of gravel. Yet below the camp was the evidence that what Batöldzii said was true. We stopped at a spot where a camel had died, and been gnawed apart by lynxes or wolves, leaving three leg bones, hooves attached, well separated on the desert floor. There were no remains of the fourth leg or the rest of the camel. A few yards beyond were chunks of a pump, once used to extract water from the wealth that lay not far beneath the surface.

The water was there all right. You only had to raise your eyes to see that, for further down the long, gentle slope, the landscape, if you framed it in a viewfinder, turned into a study in horizontal strips of colour, something Rothko might have done if he had drawn inspiration from the Gobi rather than colour itself. At the bottom was the grey of gravel, at the top the sheer blue of sky, and in the middle the yellow of sand above green.

The grey, blue and yellow had been clear from a distance.

The green, though, was a surprise, and a mystery until we were close enough to see it for what it was.

The Singing Sands stretched along the horizon in a glowing line of buttery yellow which became almost white where it took the full glare of the sun. As we dropped down the long slope towards them, the dunes merged into a single feature, one immense ridge several hundred feet high, stretching out of sight to east and west.

Along the base, ever clearer, ran that strip of green. It was pasture, dotted with camels, cattle and horses, and a scattering of gers. I couldn't understand it: was this the result of a river which for some reason flowed parallel to the dunes?

At the gers, two worlds met. Outside them stood two tethered horses, a wind generator, and a satellite dish. At the first ger, a middle-aged woman in a nylon shirt and pop-socks came out. Ariunaa asked about the ranger. As the woman pointed to the next ger, I couldn't help noticing that her shirt and tights did nothing to disguise rounded shoulders and drooping waist. I wondered why a woman who was raised wearing something as graceful as a deel chose such back-street garb, and suspected the influence of television. She proudly explained that she could watch CNN and MTV beamed in from Hong Kong, as well as Russian and Mongolian channels. With the world pouring in upon her, she had acquired new ideas about how she should dress. Who was I, who had never lived in such harsh isolation, to insist the old ways were better?

The second ger was a masculine hangout. Amidst a litter of machinery, two men in grubby shirts and trousers were working on a dismantled motorbike. To one side, sipping a dish of tea, sat a sad old man in a tattered shirt and vest. As we found space on the floor, I found myself focusing on the two younger men, one of them small and wiry with a crew-cut, the other solid as a weightlifter, with a bald head and shrewd gaze. He looked a natural leader.

I was completely wrong. When Ariunaa explained our purpose and my interest, it was the old man who responded. As we drank tea, he transformed himself, putting on a purple deel over his shirt, a saffron band around his waist, an incongruous white Panama hat, and finally a pair of golden-framed glasses. The tramp was now a sage: Shirav, park ranger, the Old Man of the Singing Sands. He was seventy, he said, and had been the ranger here for thirty years. Then, with slow, gentle gestures, he unwrapped a cloth bundle, containing permission forms and receipts. I was not his only visitor that summer, I noticed as he inscribed my name and checked the authorization issued in Dalanzadgad. Only five days before, two Americans had come through.

In the jeep, bumping across the tussocky pasture with the Singing Sands rearing up ahead, Shirav explained what I saw before me. The dunes ran for 100 kilometres, and they were, as they seemed, a strip only a few kilometres across. These were among the highest, if not the highest, dunes in the Gobi. Passing camels shaggy with unshed wool, we forded a stream hemmed with an astonishing and incongruous line of blue – they were irises, in a display of country-house splendour. This was another of those rich enclaves, almost invisible until you come upon it, then a whole separate world, with horses made sleek by meadow grass. A grey crane paced sedately from clump to marshy clump.

Water from several springs came together to form a river, the Khongorin Gol, the River of Sweetness, which vanished into a muddy lake a few kilometres westward. We stopped near one of the springs, a fenced-off area where water welled up into a cool pond a metre across.

'Is it safe to drink?' I asked.

'It is good. People use it as a cure for stomach ache.'

I cupped my hands, and drank. It was deliciously cool, leaving a faint taste of some mineral I couldn't identify. I splashed water over my face, and picked my way over the soggy ground back to the car.

And then suddenly, within a metre, the grass and the irises ended, and the sand rose in front of us, smooth as the surface of a tidal wave. Batöldzii brought the jeep to a halt as the wheels dug in. Looking up, I felt disoriented, not just because of the sand's brightness in the overhead sun, but because the sun wiped out all shading and left no terms of reference. The dune formed a uniform sheet until it cut off against the blue, like an American abstract painting come to life, with no clue to indicate depth or distance or height. It was an enigma. Sand simply does not form such regular ridges. Sand moves, in separate dunes. Sand should not form a sheer, steep barrier like this. I felt at a loss, and could think only that if I climbed, an overview would give me back a sense of proportion, and perhaps some understanding.

'How long will it take to the top?'

The old ranger sized me up. 'For you, maybe an hour,' he said.

We set off, shoes sliding and sinking into the soft, hot sand. Behind me Ariunaa and our driver laboured upwards, as if responding to the challenge. Below, the jeep parked on the sand's rim and the camels on the pasture beyond provided reference points, but when climbing, bent over with the effort, I found myself removed from time and place, as baffled as if walking up a snow-face. On the sand by my feet, tiny tracks showed that a lizard had been here, but in my immediate surroundings there was nothing – no bird, no plant, no shadow – to give a sense of slope or distance.

I glanced up again. Strangely, two figures on horseback had appeared from an invisible dip, joining us in the climb. The sand was not all soft: in places, it was sealed with a thin crust, which for several paces at a time provided a firm support. Above, still at an indefinable distance, the crest of the ridge took shape, a regular arc of white, like the rising of some vastly magnified full moon.

Then, quite suddenly, after only half an hour, I was at the top, panting, sweat evaporating fast in the dry air, readjusting to everyday dimensions. I was on a saddle between two high points, on a ridge shaped by wind into a knife edge, looking out at mountains. I had been expecting a succession of ridges, a cliché'd expanse of wave after wave. In fact, this was it, the first and only ridge of the Singing Sands. A few hundred feet below me, the sand rippled away for a mile or two, merging into rising ground of gravel, foothill, and finally the mountains, the range we had seen from the top of the Three Beauties. I was on a strip of sand as crisply defined as a beach.

Stretching away on either side, it looked an impenetrable barrier, but a few kilometres to the west, invisible from my vantage point, the rampart is breached by a natural highway of low-lying sand. Here, an underlying feature – a dome of uplifted rock, perhaps – encouraged prevailing winds to blow away lightweight sand before it had a chance to lay down deep drifts, preserving a north–south route semi-petrified by age that has been in use for centuries.

On either side of the road, the sands are forbidding. When the British geologists Brian Windley and Lewis Owen crossed the dunes in 1995, they turned off the track to explore a canyon, hoping to see strata that would throw light on the area's prehistory. After plodding through several miles of sand, they spotted something white. It was a human skull, with no sign of a skeleton, its age indefinable, except that the teeth were without any of the gold fillings common to Mongolians, Chinese and Kazakhs this century. There was no telling how its owner had died, but twenty to thirty metres away were the bones of a camel. I imagined the dunes in winter, an icy wind roaring from the northwest, man and animal seeking camp after a day's travel, wandering off the track, disoriented by wind and snow and gathering gloom, then hunkering down to wait for the storm to pass. Before it ended, they froze to death. The bodies must simply have vanished, hidden from other travellers, deep-frozen through the winter, torn apart by wolves in the spring, the bones finally buried by the shifting sands. Only now, when all signs of flesh and clothing had long since disappeared, had the winds exposed the whitened remains.

I wondered what had seduced the traveller from his path. Mere error? Inexperience? Or something more sinister, the sound of the singing sands interpreted by disoriented minds. 'There is a marvellous thing related of this desert,' wrote Marco Polo in his *Travels*, 'which is that when travellers are on the move by night, and one of them chances to lag behind or fall asleep or the like, when he tries to regain his company again he will hear spirits talking, and will suppose them to be his comrades. Sometimes the spirits will call him by name; and thus shall a traveller ofttimes be led astray so that he never finds his party. Sometimes the stray travellers will hear as it were the tramp and hum of a great cavalcade of people away from the real line of the road, and taking this to be their own company they will follow the sound ... Even in the day-time one hears those spirits talking. And sometimes you shall hear the sound of a variety of musical instruments, and still more commonly the sound of drums.'

I was ready to go back down from the crest, but when Shirav stood, he looked up at the ridge rising another ten metres or so to the summit. Like Choinjin on Sacred Mother mountain, Shirav was drawn upwards, and was determined that I should join him. He walked ahead up the wind-sharpened crest, and I followed, teetering on the knife edge of sand. By the time I reached the very peak, he was sitting, scanning the scene below through binoculars.

'This is what I like best,' he said. 'Sitting up here, and looking over everything.'

'The Khan of the Sands,' I said, and he smiled behind his binoculars.

This was a terrific spot. A light wind carried a film of sand hissing up against our legs, and through that gentle sound came the fog-horn groans from camels far below. From up here, 180 metres above the desert floor, the thin strip of pasture looked like a lawn. Beyond, the gravel stretched away, past the distant blobs of the abandoned tourist camp, towards the grey mounds of the Three Beauties.

Then, finally, Shirav was ready to leave. He strode and slid ahead as Ariunaa arrived panting on the saddle of sand immediately below me. She was barefoot. She said it was healthy; it massaged the feet. It seemed a good idea. I took my track shoes and socks off, and began to run and jump down after Shirav like a child. The sand was hot, but if I kept moving fast my bare feet pushed through instantly to the cool beneath. Goaded by the oven surface and seduced by the speed, I covered in three minutes a distance that had taken half an hour to climb.

Shirav was sitting near the bottom, on a little prominence locked in place by a few grasses. With a rush of bare feet, I fell beside him, joined after a moment by Ariunaa. Shirav took out a long pipe, and began to smoke while I recovered my breath.

'It is beautiful here,' I said, shielding my eyes from the sun. He nodded, waiting, puffing gently. 'Do you think it is beautiful?'

'When the rain comes, and when the wind is not too strong, like today, it is beautiful.'

'I have heard mountains are sacred. Are these dunes sacred?'

'They are sacred, as mountains are.'

'And they have nymphs?'

'All places have their nymphs. So do the dunes.' He paused, drawing on his pipe. 'Do they talk about nymphs much in England?'

'Not much, these days.' Then I thought of Pan, and the Green Man, and children's poems about elves and fairies. 'But there are stories, legends.'

I asked about the song of the dunes, wondering if folktales still told of siren voices. I had once read a technical explanation for why dunes make a noise, for this ghostly phenomenon is recorded in other deserts. Some sands are made of grains that have a layer of silica. Though the exact mechanism is still obscure, the song that had once drawn travellers to their legendary doom is created when the grains are set moving by wind, vibrating together to make a deep hum.

Shirav said: 'When the wind blows hard from the east or west' – that is, along the line of the dunes – 'they make a noise. It happens about once a week.'

'Is it really like singing?'

'They call it singing, but it sounds like an aeroplane.'

'Like a jet?'

'No, no, it's like the sound of the Antonov 24, the one that flies into Dalanzadgad.' I knew the sound, and imagined the steady, throaty buzz of turbo-props instead of the hissing breeze and the groaning camels.

'How is it there is so much sand? Where do the dunes come from?' I was hoping for a scientific explanation, to do with wind direction and erosion patterns. Instead, he told a story.

Once upon a time, he said, there was a king, whose name was Shugshnim. Back then, there was no sand, only stones and fields and the king's great city. Shugshnim was a generous khan, who always helped people. Gold fell from heaven, and all the people were happy. Now, Shugshnim had a son, who wanted to be king, and killed his father. God became angry, and he sent the sand instead of the gold, and buried the city.

This was intriguing. There are the remains of cities abandoned in the Gobi, walls and roads marking ancient routes and barriers, for the inhabitants of these regions were not all nomads. Did he mean there was a city buried beneath these dunes? Shirav gave me a look. 'No, I'm not talking about *these* sands. The sands I'm talking about are in the western part of Inner Mongolia. I have no idea where *these* sands come from.'

We fell silent. At the time, this was another geomorphological mystery, like the ice of the Vulture Gorge. But later, back home, research suggested a solution. It is surely no coincidence that the dunes are aligned pointing a little bit north of west, or south of east, in the same direction as the Three Beauties and the Sevrey mountains. A prevailing wind, funnelling along a corridor between the two chains, seems to sweep lighter grains from the surrounding desert and pile them along the lowest section of the outwash plains into this great wall, with lower dunes lying behind it as if in a rain shadow.

Yet this is no static feature. The light mist of sand blowing round our feet showed its dynamism; the winds that made it could as easily unmake it. Though centuries, perhaps millennia old, the dunes are made up of the most airy particles, which should long ago have been blown away into China. As Shirav talked, I idly burrowed into the sand, finding dampness only an inch down. If it were not to dry out underneath, the surface sand must be constantly renewed, constantly cycling, vanishing in the east as it is replaced from the west. My image of a tidal wave was wrong. In a wave, the form moves, while the matter remains in place. Here, the constituent parts moved, while the form remained permanent.

That still left a mystery. What causes the springs to pop up just where the sands end? It could not be mere coincidence that the dunes rose so sharply from the pasture. I could see that the lie of the land was in some way responsible – the underlying fault line, the springs, the pasture and the sands all occurred along the same low-lying section between mountain ranges. But if the sand shifted by a fraction of a per cent, the pastures would be overwhelmed, turning the place to utter desert.

My thoughts had reduced me to a long silence. Now Shirav turned questioner again. 'What religion are you?'

I was about to say Church of England, but then, afraid of getting lost in the intricacies of Protestant sectarianism and the nature of my scepticism, I settled for an easier response. 'Christian, I suppose.'

'Is there any way you could bring a bit more rain here?'

'Me? Bring more rain?'

'Yes. Do you have any experience in making rain?'

At school, there had been divinity lessons, and instruction for Con-firmation, but no one had thought to teach me rain-dancing. 'No,' I apologized. 'I'm afraid I do not have that sort of power.'

'Oh. I have heard that people in England can make rain.'

I understood. This was no request for a miracle. A straightforward question about religious affiliation had merged into a scientific one. I explained what I remembered about 'seeding' clouds.

'Could you do it here?'

'I don't think so.' You could only make rain, I said, if the clouds were already bearing moisture, and if you had planes, and the right chemicals, and anyway with only two inches of rain a year there wasn't much to build on.

Besides, this place didn't need rain to make it a wonder. When I put my shoes on and walked back to the jeep, my feet still tingled. It was from the run, of course, and the impact of the hot sand, and absolutely nothing, I'm sure, to do with absorbing a little of something sacred.

7

The Flaming Cliffs

One of Sukhe's drivers ferried me back northwest of Dalanzadgad, along the line of telephone poles. White blobs trembling on the horizon grew and hardened into two wooden hotels, a restaurant and forty big, round, white gers, separated by a waist-high metal fence from the immensity of gravel. This was Sukhe's camp, Juulchin Gobi. I joined seven young film makers to fulfil my Faustian pact with Sukhe. Keyed up and silent – for there had been no time for introductions – I crammed myself into one of two Ukrainian jeeps. We were off to the Flaming Cliffs, the dinosaur graveyard that made the Gobi a household name in the 1920s.

I was in car No. 2. The driver of the lead car knew the way, but no one else had been here before. Scrunched up in the front seat, I sought enlightenment from my map. Fifty kilometres away lay a town, Bulgan, and fifteen kilometres north of the town were the Flaming Cliffs. A couple of hours, surely no more.

But the director in the car ahead had another agenda. It veered north, away from the main track, and we followed, slewing through soft light brown soil and scrub. I jammed myself deeper into the seat, clinging to door handles.

Ahead, the ground rose into a smooth golden hill – a sand dune; then another; then a whole regiment of crescents jutting up from the gravel surface. We stopped by one of them, under a sky burnt pallid by the afternoon sun. A solid young woman in dark glasses declared herself an English speaker. There aren't many sand dunes in the Gobi, she explained, so they too were to be on Sukhe's tourist route, they too had to be filmed. I glanced at my watch, wondering about the wisdom of this diversion. We admired the purity of the dune's geometry and the sharpness of the ridge, sweeping up in a 100-metre curve to a height of six metres or so. The film makers wandered around it, then up it, capturing images in leisurely fashion. The slanting sun picked out little ridges on the flanks. A breeze dusted sand against a lone bush, a reminder that this regiment was on a slow march across the desert.

After half an hour, we drove on, following a westward track.

'You are American?'

The question came from a slim man, thirtyish, behind me in T-shirt and jeans.

'English.'

'You make films, too?'

'Books. I'm a writer.'

'Ah. What Russian authors do you know in England? Do you know Gorky?'

In halting English, he said his name was Ayur, which he said was Tibetan for 'life'. (In fact, it is Sanskrit for 'health'.) His family was not Tibetan, but Mongolians derive their traditionally Buddhist beliefs and rituals from Tibet, and his claim recalled the ancient link, telling nothing about his background. Ayur, like most educated Mongolians, had looked to Russia for advancement. He had studied in Moscow, writing a thesis on Gorky. Now he was working on *Unen*, Mongolia's main daily newspaper. Like all of Mongolia's many newspapers – there are some 400 serving this literate, diffuse, impoverished population – it was pared to the bone. Ayur was looking after the advertising, which was why he had been included on this trip. But he also edited the literary page.

'You like Joyce? I read *Ulysses*.'

'In English?' I was preparing myself to feel humbled by his diligence.

'In Russian.' That was a relief. 'Do you know Joyce's stories?' Humiliation loomed again, this time with reason. 'Do you know his story *Araby*? I translate into Mongolian for my paper.'

There was a pause, while we stared out over the heaving desert. The driver said something in Mongol. Ayur interpreted: did I know where we were? After all, I was the one with the map.

'Perhaps they know,' I said, pointing to the jeep ahead.

They didn't. We stopped to confer, and I unfolded the map on the bonnet. The Flaming Cliffs were definitely west, they had to be. But we had come off course to see the dunes. How far off course? Were we north or south of the cliffs? There was no telling.

In the distance, a ger appeared, standing out of the desert as clear as a mushroom on the moon. As we wove our way around low bushes and gravelly hummocks, two girls, aged about nine and ten, ran out in T-shirts and shorts. The avid cameraman captured them against four baby camels tethered in a line, while the adult camels, shedding their winter wool like moth-eaten shag rugs, stared haughtily from the middle distance. This was exhausting work. We filed into the ger for tea.

Inside, the woman of the ger was distilling camel's milk, boiling it in an immense pot, capturing its essence as it condensed, drop by drop. We received tokens of hospitality: camel's curd, hard and sharp as parmesan, and a dish of the distilled camel's milk. It was nectar of a transparent purity, like vodka to look at, but with its alcoholic content disguised by a smooth and subtle texture.

Another half-hour passed.

Yes, the Flaming Cliffs were not far. Not that the Mongolians call them the Flaming Cliffs. To locals, it's not the barren sandstone that matters, but what is nurtured by the rare outwash from the gullies. The common name for the place is Bayan Zag, 'Rich in Saxauls'.

So, following a track up a long, slow slope, we climbed, trailing dust, spirits rising with the plain. We were not sure yet where we were, but at least we could get a view from the top.

As we rolled onto high ground, the rock fell away along a cliff edge, revealing arrays of pinnacles and promontories sculpted by wind and rain. I would have to wait awhile for the lowering sun to turn the rock's chocolate-brown to fiery red, but I recognized the place from countless photographs.

I was on the edge of the Flaming Cliffs, at last.

The cliffs lure people for many reasons. They are, of course, the focal point of a great and worthy enterprise, and a scientific monument. But their appeal goes deeper. The discoveries made there in the 1920s reformed awareness of life on earth. The late nineteenth century had witnessed a boom in dinosaur finds, which summoned 'vast forms and gigantic beasts from the abyss of time and the depths of the earth' – the words are those of painter and sculptor Benjamin Waterhouse Hawkins, who designed a dinosaur display for London's Great Exhibition of 1851. The creatures sprang to life, and into the awed imagination, not only because of what they had been, but also for the deeper reasons hinted at by Hawkins. They were the stuff of myth and nightmare come very nearly to life, but at a safe distance, with names that resonate like mantra and trip off the tongue like jingles. 'Ankylosaur, tyrannosaur, iguanodon, diplodocus' – children could skip rope to that, as well as delight proud parents. Dinosaurs await their laureate, but the names are as much the raw material of popular verse as Dorset village names were to Betjeman. For a century, America and Europe had the fun to themselves; then, in 1922, along came Asia, represented by a few square miles of Gobi.

The mastermind behind the discovery, Roy Chapman Andrews, was one of the last of an archetypal eighteenth- and nineteenth-century figure, the explorer–scientist, created by an age when science and empire marched together. Sir Joseph Banks, Cook's botanist; Humboldt, bio-geographer and explorer of the Orinoco; Darwin himself – men like these created a tradition that inspired the young Andrews through his schooldays in Wisconsin. He never wanted anything else but to work for the American Museum of Natural History, where he started in the taxidermy department in 1906 at the age of twenty-two. For four years, he studied whales, dolphins and porpoises, sailing the North Atlantic and Asian oceans and earning a masters degree from Columbia University. But from 1908, his ambitions lay in Central Asia, largely because Andrews' boss, Henry Fairfield Osborn, a palaeontologist of immense repute, predicted that Asia would prove to be the womb in which mammals had developed, and the base from which they dispersed throughout the world.

In particular, Osborn became convinced that the Gobi would yield up the key to human origins. At that time, the scanty evidence for human evolution relied on two small heaps of bone – Neanderthal fossils, found first in Germany in 1856, and the so-called 'Java ape man', unearthed in 1891–2. The Javanese was older than the Neanderthaler, and looked more ape-like, more 'primitive', which was seen as confirmation of the simple, straight-line path of human evolution: ape – ape-man – man. Osborn's conclusion was that, if early man lived on the fringes of Asia, a search deeper into the continent would reveal older finds, perhaps even the 'missing link' between apes and man. No one gave a thought to Africa.

In 1912 the debate intensified when a skull was found in Piltdown, Sussex, that linked a human brain case to the jaw of an ape. Sceptics pointed out a number of oddities about the find, but scepticism gave way to prejudice because the skull answered two earnest desires of European anthropologists – that there should be a 'missing link', and that it should have evolved in Europe. It took forty years before Piltdown

Man was proved a fake. At the time, the find sharpened American ambitions to confirm their own theory, one that fitted nicely with America's growing wealth, influence and intellectual standing – that intelligence did *not* arise in Europe.

In an attempt to resolve the great controversy, Andrews proposed to storm the heartland of Central Asia. Scientifically, this was almost virgin territory. Few explorers and fewer scientists had crossed the Gobi. No one had done extended research there. The only fossil from the area was of a tooth, possibly belonging to an extinct rhinoceros, discovered by a Russian explorer, Vladimir Obruchev, in 1892. In two small-scale preliminary trips, Andrews showed that it was possible to cover these regions by car, and allowed his ambitions to expand. He proposed a larger assault with a team of specialists.

The major problem was one of logistics. Previous explorers had relied on camels, yaks and horses, and as a result expeditions were slow, small in scale, plagued with health problems, unable to carry much food, water or equipment, and unable to bring back many specimens. Andrews wanted crate-loads of specimens – rocks, plants, animals as well as fossils, enough to found great new collections. He knew how to transport them: by motor car. The expedition would use three Dodge cars and two one-ton Fulton trucks. This would enable the men to carry much of their food, drink, fuel, clothing and scientific gear with them, with the rest on seventy-five camels, labouring in trains ahead of the vehicles. This combination of what was still a new form of transport and traditional methods would allow the scientists to multiply their productive work tenfold, compressing ten years' work into the five summer months during which travel and work was possible.

Andrews had several things going for him. Osborn and the museum stood behind him. He had his own experience in the field. And above all, he had the flair and drive to go out and raise the cash. The venture was an idea whose time had come, perfect for Andrews, his boss, the museum, America and science.

It was Andrews himself who made the expeditions happen, and he did it by putting his personality at the service of his dream. Project and character found a perfect match. He was, in his way, a star, in a country and at a time that was newly in love with stars. Moreover, he knew how to play his stardom. He has been called the prototype of Spielberg's scientist–adventurer Indiana Jones, but to understand his appeal, imagine the hero of *Raiders of the Lost Ark*, its star Harrison Ford and

David Attenborough rolled into one. Lean, square of face and jaw, he addressed countless dinners and lectures, knowing that his audience would see him in their imaginations staring out over some remote spot, pistol on hip and broad-brimmed hat shading his steely gaze. 'I have been so thirsty that my tongue swelled out of my mouth,' he wrote later. 'I have ploughed my way through a blizzard at fifty below zero, against wind that cut like a white-hot brand. I have seen my whole camp swept from the face of the desert like a dry leaf by a whirling sandstorm. I have fought with Chinese bandits. But these things are all a part of the day's work.'

Behind the egocentricity and the self-promotion lay a serious mind. Andrews pandered to his own publicity machine by calling the expedition the Great Adventure, but at a deeper level he was too much a professional to seek adventure for its own sake. He was fond of quoting a remark of an explorer friend, 'Adventures are a mark of incompetence.' He knew that success depended on the humdrum: knowing everything possible about the area, drawing on the experience of others, using the best equipment, planning meticulously, staying healthy. He was realist enough, and scientist enough, to know that he did not have the expertise or patience to formalize scientific discoveries. His genius lay in organizing fieldwork, choosing men who could compensate for his own deficiencies, and fundraising.

It would of course take a great deal of money – $250,000 by Andrews' estimate. This was an immensely ambitious undertaking, the largest American scientific expedition to date, at a time when workers in industry were making $20 a week. Andrews was proposing to risk the modern equivalent of $8 million, in a region that was little explored, and might prove entirely empty of fossils. In fact, the five Central Asiatic Expeditions he finally undertook between 1922 and 1930 cost some $600,000, which would be around $20 million in today's terms.

He mostly sought money from individuals. One early visit was to the multimillionaire John Pierpont Morgan, who by happy chance was Osborn's uncle. Morgan gave Andrews fifteen minutes in the library of his house on 33rd Street. That was enough for them both. Morgan donated $50,000. With 'Morgan, J.P.' as a listed contributor, Andrews soon had 650 others.

Initially, there were nine scientists – palaeontologists, geologists, a photographer, a mechanic – rising to thirty-three during the course of the expeditions. Expertise, steadiness of character, experience: these were the qualities that counted. The anchorman was Walter Granger, vertebrate palaeontologist, who had been at the museum for over thirty years. A rotund and jovial man, with a hearty laugh, he was used to deserts, having overseen dinosaur-hunts in Wyoming, New Mexico and Utah.

The press loved the subject, nicknaming Andrews and his team the 'Missing Link' expedition, to the disgust of its leader, who was proud of the full range of sciences represented. Letters from would-be members poured in at the rate of 100 a day. Three thousand men offered their services, and so did 1,000 women. 'Regarding search for Missing Link,' wrote a young woman. 'Ouija board offers assistance.' One hopeful groupie suggested herself as a 'woman friend', someone who could 'create the home atmosphere for you in those drear wastes. I am enclosing my photograph. Could you not have tea with me some day when your work is done?'

The practical problems could be faced in advance. Not so the political ones. China was being torn apart by rival warlords, in a process that would only be halted with Mao's Communist victory in 1949. Russia was in the midst of a civil war that had spread to Siberia. Mongolia was emerging from a nightmare.

Mongolia had broken from China in 1911, been retaken in 1919 by a notorious warlord known as Little Hsü, and been re-'liberated' in February 1921 by a psychotic, anti-Semitic White Russian baron, Roman von Ungern Sternberg. The 'Mad Baron', with staring eyes and wild hair, was of a German Baltic family with estates in Estonia. He claimed that he came from a line of adventurers. An eighteenth-century ancestor had been an alchemist known as 'Satan's Brother'. His grandfather had been a pirate terrorizing British vessels in the Indian Ocean before he was captured, handed over to the Russian consul in India and banished to Siberia. Baron Ungern, as he was known, had been a naval officer in the Russo–Japanese War, and then joined the Trans-Baikal Cossacks, planning to turn this band of freebooters into a clan of Buddhist warriors who would combat the forces of darkness and destruction, i.e. Communists and Jews. But he was prepared to extend his range. In exchange for $3 million, paid by Mongolia's ruling Living Buddha, Ungern agreed to support the monarchy and drive the Chinese out, on the understanding that he could use Urga as a base for an assault into Siberia. He then embarked on an orgy of destruction that turned all but his immediate entourage against him. That winter, dogs gnawed at frozen corpses in the streets and bodies swung from doorposts.

Baron Ungern's murderous five-month regime ended in July 1921 when Mongolia's national hero, Sükhbaatar, brought in Red Army help to drive out the Mad Baron and the Chinese alike. Mongolia became the world's second Communist nation. Hence the Russian presence for the next seventy years.

'A paradise for palaeontologists'

It took Andrews the winter of 1921–2 to gather the stores and people in the north China town of Kalgan, where the railway ended, just short of the final pass leading to the Gobi plateau. From here, two trails led across the desert, one north alongside the telegraph to Urga, the other northwest to Uliastai. They would have to go to Urga to seek diplomatic clearance for their fieldwork.

Though the numbers varied regularly, the expedition started out with a dozen local helpers and nine Americans, four of whom brought wives, among them Andrews' wife, Yvette. Camels were sent on a month ahead, leaving the seven vehicles to follow in mid-April, dragging themselves out of China through axle-deep mud and risking assaults by bandits and/or soldiers who had deserted from the warring armies.

Once on the grasslands, and beyond, on the gravel plains of the southern Gobi, Andrews' careful preparations paid off. Seven days and 400 kilometres out, they were approaching Erlian (also spelt Erhlien, the Chinese version of a name transliterated variously as Iren, Eren, or Ereen. It means 'motley', a reference perhaps to the variegated terrain). Today Erlian is the last stop in China for the trans-Gobi railway, and growing fast. Then, it was two houses – a telegraph post and an inn – and on that particular day a couple of gers. The telegraph was out of action – it had been cut by Little Hsü's soldiers.

Here Andrews had his first inkling of success. Eight kilometres short of Erlian, the cars rolled off level upland over a bluff of exposed strata, the edge of a twelve-kilometre wide dip, excavated by wind and rain, with a sump of salt-encrusted mud from which, in normal times, Chinese labourers loaded salt onto ox-carts for transport south. The Americans referred to the hollow by their version of its Mongolian name, Eren Dabasu (*davs*: salt). The two geologists, Charles Berkey and

Frederick Morris, and the palaeontologist Walter Granger remained with two cars to investigate, while Andrews took the others on to make camp.

An hour later, the two cars came swaying and bouncing into camp. The three men were excited, eyes shining, grinning with delight. Granger was pulling furiously on his pipe. But they said nothing until Granger dug into his pocket, and produced a handful of bone fragments.

'Well, Roy,' he said, 'we've done it. The stuff is here.'

In the cars were another twenty or so kilogrammes of fossils, all collected from the surface in one hour: rhinoceros bones, small mammals of some kind, titanothere teeth – the first evidence of this rhino-like creature outside North America. The men became giddy with joy, laughing and shouting about their good fortune and shaking each others' hands and pounding each other on the shoulder. It must have been an astonishing sight for the Mongolian and Chinese drivers, cooks and assistants.

Then, as Granger wandered off in the fading light along the grey ridge at their feet, he found more fragments. The whole place was a fossil bed. Next morning, the scientists were out at dawn. Berkey came into breakfast with another armful of bones, among them part of a lower leg bone.

Granger turned it this way and that, puzzled. 'Might possibly be a bird,' he mused. 'But it must have been some bird to have a leg bone like that.'

Not long afterwards Davidson Black, doctor and anthropologist, a temporary member of the expedition, almost stepped on the missing section of the same bone, which had obviously weathered out of the ridge above. Berkey and Granger set off to find more. Later that morning, Berkey summoned Andrews. There was Granger on his knees, working with a camel-hair brush at a huge fossilized bone. They all saw at once that this, in Berkey's words, belonged to 'the first dinosaur known in eastern Asia!' (Or something like that. When Andrews wrote up this incident later, which he did several times, details varied. Though meticulous in the field, he easily sacrificed rigour for colour in his prose.)

Never mind the exact words. They had made an astonishing dis-covery – sedimentary strata laid down during the Cretaceous period between 140 and 65 million years ago, the end of what was then known as the Age of Reptiles, in other words dinosaurs. The basin proved to be part of a much larger depression, 25,000 square kilometres in size. Some of the sediments were over thirty metres thick, proof that a hundred million years ago, this desolate place of sandy mounds and thorn bushes had been a land of lakes. Nor were they just Cretaceous beds. The lakes had lasted for more millions of years, their shores and shallows supporting successions of reptiles and mammals. In more recent sediments, dating from about 38 million years ago, lay the skeleton of a giant hornless rhino, Baluchitherium, named from fragments found in Baluchistan. When the creature was restored in New York, it turned out to be the largest land mammal ever, standing five metres at the shoulder, with a head that could nibble leaves seven metres above the ground.

One older bed of red sandy clay contained countless smooth, curved platelets. They looked for all the world like bits of egg. Were they turtles? Birds? No one knew. They were labelled 'doubtful material', and set aside for later analysis.

Andrews and his team were ecstatic. The finds more than justified the leap of faith, the effort, the expenditure. More than that, though; these fossil-rich sediments must extend throughout the Gobi. There had to be other treasures beneath their feet, and more ahead of them. Andrews agreed to divide the expedition, the geologists remaining to work in Eren Dabasu for ten days, while everyone else pushed on to Urga, past ruined monasteries and over abandoned plains, to catch up with the camel train and negotiate work permits from officials.

This required careful diplomacy. Andrews and his capitalist-imperialist entourage had emerged with apparent ease from the land of Mongolia's former master and present enemy. Mongol officials, now tightly under Russian control, were deeply suspicious. It took two weeks for Andrews and his Mongolian fixer to win them over. They managed it only by promising to capture a legendary 'worm' that lived in the Gobi, a sixty-centimetre-long sausage-shaped beast 'that has no head nor legs and is so poisonous that merely to touch it means instant death'. A cabinet minister swore that a cousin of his late wife's sister had actually seen the animal (in Mongolian, it is the 'olgoi khorkhoi', the 'colon-shaped worm', and it is still believed by some to exist). Andrews promised that if he saw one he would seize it with his collecting forceps, wearing dark glasses as a protection. That settled, they were on their way.

From Urga, the expedition headed southwest, to the eastern end of the mountain massifs, the three Bogd ranges. Success built on success.

Living animals were shot, the fossilized exhumed. Another Bal-uchitherium, its skull spotted by Andrews himself; bits of fossil rodents so abundant 'it seemed as though they had been sowed like grain with a lavish hand'; a mastodon with serrated teeth; corals dating back perhaps 350 million years – all went into the crates and onto the trucks and cars for shipment to New York.

And still the best was to come. It happened by chance. The expedition was in the high plains spanning the gap between the final Bogd range and the Three Beauties, a few miles north of the spot where Ariunaa and I had found the wrestlers. It was the first day of September, and the nights were frosty with the promise of winter. Scanning the new snow that already capped the Bogd, Andrews declared that their departure would be halted by nothing less than the discovery of the 'Missing Link himself' (in 1922, on such a masculine enterprise, no one spoke of female fossils).

The Americans were heading north, planning to join the trans-Gobi trail leading back to the Chinese border. But they did not know where they were. Spotting a collection of gers, Andrews walked over with his interpreter to ask the way. They were at a spot which sounded to them like Shabarakh Usu (more properly, Shavart-Us, 'Muddy Water'). While he did so, the expedition's photographer, J. B. Shackelford, wandered in the opposite direction, and found himself standing on the edge of a sandstone basin, just the sort of place for fossils.

Promising himself that if he found nothing in ten minutes he would return to the cars, he climbed down the steep slope of soft rock, and at once saw a fossil on the top of a little pinnacle. It was a tiny skull, six inches long, lying almost fully exposed, on the point of being eroded out by the next storm. He simply scratched away its soft matrix, picked it up and carried it back to the others. No one had seen anything like it, but Granger declared it was a previously unknown type of reptile, news that was enough to demand a day's further research.

They made camp on the edge of the sandstone depression, and spent the rest of the afternoon walking, climbing and probing this odd and beautiful formation (technically, the Djadokhta Formation, after the Chinese name for the area). The place was a treasure trove of fossils – including some more eggshell-like fragments – from which they retreated only after the setting sun had turned the pink rocks to flame and the clefts to rivers of darkness.

Andrews' own words capture the site. 'This was one of the most picturesque spots that I have ever seen. From our tents, we looked down into a vast pink basin, studded with giant buttes like strange beasts carved from sandstone. One of them we named the "dinosaur", for it resembles a strange Brontosaurus sitting on its haunches. There appear to be medieval castles with spires and turrets, brick-red in the evening light, colossal gateways, walls and ramparts. Caverns run deep into the rock and a labyrinth of ravines and gorges studded with fossil bones make a paradise for the paleontologist. One great sculptured wall we named the "Flaming Cliffs", for when seen in early morning or late afternoon sunlight it seemed to be a mass of glowing fire.'

The Flaming Cliffs: the name proved a master stroke of PR when the expedition returned triumphant. They had covered 4,800 kilometres, mostly over open desert, with no breakdowns they could not fix themselves. This success alone was enough to transform the area, as fur and wool traders rushed to acquire cars and exploit virtually untapped regions. With their research and their 2,000 fossils, the Americans had opened new worlds in geology, palaeontology and zoology.

And they *had* found a missing link of a sort – a reptilian one. The tiny skull from the Flaming Cliffs provided an ancestry for a group most famously represented by Triceratops, 'three-horned-eye', one of many rhino-type dinosaurs well known from finds in North America. The ceratopsians posed a problem, for this late Cretaceous family had evolved rapidly into over two-dozen species, mostly massive creatures weighing several tons, all with their own style of neck-frills and horns. Yet there had been no sign of a progenitor. They seemed to have burst upon the North American grasslands in full flower. Now the mystery was solved – the ceratopsians had arisen in the savannahs of Asia as sort of dinosaurian sheep, migrated across the Bering straits, and diversified into the equivalents of buffaloes, elephants and rhinos in the warmer, wetter lands of North America. Granger and Gregory named the ancestral ceratopsian *Protoceratops andrewsi* – 'Andrews' first horned eye'.

The following year, Andrews aimed to build success upon success, with the help of another three palaeontologists. Eren Dabasu yielded immense troves – duck-billed dinosaurs that had been piled up in the shallows with flesh-eaters; twenty-six titanothere fossils, which revealed a striking resemblance to American ones, further proof of a land-bridge between the two continents; more of those enigmatic eggshells; and the largest mammalian carnivore ever, with a skull double the size of the Alaskan brown bear. It was actually found by a Chinese assistant, Kan Chuen-pao, known to the team as 'Buckshot', who had proved so able he had been promoted to assistant palaeontologist, but Osborn named the find for Buckshot's boss, *Andrewsarchus mongoliensis*.

On, then, to the Flaming Cliffs, and so many astonishing results that the expedition ran short of plaster and the burlap used to make fossil-casts. Andrews sanctioned the use of cooking flour to make plaster and tore up his own pyjamas for binding material. Among the new finds was a fleet-footed predator, Velociraptor, now famous as the smart and vengeful antihero of *Jurassic Park*.

On 13 July George Olsen, assistant palaeontologist, made the find for which the expedition was best remembered. In Andrews' words, Olsen 'reported at tiffin that he had found some fossil eggs. Inasmuch as the deposit was obviously Cretaceous and too early for large birds, we did not take his story very seriously.' Guessing that the things would prove to be common-or-garden stones, everyone went to look at the find, three fossilized ovals twenty centimetres long. There was no mistaking what they were.

'These must be dinosaur eggs,' said Granger. 'They can't be anything else.'

They were not the first dinosaur eggs to be found, but previous discoveries had been dismissed as those of birds. These leathery-looking ovals showed they were not, and explained all those shelly fragments elsewhere.

The Americans turned up dozens of eggs over the next five weeks. One sandstone block contained thirteen eggs in two layers, as if the mother had turned as a turtle does while laying them. Moreover, some of the eggs contained fossilized embryos that looked as if they could be Protoceratops. The Americans assumed these were all Protoceratops eggs. Apparently, the area had been thickly populated with these squat, sheep-sized creatures, with their heavy heads, parrot beaks and protective neck-shields.

The link between 'protos' and the eggs seemed all the more certain when Olsen found the remains of a small, toothless, bipedal dinosaur lying right above a nest of eggs. It was, Andrews pointed out, 'strangely birdlike', a comparison that at the time seemed coincidental. It would take another fifty years to explain the similarity. When Osborn described the fossil, he wrote a scenario of its death, imagining the animal 'having been overtaken by a sandstorm in the very act of robbing the dinosaur egg nest'. He named it *Oviraptor philoceratops*, 'Egg-stealer that likes ceratopsians'. He added a warning about his own imaginings, 'which might entirely mislead us as to its feeding habits and belie its character', but his paper planted an idea that would dog research for decades.

One discovery was to prove of particular importance. Granger found a tiny skull, which he labelled simply 'unidentified reptile'. Its significance would not be known for two years.

Such success demanded more expeditions, more money, and no one was better qualified to raise it than Andrews. The discoveries made superb publicity. Dinosaurs, which had already seized the public imagination, now acquired new traits, not at all the clodhopping reptiles of nineteenth-century imaginings, less monstrous, more charming, with nesting instincts, and families, and babies. When Andrews arrived on the West Coast on his way home, he was mobbed at the port, mobbed again at each station across the continent, mobbed in New York. At his first lecture at the museum, 4,000 people queued for the 1,400 tickets, and he had to give the lecture twice. At a fundraising auction, one of the eggs was sold for $5,000 as a publicity stunt. Not for the last time, America went dinosaur-crazy.

In 1924, Andrews again went to Urga to prepare the way for the most ambitious expedition so far. The Mongolians were much sharper than before. They had read of the sale of the egg, and done some swift multiplication: 2,000 fossils × $5,000 – why, the Americans had stolen 10 *million* dollars' worth of Mongolian property. They also knew that the Americans were making detailed maps, of great value to hostile nations. They were loth to accept that the egg-sale was a publicity stunt, could not believe that 'we would come from America, have a great caravan of camels and a fleet of motor cars, bring 40 men and spend thousands of dollars, just to dig up a few old bones. That was too ridiculous for any man to believe.' It took three weeks and the payment of $3,000 to get permits, which were granted only on condition that Andrews provided duplicates of everything – fossils, maps, publications.

The following year, the largest expedition so far set off for Mongolia: 40 men, 125 camels, 18,000 litres of fuel, many tons of food. The risks were higher, too. Almost every week, cars heading into the desert were robbed by brigands. Andrews was not deterred. 'Foreigners, as a rule, shoot too well, and they do not follow the Chinese custom of running at the first sign of danger. Twenty Chinese, be they bandits or otherwise, to one foreigner, is about the proper ratio for anything like a good fight.'

There was one hiccup in their progress. The advance caravan of camels was seized by Mongol border troops. In fact, they were not *Mongolian* Mongols, but Buriat Mongols from across the border in Siberia, operating under Russian control, eager to seize anyone travelling north who seemed suspicious or rich enough to pay a hefty administration fee. The commanding officer's attention had been taken by seditious literature in the form of the *Saturday Evening Post* and flashlight batteries which he thought were bombs. News came back to Andrews and the others, digging a few miles back down the trail, that when he arrived at the border he was to be arrested, taken to Urga and shot. 'A most interesting prospect!' he observed. He was infuriated: the caravan was supposed to be weeks ahead of the cars. A delay like this could prejudice the whole venture. He pulled up at the offending officer's tent with five of his team, all armed, and threatened to arrest the head man and take *him* to Urga, unless everything and everyone was allowed to proceed instantly. The man complied, quivering. The swaying camels set off again, while Andrews returned to complete work in China.

In May, back at the Flaming Cliffs, yet more new discoveries emerged, this time evidence of human presence – flints, scrapers, stone drills, arrow heads, flakes of jasper and chalcedony, pottery, layers of ash and charcoal. There were no bones, and the Stone Age artisans were not ancestral humans, but they were the first prehistoric finds. The artefacts, now dated between 12,000 and 7,000 years ago, showed that the Americans were not the first to find dinosaur eggs. Bits of their shells, mixed with ostrich-egg shells, lay around the ancient campsites. Apparently, the Mesolithic campers – 'Dune Dwellers', Andrews called them – had brought them from the Flaming Cliffs two miles away and used them as decoration.

Finally, news came of the 'unidentified reptile' found previously. W. D. Matthew, back in the Natural History Museum in New York, wrote that the skull was one of the oldest known mammals, a shrew-like creature that he named Zalamdalestes. At the time this was thought to be only the second mammal skull from the Age of Dinosaurs ever discovered (the first, Tritylodon, which came from South Africa, has since been dethroned as a putative mammal ancestor). In his letter Matthew wrote, 'Do your utmost to get some other skulls.'

'I guess that's an order,' said Granger as he finished the letter. 'I'd better get busy.'

It was a difficult assignment. What he was looking for was not the smoothness and paleness of an exposed fossil, but minute nodules of sandstone that might, like a berry, enclose a seed of petrified bone. The floor of the Cliffs was scattered with millions of nodules. Yet an hour later he came back with another little mammal skull. 'Such things do not sound possible, I will admit,' Andrews commented. 'But they did happen.' A week later, Granger had seven such skulls. By the end of the dig, he had bits of eleven of these rat-like, shrew-like, rabbit-like creatures, which showed that already in dinosaurian times the mammals had divided into placentals (those that bear live young) and marsupials (those that raise young in a pouch). There were also two members of a third mammalian branch, multituberculates, a diverse group of rodents and herbivores of obscure origins that died out without descendants some 60 million years ago.

That was the height of Andrews' success. In China, civil war between Nationalists and Communists fanned xenophobia, and two further expeditions were fraught with risk and political problems. Palae-ontology was equated with robbery. In 1928 Andrews paid $10,000 in new 'taxes' just to get to Kalgan, then was not allowed beyond Eren Dabasu. All his finds were confiscated for weeks. In 1930, as conditions became worse, Osborn declared the dangers and the expense too great, and the Central Asiatic Expeditions ended.

Writing after the end of the expeditions, Andrews said that, of all the discoveries, 'Those [mammal] skulls were the most precious of all the remarkable specimens that we obtained in Mongolia.' It seems a graceful admission, given the fame conferred upon him by the dinosaur finds and the unappealing nature of these minute fragments. But they ful-filled an important function for him, and for the expedition's mentor, Osborn. Osborn had predicted that Mongolia would provide a key to the understanding of mammalian radiation, in particular of human origins. Here was the world's first collection of early mammals. In a totally unexpected way, the Gobi had divulged missing links after all. The rat-like skulls of Deltatheridium and Zalamdalestes – I can hear the patter of their paws in their mellifluous names – humans saw ancestral forms that linked them to all mammals, from the pygmy shrew to the blue whale. In the Flaming Cliffs lay humanity's deepest roots.

To see this palaeontological shrine, I would have walked for days over burning sands. Instead, I was about to be whisked right into the sanctum itself with an ease that Andrews would have envied.

It was early evening already, well after 7.00, but sunset was late, and it would remain light enough to film for an hour or so. I prepared myself to feel as one should when ambition is fulfilled: humble, awestruck, poetic. There would be words to camera. No one here would have a clue what I was saying, but I surely had a responsibility of some kind to this historic site. I rehearsed weighty phrases about roaming dinosaurs and eggs still eroding from the crumbling cliffs. My scripting was broken by another thought: what if tourists really *did* come? I had a guilty vision of plastic dinosaurs and Coke tins and a mass of bottles cluttering the pristine landscape.

Then I noticed, with surprise, that we were heading round, and down, parallel with the edge of the escarpment. Ahead and below was a plain of dark green against the grey of the surrounding desert. The saxauls. We swirled round at the base of the sandstone escarpment, past a single tent – securely locked, abandoned for the summer while its owner sought better pastures in the mountains – and halted on the edge of the saxaul 'forest'.

The film crew carted camera and tripod off among the saxauls. I wandered about on my own. The trees were gnarled and ancient and small, as if the aridity and coarse soil had bound their roots and turned them into bonzais. But they liked it here. Growing about three or four metres apart, they locked this section of Gobi fast, their roots forming little mounds at their bases. This square mile was a borderland, where the little trees could profit from the water flowing from the cliffs yet far enough from them to avoid being swept away by the occasional slurry of flood water and sand.

The surface was puzzling: baked by the sun, the red gravel was covered by a dark patina a few millimetres thick. Our tyre marks scoured it away, leaving livid scars. I wondered how long they would last, and remembered a line from Andrews' account of his second journey to this spot: 'We found the tracks of our motor cars, made ten months before.' If I returned in a year, would these tracks still be here, evidence of a little violation?

From far away there came a surprising sound, like distant artillery. I looked up, and saw an answer to my question. There would be no marks this time next year, because we were in for a storm. Below the lowering sun, dark clouds were forming. What I had heard was distant thunder.

I became nervous. Andrews had found Gobi storms to be brutal, powerful enough to turn grains into flying splinters that cut tents to ribbons and flayed exposed skin. On one occasion, he wrote, 'I could hardly breathe. Seemingly a raging devil stood beside my head with buckets of sand, ready to dash them into my face the moment I came up for air out of the sleeping bag. There was something distinctly personal about the storm. It was not just a violent disturbance of the unthinking elements. It acted like a calculating evil beast. After each raging attack it would draw off for a few moments' rest. The air, hanging motionless, allowed the suspended sand to sift gently down into our smarting eyes. Then with a sudden spring, the storm devil was on us, clawing, striking, ripping, seeming to roar in fury that any of the tents still stood.'

'Why are we filming here?' I asked the girl with the dark glasses, in rising anxiety.

Wasn't this our destination, she said – Bayan Zag, the place that was rich in saxaul trees?

The director was already lining up a shot. He beckoned, and directed me to a little rise behind a wizened tree.

I hesitated, and spoke again to the assistant. 'You better tell him that this is not what tourists would come for. They come for dinosaurs. I'm sure Mr Sukhe would want him to film the place where the Americans found dinosaurs.'

'Dinosaurs not here?'

'No!'

'But dinosaurs are at Bayan Zag? This is Bayan Zag?'

'Yes. But the dinosaurs are over there! In the cliffs!'

There was a brief discussion.

'He says: talk about dinosaurs here.'

I wondered if I should make the point more strongly. These idiots had wasted half the day, and the sun was setting, and they'd got the wrong subject, and now clouds were about to cover the sun. We had, I guessed, half an hour before daylight died and the storm struck.

On the other hand, the director had made a decision. If we argued, we'd get nothing. If we moved fast, perhaps we could get both saxauls *and* cliffs. I gave in, and nodded.

'How long you speak?'

I glanced at the gathering clouds.

'I don't know. I'll try for forty-five seconds.'

I can't remember my words, but two minutes later we were back in the cars, heading for the cliffs. Where the gravel turned to rock and a gully enticed us towards the heart of the escarpment, a beam of sunlight set the sandstone afire, just as Andrews had described. But that gleam would be the last of the sun. Behind us, thunder boomed. The clouds were gathering faster than I realized. How long did we have? Ten minutes?

With car no. 2 a couple of hundred metres behind us, we bounced into the floor of the gully.

'Where?' said the driver.

'Here!'

The cameraman jumped out, and ran over to a low ridge to check an angle. I looked back, and saw something I had not seen before. Below the dark thunder cloud, silhouetted by it, was another cloud. It was lighter, a dirty grey tinged with yellow, and it formed a perfect arc. That wasn't just a storm. It was dust. Above, the sky was still blue, but that thing blotting out the horizon was coming for us fast, and it was hungry, with thunder in its belly and lightning in its eyes.

Behind us, just where we had descended from the rim of the escarpment, the other car stopped. There was a pause, a silence. You could almost hear the gears clicking in our brains. A light breeze brushed sand round my ankles, and I thought: this gully was made by rain. This stuff underfoot was dried mud. If we didn't get out instantly, we wouldn't be going anywhere for a long, long time.

From the other jeep, someone pointed, beckoned and shouted. The cameraman, fifty metres away, looked up, and ran. By the time he reached us, his feet were hidden by a rising cloud of sand flowing like liquid oxygen. The first heavy drops smacked the windscreen.

Revving and spinning the wheels, the cars headed back, and up, over sand already wet with rain, to the edge of the escarpment.

We climbed, fast. I glanced back, and saw –

– a blank, a nothing. It was as if a sheet had been drawn across the cliffs, the drop we had just climbed, the saxauls, the plain beyond. The beast had us in its jaws, and they were closing fast, surrounding us with its grey-brown breath. All the world now was the track of the jeep in front, the only lines in a universe without dimension. In snow storms, you get a white-out. This was a grey-out.

The car ahead stopped. In wind and gathering rain, a quick agreement on what to do: flee.

'This is a "black wind",' yelled the girl, sounding panicky. 'Maybe once a year. Very dangerous. The wind, it blows at a hundred metres a second.'

We sped away, with the storm rumbling behind us, drowned out by the squeak and judder of the jeep as we fled over flat ground, out of time, out of place, cocooned in grey.

I wondered about their urgency. A hundred metres a second. That's 6,000 metres a minute. Six thousand metres is about, I pondered, four miles. Hang on. Four miles a minute was 240 miles an hour. That was crazy. Winds don't come that powerful. But if that was what they were telling each other, no wonder we were fleeing.

An oasis sprang out of the grey, a flash of green, and half a dozen tents, their doors shut, their airholes all battened down by weighted ropes.

But all at once the storm seemed to be passing. The rain stopped, the wind was dying. The flying dust now came only from the wheels. Ahead, the fog was lifting, clear sky emerging, and then a shadowy horizon, rimmed by the Three Beauties, fifty kilometres away.

There now, I reassured myself. What was all the fuss about? I felt a bit let down by these pusillanimous townies, scaring themselves with talk of flesh-stripping winds, blowing our reactions out of all pro-portion. Ahead, the sky became an eggshell blue, and the saw-toothed ridge of the Three Beauties stood out stark and crisp.

For the last fifteen minutes, we had all been staring in front, hyp-notized by the track, and the car ahead, and the lure of clearing skies, and limited also by the darkened glass of the windows. It was like driving in blinkers. Now, as the immediate threat receded, I glanced sideways, and saw something that did odd things to the pit of my stomach.

It was the hard edge of a cloud, curving up and back from the surface of the desert. I pointed, and we all stared.

At that moment, the car ahead stopped. Two people got out and threw open the bonnet. We drew up alongside. Someone yelled for a spanner: blocked fuel filter. We piled out, and then, all at once, we could see the storm, entire. What I had thought was the storm clearing was a consequence of our flight. We had simply out-distanced it, emerg-ing into a place of temporary peace, but leaving the clouds to gather behind us, as if galvanized by our escape. Now the storm was coming for us with a sort of focused rage that had not been there when I first noticed it.

To our left, that hard blade was the leading edge of a great grey-brown dome of dust that formed a semicircle, perhaps fifteen kilometres across and nearly a kilometre high. It was the mouth of the beast, and it was ringed above by a mantle of charcoal clouds, and inside it thunder boomed and lightning flashed.

I stood, hypnotized by power and majesty, knowing I would never see such a thing again, wondering if we were, after all, about to be swallowed and flayed alive. Beside me, the others had similar thoughts and fears. The driver whipped out the filter, splashed it with petrol, blew on it, cleaned it, replaced it.

Round us, the desert stirred with the storm's first menacing breath. It was coming at us fast, at a gallop. As the edge of the disc ate up the desert to either side of us, the sky darkened, the distant mountains vanished, and the cloud began to close around us.

'Let's go!'

Doors slammed, I jumped in. Beside us, the stricken car whined, coughed, died. We waited, helplessly, either for release or execution. The engine whined again, roared into life, and we were off, through raindrops as heavy as hail, driven by a wind that licked at the roof and the rattling doors.

But now we had regained our breath, and the going was good. Again we burst clear of the engulfing dust, again the mountains emerged, and spirits soared. This was exhilarating. Alongside us, now near, now half a kilometre away across the open desert, our companions ran at the head of their own cloud, silhouetted against the larger, overarching one.

Ahead, perhaps eight or ten kilometres away, white dots emerged: the camp.

The mathematics were simple. On the level, we could manage fifty, perhaps sixty kilometres per hour. The storm, I guessed, was coming on at about thirty kilometres per hour. If we could keep a straight course, we could win. But the course was not straight. Here and there were dry watercourses. At every twist of the track, at every gully, we would slide and slew and change gear, and lurch down, and round, and up, and the storm would reach out for us, until we drew clear.

Five kilometres, five minutes to home. Now the storm's outriders, like a breaking wave, seemed about to surge over the camp itself. But bumping up from the last gully, I saw that the leading edge was beyond the camp. Around us, and between us and the tents, all was still. We tore through the gates with two minutes to spare.

I stared one last time at the rolling clouds, waited until the edge of the camp dissolved into a fury of whipped sand and seething rain, and fled into my tent. Actually, it was Sukhe's tent as well. He was in there, his paunch chicly clad in massive shorts, Nike trainers over white socks, talking with a big, bald, mustachioed Russian travel agent, who had arrived in a four-wheel drive Mitsubishi crammed with camping and travel gear. This fearsome exponent of the new capitalism had driven several thousand miles across Central Asia, heading across Mongolia into China in pursuit of new destinations. The two were deep in deals and vodka toasts, and didn't need to pay attention to any storms, because in this haven of heavy canvas – its rounded shape shouldering the wind, airhole secured, wooden door locked tight – storms battered in vain. I felt a childish shiver of joy.

To the west, the storm was washing the Flaming Cliffs into a slurry, scouring away the marks of our presence, restoring the wilderness, and remodelling it.

Sukhe held up a vodka glass. 'The Flaming Cliffs, they are beautiful?' he shouted above the wind. 'You want to go back?'

Yes, I nodded. I had a wilderness to see and an explorer's footsteps to follow, sooner rather than later, for if Sukhe had his way, later would be too late.

So two days later I set off again, this time with the patient Ariunaa and our driver Batöldzii, who had piloted us around the Three Beauties. We swung northwest, with the Three Beauties on our left, over an immensity of grey washed by a pastel green. Andrews had crossed a plain like this, nicknaming it 'The Hundred Mile Tennis Court'. Trailing dust, we skirted the tourist camp, bypassing the few puddles that remained of the brief downpour. After another hour, well beyond where Sukhe's film crew had veered off northwards to see the dunes, the track lifted, and breasted a rise. Below us was Bulgan, a town with a core of white buildings surrounded by stockaded gers. We needed to stop here for two reasons: fuel, and if possible to find the warden of Bayan Zag, in the hopes that he would come with us.

I should have guessed what to expect, for Siggy had mentioned

Bulgan as the site of his plantation. Below lay apple trees, fields of vegetables, rank grass. From a nearby field a pipe led back up the slope towards us, vanishing over a low hill. As we swung around the flank, I saw what made Bulgan an oasis – a small lake, set in the lee of the hill, and fed by a spring that ran strong and clear, unaffected by the lack of rain. Subterranean pressure forced deeper-lying water up through a fault, feeding the town.

Descending, Batöld pulled into a one-pump fuel station. While he was filling up, there occurred one of those coincidences that mark life in the Gobi. Down the hill in our wake came a smart red motorbike ridden by a burly figure of seventy or thereabouts. Man and machine made an incongruous union of ancient and modern. Wrapped in a brown deel with a gold waistband, he was wearing a traditional onion-dome hat and long leather boots ornately incised, with retroussé toes and red trimming.

Ariunaa overheard his name as he exchanged words with the driver of the truck. 'This is Baitsert,' she said, 'the man you want to talk to.'

Baitsert was the guardian of the Flaming Cliffs. Overcoming my surprise, I asked if he could accompany us. He looked at me, and I saw that he had a wonderful face, made for laughter. His smile raised mountains of wrinkles that besieged his eyes, and turned him into the epitome of joy. Unfortunately, no, he was expected somewhere else right now. But we were welcome just to go. Was there anything I wanted to know? He smiled radiantly, awaiting questions.

I wondered what guarding the Flaming Cliffs actually entailed. Could he tell me what he actually did, as work, on a daily basis?

'I wish I could!' His eyes seized up into slits and he began to laugh, I suppose at the very idea that driving around on a red motorbike looking at rocks and plants was *work*. The laughter spread like a happy contagion, to Ariunaa, to the driver, to the fuel pump attendant, to the driver of the truck. 'I would be very interested to discover the answer to this question!' he said, wiping the tears from his eyes on his sleeve.

At last he became serious. There were so many tourists these days, from all countries. And the geologists! Sometimes twenty people a week, sometimes a hundred, came here. It was his job to see they did not damage the saxauls, or dig around too much in the Flaming Cliffs.

He kick-started his bike. 'Don't take any eggs!' he warned, adding,

'The Americans say they discovered the bones, the eggs. But people round here knew about them long before. We called them dragons!'

In fact, it wasn't going to be all that easy to find the way. To be certain, Batöld called in at a friend's house, and sought local help. With another young man aboard, we set off, over more of the Hundred Mile Tennis Court.

Fifteen kilometres out, the plain rose gently. Two days previously, I had approached from the opposite direction and left blinded by the storm, but I knew where we were. As we skimmed up the hard slope, the frustration of that cursory approach, the sense of loss as I was snatched from the cliff edge, the drama of our precipitate departure, all dropped away. The sky was clear, the breeze gentle, and we were alone. We drew up on a platform at the edge of cliffs.

I had in my mind that the drop would be a sharp one, as if this were a miniature version of the Grand Canyon. But these rocks were not hard enough to preserve sheer falls and sharp edges. Opposite, the sandstone jutted up in proper cliffs, but in many spots the edge simply fell away into an angled descent made by rain-washed, windblown detritus. Below, a peninsula of sandstone reaching across the valley floor fell away at its tip into a rubble, which merged with the alluvium, washed smooth by the storm. A mile to the south, the ochre turned to green where the saxauls grew.

The cliffs are made up of wonders – the variety of fallen rock, and the interplay of ochres, reds and grey, and the shadowed and secretive clefts. Andrews captured the sight well: 'Like a fairy city, it is ever changing. In the flat light of midday the strange forms shrink and lose their shape; but when the sun is low the Flaming Cliffs assume a deeper red, and a wild mysterious beauty lies with the purple shadows in every canyon.'

But there was more here than picture postcard beauty. I felt as if I had been granted a sight into the heart of the Gobi, and found it to be alive. Weeks before, far to the west, the granite flanks of the Sacred Mother had made me feel I was on the rock of ages. Here, there was no such sense of timelessness. These soft rocks were young and vulnerable, with the processes that constantly unmake them on show. It was as if the desert had created a model of itself, to reveal in one square mile the processes of a million, and in days the work of aeons – underlying rock cut open by rain and wind and frost, boulders broken down into stone and sand, the sand washed away, the water vanishing into substrata, wind seizing the grains to wear away yet more of their origins, and then dispersing them.

To feel the atmosphere of the cliffs on my own, I began to walk down the slope into the valley. My feet crunched and slid. My hand reaching out for support broke off a cornice. The view must already have changed since Andrews' day – as it had, minutely, since yesterday morning – for the whole place was like biscuit, made crusty under the oven sun, but easily dissolved. There was no trace of the recent storm, except that the carpet of coarse sand still looked newly washed, and I saw not a single sign of human presence, not a stray piece of toilet paper, not a can. It was a place of silence and emptiness.

Berkey's explanation of how these cliffs arose leapt to life. Once, the area had been very much damper than it is now. Several thousand years ago, there was a river here that poured over the edge of the plateau and cut the canyons. The walls and floors of the valleys were protected from erosion by grass, bushes and trees, which provided lush living for what Andrews called the 'Dune Dwellers' – not dune dwellers at all, as he realized later, but plains people. Gradually, as the climate changed, the people were driven out, and the vegetation died, exposing the soft rocky base. Rainstorms washed the soil down into the valley floor, clogging it with debris and mud, covering the ancient hearths. When it dried out, winds whipped the debris into dust, gathering it to sand-blast the cliffs into their present form, and blowing away the finer grains entirely.

The path down had been made smooth by others, though after the storm there was no trace of a footprint. All would have been on the look out for fossils. On one side of the path, where the wall rose more steeply, a shell-like shape protruded. Where the cone vanished into rock, the matrix was smooth where curious fingers had explored. One day, after more storms and more probing, some Japanese will prise it out with a cry of triumph, only to find it is no egg, but an egg-shaped concretion of rock. Another lay at my feet as I reached the bottom. I picked it up, felt how soft it was, and dropped it. It collapsed into half a dozen pieces.

I wandered over the valley floor, over low, dust-covered dunes, past scattered bushes, scouting for fossils. Everywhere there were possibilities – shapes suggesting femurs, knuckles, skulls and eggs, but all were mere rocky accretions. You need a good and experienced eye to spot the real thing.

The shapes were enough to remind me that this was a cemetery, with bones being continually eroded out. I scrounged around a new fall beneath a cliff at the far side of the valley, and saw that this was a place of the living as well as the dead. There were droppings of horse, camel and gazelle. Little bushes offered scanty grazing. I knelt, feeling the sun strike through my shirt. Little enigmatic lines criss-crossed the desert floor, bordered by pinprick indentations. A foot from me, I saw a lizard, its tail dragging, dividing the prints of its splayed feet. We both froze.

I imagined the little animal magnified a thousand-fold. That would suit Sukhe. If he had his way this place would become Cretaceous Park, with a hologram of Tarbosaurus rearing from the sandstone at busloads of tourists on the apron of rock up above. Listening to the breeze whispering among the sandstone canyons, it seemed unlikely. This was a long way for tourist buses. I preferred to imagine the Flaming Cliffs as a living memorial to its buried creatures and a stage-set for nothing more than black winds, brief rains, and its own slow erosion.

8

Cretaceous Park

With Mongolia welded on to the Soviet empire, China barred by civil war and revolution, and both locked away by xenophobia, the only scientists who could follow in Andrews' footsteps were those from the Eastern Bloc. In the late 1940s, when the Soviet Union emerged from war, three Russian expeditions went exploring 290 kilometres west and south of the Flaming Cliffs, across the Three Beauties, beyond the ranges I had seen from the top of the Singing Sands, to a valley named after the mountains that hem it in to the north: the Nemegt. They found 'the stuff' to be there beyond anything Andrews had dreamed of.

The Nemegt Valley, 180 kilometres long and fifty kilometres across, at once proved itself a wonderland for fossils. This is a region of 'badlands', tracts of soft red sandstone eroded into decaying peaks and gullies, miles of alluvial fans, hard rock pavements, scattered dunes, and plains of red gravel that look like the surface of Mars. These lead westwards to Altan Uul, the 'Gold Mountain' that guards the end of the Nemegt mountains. Altan's canyons cut through exposures of sandstone and rubble, giving way to garish exposures where former soils and plants left stripes of purple, red, yellow, blue and green. The mountain is well named: there is gold here, in minute traces. It is this area, to the south of Altan Ula, that the government cut from the proposed Three Beauties National Park to allow for the possibility of future mining.

From these forbidding regions the Russians removed 120 tons of fossils. Among their finds was the place they called the 'Dragon's Tomb', a graveyard of seven duck-billed vegetarian dinosaurs – hadrosaurs – similar to types found in Canada; and three examples of the Gobi's own 'top predator', the local tyrannosaur, named Tarbosaurus. Like T. rex, tarbos had a one-metre skull packed with razor teeth up to fifteen centimetres long, all close set to create the shape of an enormous scalpel. These creatures could use their jaws to carve into a 50-ton herbivore and cut out a mouthful faster than you or I can bite into a ham sandwich.

At about the same time, across the other side of the Soviet empire, a young Polish palaeontology student, Zofia Kielan-Jaworowska, heard the eminent Polish palaeontologist Roman Kozlowski speak of Andrews' expeditions, and daydreamed of Gobi dinosaurs. She had little to go on, for Poland had no dinosaur fossils of its own, and in Eastern Europe's shattered postwar economy there was not much hope of taking her interest further. She focused instead on fossil marine invertebrates. But in 1961, as the Eastern Bloc countries came together under Soviet auspices, Kozlowski suggested a series of Mongolian–Polish expeditions to the Gobi, putting forward Kielan-Jaworowska as one of the leaders. Three Polish–Mongolian expeditions in the mid-1960s were followed by others each summer until 1972, when the Russians took over again. The Poles – fifteen of them in all, half of whom had never worked in a desert before – learnt fast. Kielan-Jaworowska, who is now back in Poland in semi-retirement after a long stint in Oslo, became one of the world's experts in Cretaceous fossils. Her Mongolian colleagues, Dashzeveg and Barsbold, also made themselves international reputations.

The Poles and Mongolians, working together, mined more treasures, not just from the Nemegt and the Flaming Cliffs but other locations as well, some along the route I had driven with Ariunaa, another way to the west, over towards the borders of the Gobi National Park. They found more tarbosaurs, more hadrosaurs, fast-moving little carnivores, spike-studded ankylosaurs, dozens of ceratopsians, lizards by the score, dozens of species of mammals, even some of gigantic herbivorous sauropods, the first to be found in the Gobi. (The Gobi sandstone fossil beds were late Cretaceous, when sauropods were becoming rare.) So rich was one red sandstone site in the Nemegt Valley that Kielan-Jaworowska nicknamed it El Dorado.

One day, at the far western end of the Nemegt hills, Kielan-Jaworowska saw a telltale patch of white. Carefully dusting away the sandstone, she found a pair of forelimbs two and a half metres long, each ending in three thirty-centimetre claws. She named the creature to which these fearsome implements belonged Deinocheirus ('Terrible Hand'). Nothing more of the animal has ever been found, allowing the imagination free rein. Deinocheirus may have been a dinosaurian sloth, using its hooked toes to dangle from trees. But given the nature of its contemporaries it seems more likely to have been something out of a science-fiction nightmare: a tyrannosaur-like monster five metres high, able to run at sixty-five kilometres per hour, but with the tyrannosaur's stunted forearms replaced by articulated scimitars that could slice open a sauropod with a couple of slashes.

Among the finds, two were dramatic, quite literally, for they caught in stone the drama of death with photographic immediacy.

One of the animals, a tarbosaur about two and a half metres long, was found 'lying on its side, with its head thrown back, its legs drawn up, its tail bent ... preserved in the exact position in which the animal had met its death 80 million years ago. Dead camels are often found in the same posture of agony, head thrown back and legs drawn up.'

The second find emerged from the lee of a butte overlooking a salty lake at the far western end of the Three Beauties, not far from the spot where Ariunaa and I camped on our way to the Singing Sands. The spot is known to geologists as Tugrugeen Shireh, 'Round Table' (more correctly: Tögrögiin Shiree. Tögrög is the name for Mongolia's currency. The Chinese and Japanese names for their currencies, *yuan* and *yen*, also mean 'round'). What emerged from beneath Kielan-Jaworowska's tools was a bas-relief of a proto and a velociraptor locked in mortal combat. The velociraptor is wrapped around the proto's head, its arm in the proto's mouth, its hind legs with their formidable claws scrabbling at the proto's neck.

The 'fighting dinosaurs', a prize exhibit in Ulan Bator's Natural History Museum, is one of the world's most astonishing fossil images. It is as if the two creatures had both simultaneously seen Medusa. So unlikely is the original event – let alone the unlikeliness of a scientist stumbling upon such a rarity – that there have been many attempts to explain the scene away. Perhaps the two animals were not fighting at all. Perhaps the two died separately and were simply washed together by a torrent. But this won't do. The proto's mouth is actually closed on its enemy's arm, and the proto is fossilized in a standing position. There is no getting away from it. Something killed these creatures virtually instantaneously even as they were killing each other. It would take another fifty years to understand what struck them down.

*　　*　　*

Every year finds like these opened wider the window on the past, providing evidence, posing mysteries. Andrews' discoveries, which had appeared so rich and possibly unique, were vastly exceeded by the troves of fossils to be found nearby. By the 1950s, it was clear that the Flaming Cliffs was merely part of a whole assemblage of sites in an area that was at least 320 kilometres across from east to west, and 160 kilometres deep, embracing all the eastern end of the Gobi-Altai mountains.

All the outcroppings and the finds had similarities. Though the lack of radioactive content makes the red sandstone outcrops impossible to date with accuracy, the fossil-rich strata – the Djadokhta Formation, as Andrews' team called them all – seem to have been created by similar deposits of sand at roughly the same time, give or take an aeon or two. They contain similar arrays of diverse forms, from shrew-sized mammals to dinosaurs with thigh bones like pillars, a mass and range of fossilized material that matches the best sites on earth.

The fossils are generally beautifully preserved. They lie in sandstone, but not sedimentary sandstone. The creatures were not fossilized after dying in shallow water or being flooded by streams and rising lakes. Where this happens, fossils are often torn apart by predators or dislocated by flowing water. The Gobi fossils are petrified with immense delicacy, still connected at the knee or elbow, retaining minute bones, like those of the inner ear, and microscopic surface features that mark the routes of nerves and blood vessels. If they are broken it is not usually by the action of ancient waters, but by the creation of the mountains that raised them above the floor of the surrounding desert or by the recent rains that leave them weathering out of the sides of ravines.

They lie there like the bones of a graveyard through which a flood has washed, awaiting the attention of scientists who can use them to paint a picture of the past of 80 million years ago. Already by then, ancestral dinosaurs had dominated life on earth for over 100 million years, overshadowing and outweighing the array of little mammals that probably survived as nocturnal hunters and burrowers. Both appeared during the Triassic period, at a time when the continents formed a unified land mass, known as Pangaea, and continued to evolve as Pangaea's constituents broke apart during the Jurassic and began their 200-million-year drift into their present positions. Separated as island continents, each region became a forcing-house for evolution, breeding its own range of creatures. Cone-bearing trees like pines, spruces and firs were joined by the flowering plants, deciduous trees and grasses, inspiring a further explosive diversification in dinosaur species. This period, the Cretaceous, was the great age of the Ruling Reptiles. Michael Crichton and Steven Spielberg might have named their creation Cretaceous Park, and gained in accuracy – Velociraptor was a creature of the Cretaceous, not the Jurassic. (Incidentally, in real life it was a good deal smaller than in the film, not that you would have much time to notice if you met one face to face.)

On several occasions during the 75 million-year span of the Cretaceous, depending on sea levels, eastern Asia was joined to western North America across the Bering Straits, which allowed an occasional flow of animals, mostly from Asia to America. The Very Old West revamped its fauna, not only the frilled and multi-horned ceratopsians but also velociraptors, armour-plated ankylosaurs, and pachycephalosaurs with battering-ram heads. Therapods of many species hunted across both land masses, leaving their massive three-toed tracks. Perhaps the pet American monster, *Tyrannosaurus rex*, owed its genes to the Mongolian tarbosaurus.

The Gobi offers a cross-section of this sweep of earth's history which could, once enough is found, cast light on many great mysteries: the decline, and perhaps death of the dinosaurs; the origins of mammals – the ancestors of our human ancestors; and the origins of birds. Finally, an understanding of why these fossils formed with such perfection is beginning to reveal the past of the Gobi with a rare intimacy. Like forensic pathologists examining the bodies of murder victims, scientists can make these bones speak.

Re-enter the Americans

You would think that the Gobi beds would be mined out by now, like the great fossil grounds of the American West. Far from it. The bones are speaking now as never before, thanks to a series of expeditions that stand in a direct line from Roy Chapman Andrews' Central Asiatic Expeditions. In January 1990, when the walls of the Communist empire had just tumbled and Mongolia was embarking on her second revolution, a Mongolian delegation arrived at the American Museum of Natural History in New York to invite its scientists back to the Gobi. That summer, Michael Novacek, the museum's Provost of Science and

Curator of Vertebrate Paleontology, led the first western expedition into the Mongolian Gobi since Andrews was last there in 1928. It was the first of six annual expeditions, which again – for the third time since 1922 – produced a flood of new material, revising old ideas, and suggesting new ones.

The first year was enough to show the stuff was still there. Transported in two unreliable Russian trucks, Novácek, with two museum colleagues – Malcolm McKenna and Mark Norell – and the experienced Dashzeveg, scouted Kielan-Jaworowska's El Dorado. There, they found a fine ankylosaur and the twenty-centimetre skull of a previously unknown lizard, resembling the 'dragon' unique to the island of Komodo in Indonesia. The new lizard, Estesia (named in memory of a colleague, the fossil-lizard expert Richard Estes), had canals in its teeth through which it could inject poison into its prey, as the Gila monster of the American southwest, the world's only venomous lizard, does today.

That minor success opened the way for a wider-ranging trip in 1991. For this they acquired three four-wheel drive Mitsubishi Monteros, containers of equipment (including 200 toilet rolls, vital for protecting fossils), freeze-dried food, and hi-tech gear – laptops, GPS navigators, solar cells and caseloads of batteries. The cars took twelve people in all, seven Americans, three Mongolian scientists, a *New York Times* journalist and a photographer.

They worked their way back to El Dorado, then westwards to the end of the Nemegt, up on to the candy-striped exposures on Altan mountain, around the Three Beauties to Tugrugeen Shireh, the spot where the 'fighting dinosaurs' had been found, then back down into the Nemegt's lowlands. This was at a time when Mongolia was suffering the worst effects of the transition to capitalism. Fresh food was scarce. The heat in the lowlands was a misery. And there were flies, flies, flies, settling on their eyes in maddening, muddy clouds. There were some good finds – a lovely little Zalamdalestes, another Velociraptor – but hardly enough to justify such efforts and expense. Perhaps it would be better, the next year.

It wasn't. A caravan of eight vehicles and twenty-five people included a five-man film crew making a documentary for the BBC and WGBH in Boston. The sheer logistics – the struggle to find fuel, buy food, repair vehicles – worked against them. There were no great new finds (or so it seemed at the time: in fact, one little creature, an unnamed therapod, would later prove of immense significance).

It was only in the fourth year, 1993, that the investment, the commitment and the accumulating experience paid off, in ways that would have staggered and delighted Chapman Andrews.

To learn more about this work, I went looking for one of Mongolia's most senior palaeontologists, Altangerel ('Golden Light') Perle, whose name I had seen on a number of scientific papers. Perle was an Associate Professor in the Geology Department at the State University. I had to find him on foot, because I did not have his phone number, nor could I discover it. Ulan Bator has no phone books. People build their professional and social lives by exchanging cards and creating their own fat little directories. The system works, partly because local calls are free, partly because there just aren't all that many people you need to see. In a world where everyone may have 100 or more contacts, a conversation or two can lead you wherever you wish. But at that moment I had none.

The building that housed Geology, a concrete monument to the 1950s, would have been a corpse but for the flow and chatter of students leaving for the summer holidays. In the echoing entrance hall, there was no supervisor, no scattering of notices, no lockers, no furniture to fill the shadows. A young woman pointed up a broad stairway smelling of damp cement and toilets. The voices died behind me, for the end of term had left the upstairs offices empty. A bad and ancient mural of a dinosaur showed I was on the right track, and I followed a dim corridor past a line of locked doors painted in ancient institutional green, my feet making the scuffed wooden floor-blocks clatter. A door ahead stood partly ajar, inviting entry. Inside, an empty room was hemmed with cupboards on which stood bits of rock and the cast of a triceratops head. In the corner was another door, leading into an inner office, from which came the soft murmur of two voices.

'Professor Perle?'

'Yes, one moment.' He spoke in English. 'Please wait.'

Perle, in a grey suit, no tie, and a shirt buttoned at the neck, was reviewing the work of a young woman student, who was just leaving. For a professor in his fifties he had a remarkable air of youthfulness, mainly because a schoolboyish shock of hair fell to the top of his glasses. He at once revealed a rich if individualistic command of English, with a contorted pronunciation I took to be from lack of practice. It was a good moment to talk. Term was over. No one else was waiting to see him. I seized upon him as a missing link between Andrews and the present.

Remembering the fuss over the sale of the dinosaur egg and the rising xenophobia that put an end to Chapman Andrews' expeditions in 1930, I couldn't help wondering if he, and Mongolian scientists generally, felt any resentment that the Americans had been the first to reveal and exploit the Gobi's fossil wealth.

'They came to make only palaeontological explorations! They found very many enormously-interesting-for-the-science naturals, many historically important finds.' He spoke with an enthusiasm that constantly pressed at the limits of his English, working his exuberant thoughts into the Procrustean constraints of a foreign language. The effort gave him the impression of being just the tiniest bit drunk. Perhaps he was. It would not have been surprising, given the contrast between his expertise and its scant rewards.

'I heard of Roy Chapman Andrews when I was fifteen. Then in my student time, I began to study in State Library, and saw a small article written by him in which he asked, "Where are the dinosaur *nests*?" I began to be fascinated.'

'So Andrews was a source of inspiration?'

'You are right! When I make my lovely find, I name it after Mr Andrews.'

I didn't know anything about his lovely find. He explained. It happened in 1973, when he was part of a Russo–Mongolian expedition in Baishin Tsav, in the southeast Gobi.

'First I see a piece of white, just this big.' He held up his pen-top, and turned it end on. 'During bulldozer excavation, after it passed, I followed, and I see this piece of white–'

'A *bulldozer*? Going over fossils?'

'The driver is very skilful. When we say: take 3 centimetres off to reveal new strata, he can do it. Just 1 centimetre even. The fossils survive, because they are in the rock. Then I dug down another 20 centimetres, and there was my found-by-me animal. I name it after a strange and tragic being in Mongolian mythology, the "erlik".'

Erliks often crop up in Mongolian fairy stories. The tyrannosaur of all erliks rules the underworld, while his oviraptorid assistant erliks go out and catch the souls of unsuspecting mortals. It was a good choice of name for an underworld creature, completed with a nod of thanks to his intellectual mentor – *Erlicosaurus andrewsi*.

'I can show you,' Perle went on.

He rose from his desk, pulled open a squeaking iron cupboard and lifted out a cardboard box. From a bed of tissue paper, he raised the skull and jaw of Erlicosaurus. The fossil was just over thirty centimetres long, with a thin lower jaw that closed on the peg-like teeth of a herbivore. The skull itself was a delicate tracery of bone outlining big eye-sockets and a huge nasal passage. I liked Erlicosaurus. This was no mean velociraptor with a vicious set of steak knives in its mouth.

'Seventy million years ago this animal died. Just a single skull, the only one in the whole world. You hold it.'

I hesitated. The bones looked as fragile as porcelain. I was stricken by the same fear that seizes you on a cliff edge. What if suddenly, for no reason, you go mad and throw yourself off? In this case, what if my brain seized up, and I dropped it? How much was it worth?

I took it, of course. It fitted comfortably into my hand, the snout lying up my forearm.

'You could have named it after yourself – *Erlicosaurus perlei*.'

He gave a self-deprecating, dismissive little laugh. 'It's not important. It is the creature that is important.'

'But you have made many discoveries.'

'Ten new species and genera, but this is the most lovely, because *Erlicosaurus andrewsi* gave me my life.'

It took many years for Erlicosaurus (sometimes spelt, more correctly, with a 'k') to find its place in scientific literature, because it was, and remains, a puzzling creature, with a mixture of traits that make its origins hard to establish. In 1980 Perle devised a new 'infra-order', Segnosaurs, for this and a couple of comparable finds. In 1994, in an American Museum of Natural History paper, Novacek's colleague Jim Clark, Mark Norell and Perle proposed to place it in another group, Therizinosaurs. Frankly, they admitted, no one knew how these creatures evolved. They still don't. Erlicosaurus remains a one-off.

Years of collaboration with Russians and Poles followed. Then in 1990, to Perle's delight, the Americans returned, bringing with them almost everything he had lacked for the previous twenty years: money, equipment, drive, wider recognition, the promise of a great new era.

*   *   *

To see their discoveries in perspective, I found Mike Novacek and Jim Clark preparing for their next Gobi adventure. They and their team – minus one of their usual stalwarts Mark Norell – were staying in the city's second best hotel, the Ulan Bator (the best is the Genghis Khan, new and so opulent and inconveniently placed that it is always virtually empty). We talked over a western-style breakfast, across white linen and Nescafé. Though Andrews' direct successors, they looked anything but. Full-bearded with tousled hair and sunglasses, they could have passed for roadies in a rock show. And this was *neat* for them. In the field, the wardrobe is shorts, T-shirts, open sandals and baseball hats, a far cry from Andrews' Sunday-best uniforms.

It was Novacek who did most of the talking. Six years in the Gobi and countless reviews of his team's work had done nothing to blunt his drive, his fierce belief in the significance of his work, his perverse addiction to this gruelling occupation. Six years, after all, was not much compared to what he had been through over the previous twenty years of digging in Baja California, Mexico, the Andes, and Saudi Arabia. Since we spoke he has published his own account of his team's work in the Gobi, *Dinosaurs of the Flaming Cliffs*, the final pages of which summarize the pull of the wilderness and its secrets: 'I can't think of anything more pleasurable and fulfilling than the danger, discomfort, frustration, debate and criticism that come with the work.'

This was a close-knit team. Novacek, Norell and Clark all had a similar background in Los Angeles (indeed Clark and Norell were in 9th Grade together). They all went out into the desert, scrounging around picking up rocks, minerals, anything. And they all grew to love deserts.

'Not attracted to rainforests?'

'Nah. Too many trees, they block the view. They're habitable, so the mark of human operations is much stronger. Deserts are mostly in areas where people don't invade. They have a pristine quality I find very appealing.'

I became interested in the aesthetic attraction of deserts. Not many British writers have been attracted to deserts for their looks. Charles Doughty, St John Philby, T. E. Lawrence were drawn to deserts by the people and their history. You have to look to America for desert aesthetes, to those who first saw the beauty in the wildernesses of Utah and New Mexico, finding there a silence and a purity that countered the hectic urbanism spreading from both shores. That was what Novacek had liked in the American southwest, that was what he liked in the Gobi. 'Because the rocks are so stripped clean and easily seen, I think Jim and Mark and I would love deserts even if we weren't collecting fossils. This is the place on the surface of the earth you can really experience the sky and the land, and have a sense of the whole thing. The sweep of it is fabulous. I even like the heat. I like those cold nights, those incredible skies.'

To work in those conditions – to appreciate the desert free of fear and overwhelming discomfort – you need the right backing, financial and practical. Novacek was well aware how lucky he was, being able to run downstairs to dip into one of the world's greatest collections and have the benefits of modern technology – GPS, helicopters, good maps, satellite images, CAT scanning, visual imaging – and call on backing of $150,000–200,000 for each expedition.

This induced no sense of complacency. In real terms, the money – around $1.5 million so far – is a fraction of what Chapman Andrews spent; and with the whole region opened up by others the risks were less; and the rewards many times greater. Besides, whatever help science now offers, the business of 'finding bones' has not changed. 'Andrews' team and us, when it comes down to it in the field, we still do the same things. We still get a feel about a place, we still have to spot the little flecks that show the presence of a fossil. It takes an eye, and persistence. Most of the time, you're picking up anything that looks like a fossil, and nine times out of ten it's not. You just walk around, pick things up and throw them away. The main thing is to *find bone*.'

For that, there's no shortcut.

In Xanadu

The team that summer of 1993 was back down to two Mongolian scientists, two drivers and ten Americans, maximum (numbers fluctuated as people came and went on their own research schedules), with five vehicles. This time, they aimed at self-sufficiency. One of the vehicles was a 9,000-litre petrol tanker and an imported container held food enough for weeks, including olives, hams, sausages, cheese, even Californian wines.

At Tugrugeen Shireh, they found another of the strange little therapods unearthed the year before. By now, they knew what they were looking at, for the 1992 find had been named Mononykus ('single claw'). It was an intriguing animal, as much bird as dinosaur. About the size of a turkey, it had the big breastbone that in birds carry the wing muscles and a number of other avian features. But it had no wings. Instead, it had stubby little mole-like arms, each with a large claw.

On, then, to the Nemegt. The convoy began a long, slow haul aiming to pass a range of rusty foothills, Ukhaa Tolgod, which climbed towards Gilvent mountain. (Ukhaa Tolgod has been translated as 'Brown Hills' in numerous specialist papers; in fact, *'ukhaa'* means 'light-red'.)

The team now consisted of Norell; Novacek; Clark; Luis Chiappe, a tall, blackbearded Argentinian expert in fossil birds; fossil preparator Amy Davidson; and the veteran Mongolian palaeontologist Dashzeveg. They were aiming westwards, to sites they had explored before, when the fuel tanker sank into sand. Before them, an expanse of red sand led up to a bowl fringed by a couple of pinnacles that looked like the drooping humps of a hungry camel. Forced to camp, they decided to see what the red hills up ahead had to offer.

The following morning – 16 July – dawned hazy and windless. It would be hot, but in this high, dry air not unbearable. They took two Mitsubishis up onto a saddle between two low hills. At once, they spotted a lizard and a proto skull. This looked like as good a spot as any to scout around. While the others went off on their own, Norell, Novacek and Clark remained walking slowly about on the saddle, arms behind their backs, the rough rock crunching beneath their sandals.

Within minutes, Novacek recalled over our breakfast, they began to see that there was something special about the site. 'At first we thought, "Wow, isn't this fifty square feet an incredibly rich place?" Jim, Mark and I were just sort of wandering around like monks, with our arms behind our backs, bent over, and there were these white splotches all over the ground. It looked like someone had spattered paint from a distance. But every spot was a dinosaur skeleton.'

He took a sip of coffee.

'Now you have to realize we had gone to many localities over the previous three years. If we found a couple of nice lizard skulls and maybe two or three mammal skulls over a period of five days, we were very successful. But here, every time Mark said, "I got a skull!" I found one as well.'

For a while, each kept their own counsel, as if by expressing joy and astonishment they would be tempting fate, inviting some catastrophe or reinterpretation that would destroy what each now believed was the grail they sought.

'When Mark and I stopped for lunch (I think you were off somewhere else by now, weren't you Jim?), we poured all these skulls out on the hood of the car, and went: "Oh, my Go-o-o-d." Within three hours, we had got about thirty skulls, mammals, lizards, dinosaurs. So we realized: this is it! We'd hit it big!'

In those three hours, the two men had found sixty individual animals. On the scorching paintwork lay twice as many mammal skulls as Andrews' team had found in a week.

'Then we saw Dashzeveg over the way, and Mark ran over to him. I decided to start prospecting some more. And I saw Mark come back, maybe fifteen minutes later, and he's sort of shaking, and says, "I just found something incredible." He took me over, and there was a nest, with eggs, and an *embryo*.'

Minute and intricate as an ivory carving, this was the first detailed dinosaur embryo, nestling inside an egg typical of those found by Andrews, those assumed ever since to be proto eggs. Alongside were two other tiny skulls of some carnivorous dinosaur, probably baby Velociraptors.

By the end of that glorious day, the team as a whole had marked seventy-five mammal and lizard skulls and forty dinosaur skeletons. Here, in the space of a football field, they had (as Novacek later wrote) 'found a treasure trove that matched the cumulative riches of all the other famous Gobi localities combined'. For this site, they decided, there was only one possible name: Xanadu, the palace of legendary opulence built by Khubilai Khan, the 'stately pleasure dome' that was the dream-subject of Coleridge's poem.

'Palaeontologists are content working with such *garbage* usually. Table-scraps. Spare parts. They'll take what they can get. But this . . . We're spoiled for ever. We'll probably never have another experience like that. I've worked in the field for twenty years, and I never had a day like that.'

There was more the next day: a dozen ankylosaurs, most of them splayed out as if steam-rollered into the rock; a delicate little carnivore, a troödontid, fast as a Velociraptor but smaller, probably a specialist hunter of lizards and mammals; the headless skeleton of a Mononykus; a three-metre oviraptor, though without its oddly inflated skull, which may have been a sound-chamber used to produce loud cries or fog-horn blasts. By the time the team left four days later, they had found 100 dinosaur skeletons, 76 lizard skulls and 61 mammal skulls.

Nothing could quite match the discovery of Xanadu. But the next two seasons, 1994–5, filled out earlier finds, with more lizards (lizards seemed to have been the most abundant four-legged creatures in Late Cretaceous times), crocodiles, turtles of many species, and more oviraptors, in several different strata, showing that Ukhaa Tolgod had been a nesting ground over long stretches of time. And eighty more mammal skulls, including a Deltatheridium, the rat-sized creature picked up by Andrews, which Novacek's team now recognized as a marsupial that would throw light on the spread of opossum-like marsupials to North America and Europe.

All this was big news. *Time* magazine featured Mononykus on its cover. The *New York Times*, *National Geographic* and the TV documentary all ensured enormous exposure for the discoveries. The museum began urgent work on the finds. The paper in which the team – the whole team, all ten of them – formally listed their discoveries appeared in *Nature* on 30 March 1995. The task of assimilation had begun.

Such a haul will take years to assess. But the first results came rapidly, revealing three great advances.

The first was in the realm of dinosaur behaviour. When examined under a microscope, the embryonic creature of Ukhaa Tolgod was found to be an oviraptor. Moreover, the large oviraptor, carted back locked into an immense block of sandstone, was found to be sitting on a magnificent clutch of eggs. The conclusion to this piece of detective work overturned the seventy-year-old assumption that all those eggs found by Andrews were protoceratops eggs. They weren't; they were oviraptorid eggs. In turn, that meant that the 'egg-stealer' found by Andrews in the act of 'raiding' a 'proto nest' was no such thing. She was a mother, sitting on her own nest, hatching her young. 'Big Mama', as she is called, is now a prime exhibit in the Museum of Natural History.

'So,' I asked Jim Clark. 'When are they going to rename Oviraptor?'

'You *can't*.' He gave a wry smile, as if to say: like to, but sorry. 'It's against the rules.'

Secondly, there was the odd, turkey-sized, bipedal, mole-armed, claw-handed Mononykus, which has been a major contribution to one of the great scientific debates of the last century, that concerning the origin of birds. For many years, it has been clear that birds were in some way related to dinosaurs. But feathers were seen as a stumbling block. How could feathers possibly grow on reptiles? How could a dinosaur grow a wing? The answer may well turn out to be that feathers did not evolve for flight, but for some other reason, insulation for example. The argument receives some support from the Jurassic fossil bird, Archaeopteryx, found pressed like a flower, feathers and all, between two sheets of slate in a Bavarian quarry in 1861. Often seen as a classic example of a missing link, it may be no such thing, for it may be less of a bird than it seems. If it could fly at all, it could not fly well – it lacked a solid breastbone for flight muscles, and its shoulder did not have enough flexibility to allow it to flap. It can just as easily be seen as a feathered dinosaur as a reptilian bird. That leaves unsolved the relationship between dinosaurs and birds. (By the way, the other flying animals of the Cretaceous are no help at all in this debate. Reptiles took to the air several times, but the larger flying forms, the pterosaurs, derive from pre-dinosaurian lineages, and vanished at the end of the Cretaceous.)

This issue has become an increasing puzzle because scientists have become ever blunter about the relationship between birds and dinosaurs. Many now claim that birds did not simply evolve from dinosaurs: birds *are* dinosaurs. In other words, dinosaurs did not become extinct at the end of the Cretaceous; they lived on as birds. It is therefore a matter of passionate interest among palaeontologists to know which dinosaur types first grew feathers and took to the air, and when.

The chief suspects are the therapods, which include the massive tyrannosaurs and the lean, mean little predators like Velociraptor. They, like birds, have an S-shaped neck and three-toed feet as well as many other more specialized similarities. The relationship between Archaeopteryx and therapods is well established (in fact a featherless Archaeopteryx was actually mistaken for a type of therapod in 1951). Again, though, when and how did the division occur?

Mononykus has now emerged as a major contributor to this vexed question, because it is much later than Archaeopteryx, and also much more bird-like. It may well be that the apparent lack of feathers is nothing more than a fault in the fossil record. In any event, Mononykus looks like a small Cretaceous ostrich, whose ancestors had been flying dino-birds but had become wingless, its 'wings' acquiring that vicious claw which it used perhaps for tearing bark off trees or digging up termite nests.

The discovery of its whole skeleton had a particular meaning for Perle, who had discovered parts of a Mononykus back in 1987, and has a cast of it on his office wall. In his words, 'Archaeopteryx is just one of the experiments with flight and feathers, a side-line. Mononykus is more closely related to modern birds. Archaeopteryx has been famous for a hundred years. I think Mononykus will be famous for a hundred years as well.' His 1993 paper, in which he shares authorship with Norell, Chiappe and Clark, refers to Mononykus as both a dinosaur *and* a bird. Somewhere buried in the Gobi, there could be an ancestral Mononykus, with wings and feathers, a creature that could fly a lot better than its older, dead-end cousin, and which will reveal exactly when dinosaurs learned to fly.

A third surprise in the Nemegt fossils concerns the mammal skulls. Usually, scientists are lucky to find a few teeth of these tiny creatures. A skull is a treasure – in all North America, not a single Cretaceous skull has ever been found. By the time I spoke to Novacek, he and his team had 250 of them. At Ukhaa Tolgod, Novacek and Amy Davidson, lying beneath a blue sky fanned by a gentle breeze, had even dug out a whole family of twenty-centimetre placental mammals.

These discoveries open a window onto one of the most obscure and important corners of evolution, at least for humans. Late dinosaurian times saw the emergence of an array of mammal rodents – insectivores, primates, carnivores and a whole range of herbivores. Within ten million years or so of the end of the dinosaurs, mammals were radiating explosively to fill the new niches suddenly available to new species. But what came from what, and when? As Novacek says, 'These Gobi placentals are a key to untangling the great mammalian radiation.'

'So this is the best site in the world for them?'

'By far! Orders of magnitude! Probably the best Mesozoic mammal site in the whole world, no question.'

There is a poetic justice in these discoveries, for it was the mammal skulls that Andrews considered the most important part of his work. These were not exactly the ancestors of modern man predicted by Henry Fairfield Osborn, but they were the 'ancestors of man's ancestors'. Osborn would have been gratified.

Decoding the Great Death

The land these creatures lived in, the Gobi of 80 million years ago, was not like today's Gobi. For one thing, it would be another 60 million years before the Altai mountains even began to form. Nor was it totally unlike today, either, in parts. This was a continental interior, but still within reach of ocean winds. Research on the Aral Sea as it was in Cretaceous times reveals a winter daytime temperature of 18–20°C, and no lower than 11°C at night. Summers would have been dry and hot.

The world of the Gobi dinosaur – a panorama Novacek has often seen in his mind's eye – was something like the savannah of East Africa today, a world of grasses and scattered trees, with lakes and marshes like those that dot the Great Rift Valley. Such environments, like the Serengeti today, or the Great Plains of a century ago, have always sustained the richest range of animals, and the largest ones. By comparison, rainforests are rich in insects, but large animals are rare because the bulk of the food is scattered, or hidden, or aloft in the forest canopy. Where rainforests may produce 400 pounds of biomass per square mile, savannahs sustain 100,000 pounds. At its peak of richness in the Late Cretaceous, the Gobi, like the Serengeti today, was 250 times as productive as today's Amazon.

In this Late Cretaceous scene, patches of loose sand mark the most arid spots. At a few places, rivers wind out of low hills through a mixture of desert and savannah, creating rich marshlands, mudflats and shallow lakes, whose shores are dotted with shrubs like sour-gums and dogwoods. Here and there stand clumps of woodland, with conifers forming an overarching canopy. In the distance, dust rises from herds of ankylosaur, while protoceratops graze nearby. Oviraptors huddle over their nests – which like other reptiles they prefer to dig in soft, sandy soil – while velociraptors prowl like cheetahs, awaiting an opportunity to strike, cutting a weak individual out of a herd or taunting an oviraptor away from its nest before rushing in to snatch an egg.

But this generous patchwork of landscapes is not as generous as it once was. Somewhere over the horizon, the desert is growing. Every year, mainly in the spring, like the Gobi today, rising columns of hot air over the baking grasslands pull in winds from cooler regions. Normally, like camels, these creatures will hunker down and ride out the shrieking wind and the sandpapery blasts of grit. The tiny shrewlike mammals flee to their burrows or shelter under rocks and tree roots. But every now and then, an extreme form of 'black wind' strikes. The cloud that rolls over the horizon is like a tidal wave of sand, a brief, violent, highly localized storm, like those known as *zibars* in Iraq and Iran today, in which an ocean of sand is swept up, carried a few kilometres and dumped in a few minutes. Sand pours from the sky, collapsing the sides of dunes, drowning oviraptors stubbornly protecting their nests, mammals in their lairs, even on one occasion dinosaurs locked in mid-combat – the 'fighting dinosaurs' were stricken so fast the proto was supported by raining and falling sand even before it could fall over. Overwhelmed as if in a snowdrift, a tarbosaurus scrabbles at the avalanche of sand, back legs pedalling uselessly, reaching for air, finding none.

When the storm passes, the landscape is transformed. There is no more lake. The river must carve another route from the hills. As it does so, it brings minerals from the distant hills, filtering them down through the soft sand, sealing it into a cement. Hidden flesh rots slowly away and bone safely cradled in the soft new strata reacts in its own way with the doses of minerals, and turns to rock as pale as porcelain, and sometimes just as delicate.

This was not the great disaster that wiped out the dinosaurs. That would not come for another 15 million years, and meanwhile the dinosaurs continued to evolve and die in a slowly changing world.

For the American–Mongolian research reveals that the Gobi did not remain an arid place, always subject to such brutal storms. The later, younger beds record a wetter climate, much more like the Cretaceous of North America, with big river channels and lakes, more and bigger trees. Perhaps it was this succession of wet and dry that forced the evolutionary pace, until the end.

Mongolian scientists – Perle and his colleagues Dashzeveg, Batsukh and others – should be a part of this welter of discovery, and will be if the relationship with the Natural History Museum continues. But listening to Perle talk, I began to wonder if they can be so only as junior partners. There is a generosity in that great institution. Perle and his colleagues have been flown over to share in and contribute to its work. But there is a deeper problem, which mere generosity cannot address.

It revealed itself when, in Perle's dim and dingy office, I offered him my card. He made as if to offer me his, then said, 'My last card. I cannot give. It is very difficult . . .'

'Difficult?'

'We are scientists, and we have expenses. But we are getting from the state just our salary, and absolutely no other expenses for science. In this time, in America, professors get, who knows, perhaps

$100,000 a year. I receive $110 a month ...' he shrugged.

'It's very difficult to send my friends a fax, you know.' I knew: faxes cost $10 a minute, and a minute was a minimum charge. 'From Australia, my good friends send me this book. Look: it cost $60, and to send by the post another $12. I have some books for them. How to send? It must be from my own pocket. Two weeks' salary to send a book! Even in Russia and China, they have donations for science expenses. For us, not a single coin. I have very valuable information, gathered over twenty, twenty-five years. I have a fine collection –' He broke off, waving a hand towards Erlicosaurus in its cardboard box, the Mononykus cast on the wall. 'Priceless! Absolutely! I have five children, my wife is teacher in Technical University, but our salaries are not enough to pay for scientific work. Where am I to get the dollars?

'I remember all my friends in England, America, China, Russia, Australia. I have many colleagues with whom I should exchange information, but to answer I must make calls, write letters, send faxes, have computers to send e-mail. But no money! From the state, nothing! When I work on science, if I must call to Australia, how can I?' His voice was rising now. 'Simultaneously, I know that my American colleagues –' he swung his legs onto his desk, simulating American nonchalance '– call to Australia, to Canada, to England.'

He fell silent, until I commiserated: 'But you have such a good reputation.'

'Reputation!' he burst out, not in accusation, for there was no one to accuse, but in a protest against the nature of the revolution that trapped him. 'Today, in Mongolia, who is living? Who is working? Reputation does not make work. We are people! We are men! We have family, we have children! For us, for my children, for me, reputation is just background, history, past.' He paused, almost in tears. 'I'm sorry. It is not to do with you ...'

'It's a terrible thing,' I said lamely.

'Yes, a terrible thing. Tell me, how in Mongolia it will be developed, the science? Absolutely, it is impossible.'

'Perhaps there is something I can do ... perhaps publicity...'

'It's not for you. Just, I am sad. You know, in Mongolia now, there are very many political parties, very much democracy, and for companies very much capitalism. But for scientists, nothing yet.' His voice became a whisper. 'Nothing yet.'

*　　　*　　　*

If I had no dream before, I had one now. How could anyone see and listen to such pain and not hope for something better? The dream is that there will be another great era of Gobi palaeontology, and that Perle and his colleagues, or their intellectual heirs, will not simply be co-workers, but will by some miracle become part of a thriving economy, acquire all the techniques of modern science and bring them to bear to solve one of life's great mysteries – what exactly happened to the dinosaurs, and why did life as we know it today come through?

There has been a revolution in thinking and fieldwork about the subject over the last two decades. In 1979 the US physicist Luis Alvarez pointed to a thin layer of iridium-rich asteroid dust near Gubbio, Italy, and suggested that the dinosaurs died as the result of a massive asteroid strike. Not many people took him seriously. The slow and uniform forces of geological and animal evolution held sway. Catastrophes were for the lunatic fringe and Bible-thumpers who still believed in the Flood. Then a number of strands of research came together. Astronomers refined their head-counts of wandering asteroids, and concluded strikes had to happen now and then; the mineral content of asteroids was better understood; and finally in 1990 scientists identified the smoking gun itself – a 65-million-year-old, 200-mile-wide impact crater in Mexico's Yucatan Peninsula. Now, asteroid impacts are all the rage.

But still the fate of the dinosaurs holds secrets, for they were part of a whole complex of extinctions. In all about fifty genera, each with their own clutch of species, disappeared. Ammonites, shelled molluscs that coiled into spirals, became extinct; and many other macroscopic marine species; and a whole range of tiny shelled creatures that constituted Cretaceous plankton. But there was something, or things, about the dinosaurs that marked them out for mass extinction beyond anything their contemporaries suffered. Of the fifty genera that vanished, twenty-two were dinosaurs – several hundred known species, almost all the great beasts of the time: the last of the giant sauropods, the herds of horned dinosaurs, the plant-eating iguanodons and hadrosaurs, tyrannosaurs, ankylosaurs, all gone, along with their remote relatives of the sea and air, icthyosaurs, plesiosaurs, mosasaurs, pterosaurs.

Catastrophe alone is not a sufficient explanation for the Great Death. Scientists are generally agreed that other background changes were in progress. Suggestions include the seas in retreat, continental drift slowing, and the earth cooling, all these forces and others combining to diminish opportunities for life and impose new stresses. In this scenario, the Yucatan asteroid was like a *coup de grâce* after a severe beating.

Yet the mammals came through, along with small, feathered dinosaurs – the birds. What qualified these creatures for entry into the ark of the Tertiary? At first glance, it looks as if size itself became a sudden disadvantage, for anything that weighed more than about ten kilos died out; except that crocodiles and turtles sneaked into the ark, so the Doorman apparently exempted creatures from marshes and estuaries. Or perhaps the catastrophe favoured those creatures that bore their young live; or lived in burrows; or had insulation. Whatever the criteria, large, dry-land egg-layers would have had a hard time getting insurance around the end of the Cretaceous.

But why?

This is the question that, in my dream, the Gobi can answer. Somewhere in the Gobi, a thin layer of rock has been exposed along the edge of a scarp which dates not from 80, but from 65 million years ago. Perhaps, like the wafer-thin layer near Gubbio in Italy, it too will be rich in the rare element iridium, the fallout created by the Mexican asteroid. I like to imagine some future Perle flat on his stomach with grit between his teeth and a scorching sun above, digging at a coloured ribbon of rock, easing out fossils that show in freeze-frame the rich world of the Late Cretaceous Gobi being smothered by dust, or swamped by decades of rain, or frozen into sudden silence. This would be the Cretaceous-Tertiary Boundary made manifest in stone, the Catastrophe Formation. Below, creation is in overdrive, with dinosaurs, mammals and birds all evolving together; then, for an inch of uncounted millennia, a blank, punctuated by a few tiny but revealing dots of bone; then in the stratum above, another slow flowering, as the survivors stretch evolving limbs to explore the trees, the empty spaces, the reviving forests, the lakes, the oceans, the air.

Right there, in the transitional species of the Catastrophe Formation, will lie the answers to the great questions of human evolution: what made the ancestors of our ancestors so special? How does it happen that we mammals are here to ask such questions?

9

Night on a Bare Mountain

For the mammals of yesteryear, change occurred on an extended time-scale. Today's mammals, at least the big ones, like humans, sheep, and wolves, experience it on a somewhat tighter schedule. Of the many themes that reveal how the Gobi is changing, the one that seized my attention was this: in the high valleys of the Three Beauties, the wolves are back.

Driving Ariunaa and me back from the Singing Sands, Batöld cut up from the desert into the heart of the Three Beauties. The last, most easterly of the dunes fell away behind us, and the stony ground of the plain gave way to hard-packed billows dusted with green. We came into a village, Khoolt, guarding the approach to the mountains. Batöld stopped at a ger, and I followed the two of them in. Inside, there were two children, two women and a man – I think, for I was thirsty, hungry and tired. With scarcely a word exchanged, we sat expectantly. I nibbled some hard curds from a bowl standing on the low table. The woman lifted a huge metal pot from the side of the ger, revealing gallons of yoghurt, made from a combination of milks. I casually consumed a pint of this nectar, followed by several cups of salty tea and boiled skimmings made into buttermilk, as creamy as the heart of a *crème brûlée*.

All of this was done with only the most cursory phrases. Our arrival was no occasion for surprise. We neither asked for food and drink, nor did we express effusive thanks. The gift was utterly routine, eliciting no more than a passing word. For Mongolians, there is an implicit reciprocity in this traditional hospitality. It is one half of a transaction. One day, those who supply your needs now will be in need themselves, and it will be your turn to feed them. Yet it seemed to me, an alien, to be a vulnerable system. I was the recipient, here as everywhere, of

171

generosity I could not repay in kind, only in an exchange that smacked of artificiality: sweets are always welcome. As we ducked out through the doorway, heading back to the car, I wondered how long the underlying assumptions can last, in a world where foreigners come out of the blue, and even some Mongolians, ranging far more widely in cars and trucks than they ever did on horseback, will always be receiving hospitality they will never be in a position to return. Why, in those circumstances, in which the country people give and the urbanites receive, should a system like this endure? It would be a sadness, but no great surprise, if in a decade the generosity that infuses pastoral nomadism and lightens the traveller's lot has been replaced by urban canniness. Next time I'm in Khoolt, I fear that yoghurt and buttermilk will cost more than a cursory 'thank you'.

Minutes later, we were in the heart of the Three Beauties, rolling eastwards over hard-packed hills. The afternoon sun behind us would soon be shadowing the sides of these gentle slopes. I leant forward from the back seat of the jeep, where I liked to spread out maps in a constant and largely futile effort to puzzle out our position and route. 'Where shall we stay?'

Ariunaa pulled back the edge of her headscarf: 'A hunter lives ahead.'

'*What?*'

'The woman back there told me. She said he is Mongolia's greatest hunter. He is the best shepherd in the province. Perhaps we can stay with him. He works with many tourists.'

These odd snippets of information sounded like wonderful news. I immediately looked forward to an evening of anthropological and zoological research, imagining a man of about thirty-five with a high-powered rifle and a 1,000-mile stare. How far away did he live? Were we going in the right direction?

'Perhaps we can ask,' said Ariunaa.

I looked around. We were following a track along a valley of gentle billows that rose to rugged peaks and ridges on either side. We were utterly alone. There were no gers, and certainly no tourists. The phrase 'many tourists' was, I knew from previous conversations, a relative concept, meaning 'someone came last month'. 'Not many tourists' means 'You are the first this year.' I felt that odd, and by now familiar, sense of suspension, rare in the West, in which all control is absent. The future was a blank and any concern fruitless. For a timeless moment, half an hour perhaps, I suspended animation.

I returned to this world as we roared up a barren slope topped by a flat, green plain, and two gers, attended by a herd of motorbikes and several tethered horses. A dozen people – three women, five young men, several children – emerged at our approach. They were a raggle-taggle crowd, dressed in short-sleeved shirts and denim trousers. Among them stood an old man of seventy, lean and gaunt, with a crew-cut of grey and stubble on his chin. He wore a crumpled shirt, dangling out of his trousers. Thirsty again for tea and information, we filed inside, and sat on the floor. Everyone else settled themselves opposite, staring at me in silence, while the old man sat near me, saying nothing. One of the women, working with a sewing machine on the floor, continued making a seam for a deel.

'Ariunaa, can you ask how far it is to the ger of the great hunter?'

'It is this man.' She nodded to the septuagenarian on my right.

I readjusted my perceptions. This was no deadbeat pensioner, after all. I saw experience and wisdom written in his sunken cheeks and the wrinkles that enclosed his eyes. I noticed an ornate embossed saddle hanging near the doorpost, with twelve silver medallions sewn onto it, a sign of stature and achievement. When an extremely lanky thirteen-year-old girl appeared, clad in a tracksuit, and folded herself onto the floor with her brother and cousins, I saw how the young watched and listened in deferential silence.

The old man's name was Badamtsetsen, and he was indeed a national champion, or rather had been, in 1959. He had been given the prize, awarded annually, for his bag of five wolves, fifty-three foxes and eight snow leopards. In fact, he considered himself more than just a hunter – he was employed specifically as a wolf-hunter.

This was a subject close to the heart of any herder. Wolves range wherever they can find water – even in both sectors of the Gobi National Park – though they favour the foothills. Chapman Andrews claimed that wolves had not been a problem, but he did not spend much time in mountains. Out on the plains, as he saw, wolves had a lean time of it, being forced to rely on carcasses. Once when trying to measure the speed of a gazelle, Andrews was pacing a buck at 40 m.p.h. (I still think he tweaked his speed estimates) when 'a wolf suddenly dashed from behind the rim of a ravine and tried to catch the gazelle. Evidently, it had been lying in wait, watching the buck, and when it saw that the gazelle would pass no closer, made his dash. The wolf had almost reached the gazelle before the latter saw the danger; with a few bounds the gazelle leaped to a speed of sixty miles an hour, hopelessly out-distancing the pursuer.'

Wolves were always considered a great pest by the common people and a symbol of strength by princes (indeed, a wolf, or a man called Wolf, is named as Chingis Khan's primal ancestor in *The Secret History of the Mongols*). Perhaps for this reason, wolves were not often the quarry in the great hunts that were used as a means of honing skills useful in a warrior nation; but they were killed by common people whenever possible. When Mongolia started its postwar development, without princes, herds were protected officially by men like Badam. In fact, it was a task taken on by the military sometimes. Later, in the eastern Gobi, I met a retired member of a tank regiment who said he had killed forty wolves when he first joined up in the 1950s.

Badam had been well trained. 'My brother taught me about wolves,' he said. 'And our two grandfathers taught him.'

So in all those years, he must have shot hundreds of wolves?

'In thirty years, I didn't shoot a single one.'

He saw my surprise, and explained. The policy of employing men to hunt wolves paid off. In the postwar years, in more populated areas, wolves were practically exterminated, driven back into places where few people kept herds and the wolves had to survive by scavenging or hunting marmots and argali wild sheep. 'From the early 1960s, there were no wolves round here at all.'

As a result, the wolf-hunters were out of jobs and the old skills vanished. Now, the wolves were staging a comeback. Badam himself had killed four in the previous year, the last one only two weeks before. 'I followed its footprints, and found a place where it had rested in the heat of the day. Sometimes they come back to such places, because they know they are safe. So I set this trap –' he pointed to some nasty-looking metal jaws over against the side of the ger – 'and waited. I waited for five hours. It came back, and I shot it.' He held out a hand, and one of the boys reached for a gun lying hidden behind a bed. It was an ancient small-bore rifle Badam used for close-up kills, though he had a larger Russian gun in another ger for longer-distance shots.

Once again, there was a call for the old skills. He guessed there were probably about fifty wolves now in the Three Beauties. Since each female produced up to eight cubs, the wolf population would be rising fast, especially as there were growing numbers of domestic sheep in the hills. 'There are, for instance, wandering wolves,' he went on. 'They have no fixed abode, and can wander for 300 kilometres. To kill them you have to get to know their routes, and recognize them individually.'

'Is there anyone doing this sort of work now?'

'I don't know of any. But there should be.'

The American zoologist, Richard Reading, in his report on the Three Beauties National Park, came up with similar evidence and similar conclusions. He himself had heard at least four wolves howling in these mountains, and several of his interviewees reported the loss of single sheep to wolves, claiming this as evidence that wolf numbers were increasing (though the losses may also reflect a growth in herds and their range).

To Reading, this was good news, because 'wolves are integral to a complete, well-functioning ecosystem'. But if Badam's views are anything to go by, conservation will be hard to sell to the local people. He really had it in for wolves, and mourned the lack of hunters.

'Perhaps your grandchildren will learn from you.'

'I try to teach them but they're no good. They don't have the patience.'

The teenagers opposite suppressed giggles. Badam motioned to one of them, and he placed some more dung on the fire. The lanky girl started to fold up one end of her mother's deel as the seam progressed.

'Do you teach your children about wolves?' he asked.

I admitted it did not form a major strand in British education, and explained why.

'No wolves in England?' he said in surprise.

'No. The last one was killed two hundred years ago.'

'I am very happy to hear that. Wolves are a menace. When a wolf is ill, it is *very* dangerous. They even attack people sometimes – I've never been attacked, but I have heard of them attacking people.'

He couldn't see how the old traditions were to be brought back. There was no money in it. Once, when he was a paid wolf-hunter, he used to make extra selling the skins. Now, both those sources of income had dried up. 'That's why I'm a herder. But I can't herd if there are wolves. All wolves should be killed. Other animals can stay, but not wolves.'

The return of the wolves is only one effect of change in the world of the herder. Among many others, the one that will have the greatest effect on traditional ways, is the growth of population and domestic animals.

In 1918, the country had a mere 540,000 people, most of whom were nomadic. The revolution and post-revolutionary turmoil damped down growth, but the population doubled by 1960. In the next thirty years, it doubled again, and now stands at 2.25 million, about half of whom live in towns. Of the rest, half are villagers, half are scattered over an expanse the size of western Europe. Much of the new young blood remained in the fast-growing towns, while life in the steppe and desert remained largely untouched. Now, though, that trend has reversed. With the collapse of industry and the distribution system in 1990–3, and the growth of a privatized economy, families rediscovered their roots, and a number returned to the grasslands and the desert. This was hardly a major population shift, but it did not need to be, given the fragile nature of the Mongolian pastures and the fact that the pastures are already carrying twice the number of people they did fifty years ago. What is true of the grasslands applies more strongly to the Gobi, with its rural population of about 200,000 – ten per cent of the people scattered across forty per cent of the country.

Even more crucial are the numbers of grazing animals. In 1920 there were about 10 million of them. The figure dipped in the 1930s, during a disastrous attempt to collectivize the rural population by force, a revolution that was seen by the herdsmen as pure robbery. They resisted, preferring to slaughter an estimated 6 to 7 million of their animals rather than see them expropriated by the state. Only when a more subtle programme of voluntary collectivization, building on the traditional forms of family and local groupings, started in the 1950s did the herds begin to recover. Slowly the herders, who were still allowed to retain their own private stocks, were persuaded to see the benefits of cooperation, creating the only socialist state in the world based on pastoral nomadism. Eventually, in a process that saw collectives merge into ever larger units, the whole rural economy was run by some 225 collectives, which in the Gobi formed tracts of up to 20,000 square kilometres. Now, the animal population is almost 30 million, giving nearly 13 animals to every one person. About a tenth of the stock is in the Gobi.

There is a growing interest in exactly how many animals and people Mongolia can sustain. On my first journey into the Gobi, Erdene explained official thinking on the 'carrying capacity', worked out on an eccentric system of 'sheep units'. For official purposes, a cow and a camel each eat the same amount as 10 sheep, a horse = 6 sheep, and a goat = 0.9 sheep. Mongolia's theoretical carrying capacity is 60 million 'sheep units'. At present it sustains 40 million. Therefore, logically, its pastures could take fifty per cent more animals. In fact, it is not that simple, because one-third of the pasture is used only in winter, and must be left untouched through the summer. To this must be added areas traditionally underused: the steeper slopes, the remoter parts of the Gobi. Assessments are further complicated by seasonal migrations, with usage sanctioned by ancient rights. People do not own land, but recognize land-use, with accommodation made for changes in water supply and productivity. In effect, Mongolia is one enormous common.

Now all this is under pressure, as the population grows, as herds grow, as the regulatory systems of the collectives break down. In the past, collectives were large enough to govern the back-and-forth of herders as they moved from winter to summer pastures, always seeking better pastures and springs. Disputes were common, but were settled on the basis of traditional usage. Now the collectives have gone, to be replaced sometimes by companies, sometimes by more traditional groupings, sometimes only by lone herding families. When I was at the Flaming Cliffs, for instance, I saw, drifting slowly along the gravel plains a mile away between the exposed sandstone and the mountains of the Three Beauties, a transmigration. The camels, their fog-horn groans carrying easily on the still air, were out front, followed by separate herds of sheep, goats and horses. Close up, I saw the reason for the gaps between the herds. A horse had foaled, and three men were holding back the herd, galloping about after wanderers, while ahead rode a teenage girl tending the camels. These hundreds of animals belonged to a set of three or four households, perhaps all related families, who had formed themselves into an '*ail*', the basic independent social and economic unit of livestock production. With a tradition like this to fall back on, these herdspeople at least were ensuring that the end of the collective era did not mean an end to a way of life.

The growth in human population and in domestic animals has been fuelled by two underlying assumptions. One is that nature is a cornucopia, pasture boundless and infinitely renewable. The other is that it is good to have as many children as possible. In 1997, a mother still got a medal if she had five children, and a *gold* medal if she had eight.

Tom McCarthy, working with herders as part of his snow leopard research, found the commitment to ever more children to be justified by two arguments.

Firstly, as elsewhere in the developing world, 'they say, "Since we don't have social security now, we have to have children to look after us when we are old." '

Secondly, rather more bizarrely, 'You talk to real intelligent people, and they will say, "We have to be able to defend ourselves against the Chinese."

' "Yeah? How?"

' "By doubling our population."

' "Oh, *sure*," I say. "With four million you'll stand up against one *billion*?" '

The result of such attitudes is the seemingly eccentric conclusion that the Gobi – with less than one person per square mile – is overpopulated and overgrazed.

McCarthy saw the problem exemplified in the valley near Biger where he and Schaller were based. 'There was just a universal opinion that said, "Well, overgrazing is just not a problem here." But when I went back to our valley after two years, the number of people and the livestock had gone up fifty per cent. I said, "There are a lot of people in your valley now. It's getting crowded. What are you going to do?"

' "Well, we can handle it for a while."

' "But all of you have five or six children. Where will they herd?"

' "When they grow up, they will have to go to the next valley."

' "But have you noticed – the next valley has almost as many people in it?"

' "Maybe it does, but there are other valleys."

'Well,' McCarthy gave a bitter laugh, 'there *are* no more valleys. Just the children I've seen in these communities alone – they will have nowhere to herd. Some people have started to recognize that huge tracts of land are severely overgrazed, and will *never* come back into full production in their lifetime.'

Not many though. In his report on the Three Beauties, Reading found the same evidence and the same attitudes. 'Everyone informed us that livestock in the region they lived in had increased dramatically, often by a factor of three or more, since privatization. Despite the increase in livestock, only one person believed that pasture lands were getting worse. No others were concerned about pasture degradation.'

All this suggests the Mongolians are about to receive a sharp lesson on the limits to growth. Trends frequently proclaimed in the West but disguised by complexity may emerge here in spotlit simplicity. If Mongolia doubles its numbers in people, animals, or both, the growth will threaten the very economic foundations that made, and make, the country strong. By the time the herders themselves see that their growth has limits, the remedies may be supplied by nature herself, in ruthless obedience to Malthus. If that happens, life, which for decades has become ever more charming, humane and long, would revert perforce to being nasty, brutish and short.

There was no room for us with the wolf-hunter, and the sun would not set for another five hours. No one was quite sure exactly how far away the next herder lived – perhaps thirty kilometres, perhaps sixty – but Badam was adamant we would find someone before nightfall. The sooner we left, the better.

We ploughed on uphill, following the ash-grey bed of a dry river, emerging on desert-steppe running between hills, which the light of the setting sun turned into patches of yellow-green grass and purple shadows. For an hour, we saw no sign of human life. Then, standing out from the gentle hillocks, was a collection of what I took to be stone cairns, apparently being tended by two men. As we pulled up beside them, I saw that the cairns were piles of dung, being collected for use as fuel. A single question gave us heart: there were gers ahead.

Though the rules of hospitality seem sacrosanct, not all gers are equally suitable for the passing traveller. The first one we saw looked an idyllic house-and-garden setting, charmingly set on open glebe land with the benefit of graceful hills. The disadvantages hit us even as we filed in for tea: a dung-covered site, a hell-hound of a dog, a ger almost devoid of trappings, and one withered old lady holding the fort. We made our excuses, and left. Twenty minutes later, the track, skirting a great U-shaped valley, led us to another single ger. This time, there were too many people, all of whom seemed to belong to the same family. A mentally deficient child bounced round the car with his fingers in his mouth while Batöld asked the advice of another driver. I followed the man's pointing finger. A mile away, caught in the V of a rocky cleft, was a glint of white.

We undulated over the tussock-dotted gravel, dipped across a dry stream and swung into the winding gorge. The two gers were in the strangest position, on a headland of rock jutting out from a background of hills. It looked like a perfect defensive site. Batöld, engaging low ratio and four-wheel drive, zoomed the jeep up the bulwark, and stopped. I saw that the site was not chosen as a fortress. It was just the only flat ground in the valley, and a fine spot to overlook the black-and-white sheep and goats which speckled the hillsides.

I was about to get out, when Ariunaa whispered, 'The dog.' Instantly, I forgot the view. This dog was as big as a dog can get, made even larger by a mass of yellow hair that it was shedding as if it had been crossed with a camel. Some dogs, I've no doubt, are all bombast, but this one actually attacked the car. I heard its teeth clash with the edge of the door. Batöld eased open his side-window and yelled, 'Get the dog!'. A motherly type in a deel, headband and mock-pearl earrings appeared from the ger, strode to the car, and grabbed the dog by its collar just as it was about to rip the door off. There followed an astonishing transformation. The woman threw the dog on its side. Like a wrestler admitting defeat, it went limp. She then thrust its right forefoot through its rope collar, and it lay there in an abject heap, wimpering and twitching. While we were there, it did no more than hobble about on three legs for a few yards before collapsing, never again showing the slightest interest in barking at, let alone assaulting, strangers. I actually felt sorry for it.

Following the woman's reassuring smile and twinkling expression, we followed her into the ger for tea and nibbles of hard, parmesan-like curds. With relief, I saw that this place was going to be perfect: a generous hostess, and ample sleeping space. The woman, whose name was Mekhee, disappeared again. Strolling outside, I understood why, and saw just how well-organized she was. The ger we were in was for relaxing and sleeping. The ger next door was a cooking tent, with two stoves, and she was boiling up some milk to make buttermilk. On the slope above the tents was a platform where produce was stored, out of the way of the nibbling, bleating goats. There was a pile of saxaul wood to start fires, and another pile of what I took to be potatoes, until I saw they were balls of dry dung.

'This is not a rich family,' said Ariunaa quietly, as I peered into the cooking tent. 'Look, the tops don't fit on the pans.'

If they couldn't afford decent cooking gear, it was not surprising they lacked the possessions I had come to consider as normal for herders – no car, motorbike, television, generator, or hi-fi. And here we were driving in from the desert, expecting and receiving hospitality. It hardly seemed fair.

'Ariunaa, I would like to cook supper.'

My suggestion caused astonishment. Mekhee's broad face broke into a huge smile, and she promised to let me have the whole cooking tent as soon as her milk had boiled enough. With the food we had gathered from the market in Dalanzadgad before our departure many days before, I planned a meal that would delight palates jaded by a winter of health-foods and reconstituted meat. In our cardboard box, we had cooking oil, pasta, tomato paste, onions. This would be complemented by Mekhee's dumplings and buttermilk, and rounded off with hard curds, biscuits and Nescafé.

While I waited my turn at the stove, Mekhee's husband appeared, leading two horses up from the valley below. Baatar was the second tallest and most astonishing Mongolian I saw. He looked as if he had been assembled by one of Dr Frankenstein's less-talented assistants. With a lantern jaw, heavy eyebrows and Himalayan cheekbones, he was a gangling, stooping 6' 3", his frame draped in a massive, loose-fitting deel. On horseback, his feet would have dangled near the ground if he hadn't been folded into stirrups. Emerging from shadows, he would have been a terrifying apparition, but the impression he gave was exactly the opposite. He had the lugubrious bloodhound expression of a natural comedian, and the wrinkles round his eyes were laugh-lines. When he heard about supper, he opened his eyes wide and gave me a huge grin, revealing a set of teeth in terminal decline.

Mongolian stoves have a wonderful raw efficiency. The only thing between the chef and the acrid, glowing dung is the cooking pot, which acts as wok and hotplate in one. Water – used in sparing quantities, because it has to be carried up from the valley – boils fast. The only problem is that ingredients must be prepared sequentially rather than in parallel. First came the pasta, which was then transferred to a bowl; then the onions, doused in oil and tomato sauce.

Supper was a triumph. Even before we ate, the word had somehow gone out, and we were joined by Baatar's brother and his wife from a ger down in the valley. I do not think that any of them had ever tasted onions or tomato sauce before, and it seemed to make them drunk with delight. Baatar produced a bottle of mare's milk brandy, 'arkhi', taking care to flick drops of it upwards with his third finger as an offering to the Blue Sky and then to touch the finger against his forehead to ensure more of the same in the future. Like the camel's milk arkhi I tasted on the way to the Flaming Cliffs, this was soft, delicate, and very drinkable.

Baatar and Mekhee were up in the mountains for the summer. They came here around March, in time for the lambs and kids to be born.

They would return to their winter camp, twenty-five kilometres away down the valley, in October. This was a good spot, with water constantly flowing out of the mountains. The goats and sheep had enough pasture in the hills, and could also wander over the plain below, where the rest of their animals were: horses, camels, cattle. Baatar's brother, Örnökh, with his wife and family made up eleven people in this group.

Baatar and Mekhee had three children, aged thirteen, ten and eight. But in a spot as remote as this, it was impossible to get to school daily, so they lived in a school hostel in Bayandalai, the *sum* centre, an equivalent of a county town. I said I thought it must be a difficult life, herding in the desert and the mountains. Yes, said Baatar, refilling my bowl, things had been very difficult, after the collapse of the collectives. Before, buyers and sellers would come in trucks, and the family had everything they needed, with access to goods and medicine. Then, for a while, there was no market, no vet, no doctor, no transport. They had to sell everything themselves, and they had no car or truck to transport their milk products, their sheep and camel wool. They had to borrow transport, or use the horses. It was getting better now, because they could rent a truck when they moved back and forth between winter and summer quarters. A doctor even came round sometimes.

Now traders would drive by and make exchanges. Baatar would hand over milk products, and sheep and camel wool, and receive clothes, rice, cigarettes, tea and meal in return. I had seen what this new traffic meant when swinging down to the Chinese border between the two sections of the Gobi National Park: the beer bottles along the way, the line of trucks laden with camel wool awaiting their turn to drive into China, the wiry Chinese traders hawking locally-made Pepsis.

'Don't you use money?'

'If we can get it. But it's hard to get.'

This year, they had harvested about 200 kilos of wool, 40 from the goats, 40 from the sheep and the rest from the camels. It wasn't good. They were worse off than many. But things were getting better. They had sixty new-born animals this year, and none of them died. Only two animals failed to breed.

'Will the young survive?'

'Last year, wolves took ten sheep.' Ten! So the Wolf-Man was right. 'But there have been no losses so far this year.'

'Is it good that things changed?'

'It is hard to say. Life is not so good, not so bad, just *different.*'

'What would you like to have most?'

'It would be good if we had a car. But it's very expensive. We can't even afford a motorbike. A motorbike used to cost forty-five kilos of goats' wool. Now it's gone up to seventy kilos.'

'How about a TV?'

'Oh, yes!' Mekhee smiled at the thought. But it had not been at the top of her list, a luxury rather than a necessity.

'What if you need a new ger?'

'The felt we can make ourselves. But the rest – the lattices and the canvas covering – that would cost eighty kilos of goats' wool.'

Their goats alone would buy them a motorbike or a new tent in two years, if they could set that amount of produce aside. Perhaps, in another year or two, such possessions would be within their reach. Compared to the chaos and suffering caused by the collapse of industrialized Communist economies elsewhere, the transition here, even in this remote and poor spot, even for two families that were not part of a company or an *ail*, seemed relatively painless. In the easy, smiling talk, made hazy by the flow of arkhi, I thought I saw a belief in a better future.

The arkhi got better, and I became mellow sharing the contentment my supper seemed to have brought. 'This food was like gold,' said Mekhee. 'We will not forget this ever, ever.' I felt as if my fundamental genius, so long ignored by the world, had been recognized at last.

It seemed suddenly an excellent idea to sleep out.

'Oh, no, please,' said Ariunaa, the town-dweller, sweetly. 'It is dangerous. You might disappear.'

But I was set on communing with the wilderness. It was a wonderful night, with no moon and scattered cloud veiling the stars. I gathered my sleeping bag and torch, and strode away uphill. Stopping to regain my breath, I heard a scrabbling noise. Thinking of snow leopards and wolves, I shone my torch around, and saw something to stop the heart. The silent night was full of yellow eyes, reptilian eyes, suspended, unblinking, unmoving. It took a longish second to realize that these were not the spirits of the mountain, but the black goats, utterly invisible against the darkened mountainside, intrigued by my wandering torch.

I unrolled the sleeping bag on a ridge 100 feet above the gers. The clouds were gone now, and I stared up at the stars. Below me all was silent, except for the sneeze of a goat and the wimper from the four-eyed, three-legged dog. It was cold, and the ground was hard. A night-bird whistled, once. I fell asleep.

I woke twice in the night, and heard nothing but the rising wind prowling round the hills. If there were wolves and snow leopards, they left me alone.

A raw dawn and a chill wind brought home to me my position several hundred feet above the floor of a high desert plateau. I lay for a moment, delaying the moment of departure from the sleeping bag, waiting for whatever apotheosis the wilderness might confer upon me. To the east, clouds glowing a dull red silhouetted the crags. The other side of the ravine below me, ground squirrels or fieldmice had made a warren. No animals appeared, but a surprising noise came through the gusts. I thought at first it sounded like a cuckoo. It *was* a cuckoo. Not only did it sound like any cuckoo anywhere, its Mongolian name sounds virtually the same as well: *khökhöö*. Around me loomed the black and diamantine crags, cold, uninviting, devoid of life. Across the valley below, hills ranging along the western horizon were still shadowed with night.

I packed up, and climbed higher, briefly, until my eyes were streaming in the harsh wind, then headed down past the goats, to the warmth of the ger, and the comfort of salty tea, and the reassurance of human contact.

The Gobi is harsh on the surface; but it hides a wealth that has scarcely been touched. I'm not talking of the mineral wealth that would take huge amounts of foreign investment to work, the extraction of which would leave the locals either untouched or ruined. The Gobi's real wealth, the wealth from which all might benefit, is water.

Signs of water are everywhere on the surface, in the alluvial fans, the outwash plains, the dried-up channels carved by occasional downpours. But its actual presence is a rarity, and its existence in pure, drinkable form even rarer. Yet not all that falls evaporates. A good deal of it soaks away, replenishing a water table which, under subterranean pressure, squeezes up along the cracks that fringe the Gobi's mountains, hills and rocky outcrops. The 165,000 square kilometres of South Gobi province contain 5,200 wells. A wide-ranging survey of the remoter and more arid Gobi National Park lists thirty-six springs with a combined flow of some 77,500 litres per hour – nothing much if allowed to dissipate, but a huge resource if focused. As Siggy's work in Bulgan revealed, the proper direction of these reserves can transform wasteland into gardens. There are eighteen irrigation projects in Gobi Altai province alone, and numerous private ventures.

One of these I came across purely by chance. Returning from the west with Erdene over one of the vast and simmering plains that Andrews would have termed a 100-mile tennis court, we were lost, again. Trembling on the horizon, all mixed in with dancing saxauls and a far range of hills, was a ger. Ten minutes later, as we were sipping tea inside, I marvelled that anyone would not only choose to live in this wasteland but could apparently get a reasonable living out of it, for the old man, the couple and three children who lived there said they supplemented their herding by selling potatoes, turnips, barley and carrots in Altai, 120 kilometres away.

'But where do you grow all this?'

'Over there, in the oasis.'

I followed his pointing finger to a distant shadow. Was this a new development? Oh, no. It had been there for many years. The old man had started growing vegetables thirty-five years ago, as a part of a collective, and the collective had based itself on much older practices. One old lady living in the area was ninety-eight now, and she remembered her parents growing vegetables when she was a child. The water came down from the hills, and still, if you went up there, you could see old millstones lying about, the remains of a monastic community. But it was all much better now, because of the Americans.

'Americans? Out *here*?'

We drove on, bringing the shadow into focus, coming abreast of trees, a canal with flowing water, an expanse of greenery, a fence, and two stalwart bearded figures in shorts, slouch hats and sunglasses stooping over a line of carrots. Paul Kline, from Dallas, Texas and Markus Dubach, from Zurich, Switzerland were Christians, with expertise. Kline was a vet, Dubach an agronomist.

Sheltering from the sun in the minibus, Paul explained how and why he found himself in these previously god-forsaken parts: 'I was considering working in Christian development abroad when a friend said they had a friend working in Mongolia. That was like a seed dropped in my heart.'

Markus, also impelled by faith and a desire to serve, had chosen Mongolia over Cambodia. Both were married, both had a wife and a new baby each, living in gers in Altai. And both were proud of their oasis, Khurkheree ('Waterfall'), 130 hectares of crops with a new $8,300 fence – supplied by a Swedish aid agency – to keep marauding camels and goats out. Their little group was sixteen families strong.

If these muscular Christians were there with a hidden agenda to make converts, they kept it well hidden beneath their devotion to service. (I owe them a debt of thanks: Dubach spotted a tick in my ear, and removed it gently with the tip of a disturbingly large jack-knife.) They might have come at God's behest, but they owed their presence more immediately to the Joint Cooperative Services, a Christian development agency set up to coordinate twelve Christian groups in their work in Mongolia. JCS, like other aid agencies, had been inspired by the disasters that followed 'transition', and by a particularly tough winter in 1993. Originally, they called themselves Joint *Christian* Services, but found this smacked of cultural imperialism. A change of name helped them in their stated purpose: to do good work. Now this one small agency had thirty-five people in the country.

The major challenge was not so much to use the water well, or choose the right crops, or arrange the fencing: it was to hold this little community together in the face of change. Never before had individuals had to take responsibility for their own futures. Deprived of the overarching authority of the state, each individual became a prey to odd rivalries and fears. For example, said Kline, the cooperative owned a caterpillar tractor. This year, it had ploughed twenty hectares and was just about to plough the head of the cooperative's land when it broke down. 'So the head fired the driver!' Kline finished. 'Accused him of breaking down on purpose just to spite him, despite the fact that the head had nominated the driver in the first place. It's not the oasis that is a problem – it's the people.'

If character is defined by history and circumstances, then the character of Mongolian country people is a combination of two contradictory features. One is a sense of sturdy individualism, just the sort of frontier ethic needed to endure the rigours of herding and to take decisions that involve the life or death of animals, and sometimes people. The other is an awareness of the power of that individualism when it is tightly focused. It was, after all, at the root of their historic success in the thirteenth century, when one man forged these wilful, self-assured people into a nation that conquered most of Eurasia. Later, deprived of authority, thrown back on their individuality, they were easily divided and ruled by China's subtle bureaucrats. When Communism finally succeeded, it did so by tapping into Mongolia's historic roots, building on the tradition of high authority and localized individuality. The herders lived for two generations under the wing of huge and impersonal organizations that told them what to do and provided them with an economic umbrella. Now the Mongolian herders are facing a need to absorb a new ethic of cooperation, part of which involves acceptance that leadership should be exercised not to assert power, but to achieve an end from which all will benefit. It is a long and painful adaptation. As one of the JCS administrative heads commented wryly back in Ulan Bator: 'Trying to get Mongolians to cooperate is like trying to get deers' antlers into a sack.'

The desert could be made to blossom, in theory. Whether the Mongolians would wish this to happen in practice is another question, for it would involve yet another revolution. A whole ecology would be at stake, and to initiate the change, assuming it seemed a good idea, herdsmen would have to abandon their old free-ranging lives, and cultivate gardens. If the past is a guide to the future, this would be like teaching bricks to fly. Farming is the Chinese way, regarded by the Mongols with contempt. Chingis Khan, the father of Mongolian nationality, himself warned his heirs that if ever they abandoned their nomad ways and tied themselves to the soil they would no longer be Mongols. To undermine the Gobi for its water would be to reform an ecology, a way of life, a whole sense of identity.

Yet there is a paradox: growth is changing that ecology anyway, and will eventually threaten that way of life. In years to come, Mongolians will be faced with hard choices that will bring them face to face with their deepest selves.

10

Bridging the Inland Sea

When I was driving away from the Flaming Cliffs, the teenager guide we had picked up in Bulgan asked if I knew about the road nearby, the one they called the Road of the King with the Ass's Ears. I knew of no road, nor any king.

Once upon a time (our young helper explained) there had been a king with ass's ears. He did not wish the herdsmen to know of this affliction, so he had a servant clear the way ahead of him wherever he went, and whenever he had a hair-cut he ordered the barber killed to preserve the secret. But one barber, knowing the fate in store for him, sent his daughter in his place. Her mother prepared a cake for her with ground-up meal. She cut the king's hair, but as she did so she offered the king some cake.

'This is good,' said the king. 'What kind of cake is it? Where did it come from?'

'My mother made it.'

'It's so beautiful that we are now like brother and sister. Since you are my kin, I cannot kill you. But you must swear never to tell the secret of my ears.'

The girl was true to her word, but found the secret a burden too great to bear. She returned to the king and begged to be released from her promise.

'If you must tell the secret,' he said. 'Then tell the fieldmice, and them alone.'

So the girl went out onto the steppe and told the fieldmice about the king's ears.

But the next time the king went travelling, he heard the fieldmice squeaking: 'The king has ass's ears! The king has ass's ears!'

And he was so ashamed that he went far away from this place, and no one knows where he went. But the road was always named after him, and it still is.

This version of the Midas myth, emerging far in time and place from its ancient Turkish homeland, was a reminder that the Gobi was never as isolated as its reputation claimed. It has always been as much a bridge as a barrier, its gravelly surface forming a pavement across which horses, camels and ox-wagons could make steady progress, moving between wells, springs and oases. If this were not so, there would have been no need for the Great Wall, begun in the third century BC as a defence against the Hsiung-Nu (possibly the ancestral Huns). To these and other successor cultures, always ready to turn south in search of easy pickings, the Gobi was simply not much of a problem. Inner Mongolia, with grasslands as rich as those of Mongolia itself, was historically part of the Mongol realm, and the intervening desert was treated, not as something apart, but as their poorest and grimmest pastures. Nor did the Chinese regard it as impenetrable, crossing it whenever they had the will and the ability to exact tribute or punish or trade.

When Chingis Khan invaded China in 1211; when he sent reinforcements in 1214; when Chingis himself led another invasion towards the end of his life in 1224, Mongol cavalry crossed the Gobi so easily that the histories, whether Mongol or Chinese, do not bother to record their marches. 'In the Year of the Sheep (1211),' relates *The Secret History of the Mongols*, 'Chingis Khan rode out against the Kitad [the inhabitants of northern China]. Taking Wu-jiu ... ' With one bound, our hero is across, seizing a place near Kalgan (present-day Zhangjiakou), the old frontier trading town that was the centre for Mongol–Chinese trade. On this and other occasions, routes must be inferred. One obvious course was down a river, the Ongin, which flows south into the desert, ending in a salt lake a few miles north of the Flaming Cliffs. From there, an army could cut through the Three Beauties – perhaps drawing on the waters that still flow from the hill above Bulgan – and head on south. Or, to attack further east, cavalry would have ridden across the plains where the railway now runs, and thus to Kalgan. Either way, an army of several thousand men, each with half a dozen horses, accompanied by baggage trains, perhaps with herds of sheep and goats for food, or establishing depots in advance, could have crossed 650 kilometres of desert in little more than a week. It was a commute too routine to mention. Of the logistical problems – of watering tens of thousands of animals without polluting the wells, of ensuring they got enough pasture, of feeding the men along the way – there is no word.

Running an empire demanded a communications system that spanned deserts as easily as rivers, plains or mountains. This was one of Chingis's greatest legacies. At first, in an adaptation of a much older Chinese pony express, Mongols were pressed into service as couriers instead of soldiers, being made responsible for the supply of horses, provisions and fodder. Half a century later, Chingis's grandson Khubilai built a postal relay system that was a bureaucratic archipelago. Marco Polo claims it controlled 300,000 horses and 10,000 buildings, ranging right across the Empire. He probably exaggerated; but later estimates of the 1,400 relay stations in China alone record that they deployed 50,000 horses, 15,000 oxen and mules, 4,000 carts and 6,000 boats.

The stations, each with up to twenty horses, were about fifty kilometres apart. Polo recorded that riders wore belts with bells on. 'I'll tell you how it stands,' he confided. 'They take a horse from those at the station which are standing ready saddled, all fresh and in wind, and mount and go at full speed, as hard as they can ride in fact. And when those at the next post hear the bells they get ready another horse.' A message, sometimes carried by the same man on different horses, sometimes handed on in a relay, could travel up to 400 kilometres a day, a feat which for short runs would not disgrace a modern postal system. Khubilai used to have fresh fruit delivered from Beijing to his summer palace in Shangdu (Xanadu) 320 kilometres away; it would set out in the morning, and arrive the following afternoon.

A post-road crossed the Gobi to Chingis's old capital of Karakorum, and later, after the Mongol Empire vanished and was incorporated into the Manchu Empire in the seventeenth century, other post-roads linked Beijing to what was then the Outer Mongolian administrative centre, Uliastai, and the monastic town that would become Urga, present-day Ulan Bator. It was the Kalgan–Uliastai road, heading from the southeast Gobi towards the northwest, that Andrews was aiming for when he discovered the Flaming Cliffs. Possibly, the same road became linked to the story of the King with the Ass's Ears, but myths are transferable, and there were other roads. Some ninety kilometres south of Dalanzadgad, an enigmatic line of stonework a few metres high runs through the desert. Labelled 'the wall of Chingis Khan' on some maps, it is in fact a road running into Inner Mongolia. Not much of it remains, but some sections in Mongolia are again in use by local herders and traders with cars.

A bridge for warriors and administrators was also a bridge for traders. Of the 1696 invasion which placed Mongolia firmly inside the Manchu empire, the Emperor Kangxi wrote that 'because surplus provisions were prepared at postal relay stations along the route, even the traders who followed the army did not suffer from hunger'. When the troops pulled back, the traders remained. The Mongolians needed flour, tobacco, tea, saddles, needles, cooking pots, and countless other manufactured goods. Merchants would exchange their products for horses, which the Chinese needed for their armies. By the middle of the eighteenth century, the Manchu yoke proved so high-handed that in 1756 several princes revolted, in an uncoordinated flurry of uprisings and mutinies in which relay stations were sacked and Chinese shops looted. Chinese contingents clamped down viciously, beheading hundreds, ending what later came to be seen as a heroic bid for independence. Chinese economic control remained oppressive, in part as a way to obtain taxes to pay for the relay stations. This system, which kept ordinary Mongols in a state of near bankruptcy until the twentieth century, largely explains the Mongol hatred of China, her declaration of independence in 1911, and her *faute de mieux* espousal of Russia in 1924 – all deriving in part from the ease with which the Gobi could be crossed.

After 1905, when the Trans-Siberian Railway opened up the areas north of Mongolia, the long-established routes of the postal relays were used extensively by private traders heading into and across Mongolia. In 1909, after the Chinese railway reached Kalgan, the town became a base camp and destination for over a million camels and 300,000 bullock wagons heading back and forth across the 'inland sea'. And in the 1920s, when Andrews showed how easy it was to drive across the desert, cars joined the horses, camels and bullock-carts making the journey to Urga. In 1913 Mongolia still maintained 150 horse-relay stations and the system, though increasingly made redundant by the telegraph and the car, survived until the 1940s.

The Russian presence in Mongolia introduced a new element into the equation, which reflected and affected pre-war and Cold War geopolitics. Russia, serving her own self-interest, also served Mongolia's, in three ways.

The first time was against the Japanese, in whose imperial schemes Mongolia once had a key role. In 1927 the Japanese Prime Minister,

Baron Giichi Tanaka, submitted to the Emperor a memorandum sum-
marizing Japan's foreign policy. Its immediate aim, he said, should be
the conquest of China. 'In order to conquer China,' said the so-called
Tanaka Memorial, 'we must first conquer Manchuria and Mongolia.'
The Memorial was later condemned as a forgery by the Japanese, and its
status still remains obscure; but Japanese actions reflected its contents.
Japan took over most of Inner Mongolia in 1937. Her clear ambitions
for expansion into Mongolia inspired Russia to construct Mongolia's
first railway, running from the Trans-Siberian down to Mongolia's
eastern border. As a result, in 1939, a Russian army – with significant
Mongolian assistance – defeated the Japanese in one of the biggest,
most significant and underrated battles of the twentieth century. The
battle was named after Khalkhin Gol, the Kalkh river, which guards the
eastern approaches to Mongolia. The defeat convinced the Japanese
they had better not look to Mongolia, China and Siberia to fulfil their
imperial ambitions, but to Southeast Asia and the Pacific.

In 1949 the Russians finished a branch line of the Trans-Siberian to
Ulan Bator. Then, for a few heady years after Mao won power in China
for the Communists, Mongolia and China kissed and made up, under
the Soviet Union's fraternal auspices. While Soviet advisers guided new
industries, 40,000 Chinese labourers poured concrete in Ulan Bator,
Chinese doctors staffed Mongolian hospitals, and Chinese acrobats
delighted audiences at the circus. In 1954, with a great display of
mutual enthusiasm, the two superpowers agreed to span the Gobi.

It was this stretch of line that finally linked Mongolia to the outside
world. This feat produced its socialist heroes, among them an ancient
railman, Natsagdorj. He joined the railway as a teenager in the 1930's,
the fifth person on the payroll of a narrow-gauge railway bringing coal
from a mine forty-five kilometres outside Ulan Bator to fuel the city's
first electrical supplies. Almost twenty years later, he rode the line
northwards from Ulan Bator, and finally helped administer the building
of the Trans-Gobi. Half a century later still, sitting in the apartment he
shared with his daughter and teenage granddaughter, his pride in his
role was still evident in his smart grey suit, his martial bearing, his
gracious offering of 'arkhi' in little glasses. 'Once we had the railway,
any amount of machinery could come in – like the machinery to build
across the Gobi. One railway built another!'

I imagined an epic of engineering ending in a romantic spectacle of
steam trains forging grandly southwards across the desert. No, said the

old man, it wasn't like that. For the Russians, after building the Trans-Siberian, the Trans-Gobi was a pushover. It took only two years to build, and linked with the Chinese section heading north from Jining in 1956. By then the days of steam were almost over in the Soviet empire. Perhaps, he suggested, I would like to see the engine that made the first journey?

He retrieved a neat white Trilby, and led the way out. We drove to a side-road by the station where, in a line, stood the old machines that had opened the country: a narrow-gauge steam train from the 1930s and one that had made the journey back and forth from Irkutsk in the late 1940s. Those were the great days of steam. It was something of a disappointment to see the Trans-Gobi engine, a fading green 159-series diesel electric, little different to my inexperienced eye from today's machines.

The impact of the link across the country meant that suddenly exports and imports rose sixfold. Twenty-four trains a day into China carried 170 million tons of exports in 1960, and 40,000 passengers.

By then, though, the Sino-Soviet honeymoon was over. Mao refused to kow-tow to Khrushchev, border incidents multiplied, and the two criticized each other over a number of major international questions. In 1963, separation became divorce. Russian troops arrived in the Gobi *en masse*, building a dozen or more military bases within reach of the border with their former partner.

Black gold

The coming of the railway meant that for the first time it was worth exploiting Mongolia's immense mineral resources, at least anything that lay along the line of the railway. If the Gobi were a developed country, it would be rich. There are a dozen fine deposits of coal, and many others of gypsum, silica, copper, tin, lead, gold, platinum, asbestos. The problem was, and is, how to get machinery in and the products out, cheaply enough to make the effort worthwhile. In the eastern Gobi, the railway solved both problems. Its creation was a happy conjunction of geopolitics and economics, and the Russians took full advantage.

Bob Friedline told me what happened next. Friedline ran the Mongolian wing of a privately owned Texas-based oil company, Nescor, which was prospecting in the east Gobi where the Russians used to be. Friedline's office, out to the west in Ulan Bator's industrial sector, did not have an address. I had to give the cabby instructions to find a low, brown building opposite Smokestack No. 2 of Ulan Bator's prehistoric smoke-belching power station.

Friedline was a bulky, jovial figure with a direct gaze and a joshing manner that came from thirty years' experience as an administrator of foreign aid, mainly in Africa and Asia, including Mongolia. He had fallen in love with the country, and been drawn back from retirement by Nescor's offer to work for them, and serve Mongolia as well.

When the Russians moved into the Gobi in the 1950s, they opened up an oil field and created a town, Zuunbayan, ninety kilometres from Sainshand. The oil was high in wax content, of a kind known in the trade as Pennsylvania grade – good for lubricants, but if it gets below 70 degrees, 'it's a candle'. It's hard to extract, hard to transport, not like the 'sweet' crudes of the North Sea. And Soviet techniques were archaic, allowing oil and sand to mix, contaminating both supplies and the surrounding desert.

'Then in the early 1960s, they discovered beaucoup *humungous* amounts of oil in Siberia, really sweet, not this heavy, thick stuff. They say, "Man, oh, man why are we screwing around down there?" Would you believe it, in 1965, just about the time the Russian fields went on line, there was this tremendous explosion at the Gobi refinery. Just amazing! So the Russians just capped it, and left a good deal of junk in the desert, and walked out. From 1965 to 1992, it just lay there, leaking a bit. Post-transition, the Mongolians divided the country up and – "Hey, world! Come on in here! Develop our oil resources!" '

The large oil companies declined. There was no refinery, no pipeline, no roads, and only one railway. So the Mongolians called on the independents, proposing joint ventures. Nescor took up the offer in 1994, taking on the old Russian well, fixing the holes, clearing up the mess, repairing the damage. For their $25 million investment, which made them one of the biggest investors in the country, they became part of a 50–50 joint venture with their Mongolian counterpart, Bay-anoil, with the right to explore for sweeter grades nearby.

This operation also involved a commitment. 'We're in the business of starting an industry here, training 200 Mongolians how to be oil men. Our underlying objective – drums, please, cymbals – is to turn this enterprise into a Mongolian company. It makes sense for us all.

Mongolian employees come a lot cheaper than American ones. If we can cut down American supervisors from a dozen to four, costs go down. That's the way it should go.'

There are 25 million barrels of proven reserves, but there is a long way to go before anyone gets rich. For one thing, the Mongolians had just been caught short. 'They can't figure out why they can't finance their contribution from tomorrow's revenue. Right now, we're waiting for them to put in their next $5 million. But copper's down, cashmere's hurting, it's hard for them to come up with the cash. So we're shutting down, temporarily, until they come up with their five mill.'

I was a little apprehensive about the train that would be my way out of the Gobi, via the border town of Erlian, then back west to the Inner Mongolian capital of Höhhot. I had been warned about aggressive crowds of new capitalists filling whole compartments with goods, roaming the trains in search of dollar-carrying foreigners. The business of boarding drove such anxieties into the background. The carriages, painted the subdued colour that car enthusiasts would recognize as British Racing Green, stood six feet off the ground. To enter, you have to sling your baggage above head height, then climb a ladder, the first step of which is waist height. Edging past a wood-burning boiler for the carriage's central heating, I found my compartment: basic and drab, but clean. I was joined by two Chinese who showed no interest in robbery. They were playing a pocket-calculator game obsessively and consuming biscuits and Coke.

We clacked slowly out of Ulan Bator, past Natsagdorj's train collection, past the big wheel in Friendship Park, past high-rises, across the river where children swam, out through the hills and gers of the grasslands. I was in a limbo. It was the time of the Naadam, the National Day celebrations. All offices were closed and friends had vanished. My intention was to get off in the desert town of Sainshand, but my only contact there had left. Having given up any hope of seeing Bill Friedline's oil camp in Zuunbayan, I feared I was in for a grim and lonely time in Sainshand.

The senior of the two Chinese looked up from his computer game, and spoke to Junior. Junior addressed me.

'You are American?'

'No. English.'

We introduced ourselves. The two were bankers on their way back to Höhhot.

'My boss ask: you know Chuo-ji?'

'I don't think so.'

'Chuo-ji very famous Englishman.'

'Chuo-ji?'

'No: Churr-ji.'

'Churchill?'

'Yes. What you think of him?'

'He was a great leader.'

This was relayed on in Chinese. Then: 'So why you – ?' He made a dismissive gesture that completed his sentence. 'Why you not make him king?'

My interrogator looked about my age. Presumably, not many years before, he would have demanded to know why the workers had not revolted against George VI, Chuo-ji and their capitalist lackeys, and strung them all from lampposts. Now here he was, a royalist and a bank manager. So it goes.

Sure my pack was in safe hands, I ventured into the corridor to eat a Czech chocolate bar bought in Ulan Bator. The fading grasslands were fenced off from the railway in a desultory way, with strands of wire straggling between metre-high posts, leaving ten metres or so on either side of track. I knew about this fence. In Ulan Bator, admiring Nat-sagdorj's railway engines, I had noticed the cow-catchers.

'Do the trains hit animals?'

'They used to,' he said. 'Animals used to go on the track all the time. I myself hit a camel once. We had to run patrols along the track, and forbid herders to come closer than 500 metres. Then in the 1970s we built a fence on either side all the way to China, except for the bridges where people and animals can cross under. In the old days, you know, the gazelles used to migrate from the grasslands westwards. They can't do that now.'

I was staring out of the corridor window, listening to the rail-joints pulsing beneath me like a slow heartbeat, watching the grassland slowly turning to desert-steppe, when a squat and coarse-faced criminal – I recognized the type immediately – threw down the window along the corridor and tossed out a cigarette. He spotted me, and approached. I stood my ground, warily, and felt for my wallet.

'Good morning. How are you?' he said, in English.

He was not a criminal after all, nor was his face the product of boxing school. He was a geologist, named Nasanbat, and he was simply passing the time of day with a foreigner.

'What sort of a geologist?' I was going to pick his brains about the nature of the red soil that underlay this part of the Gobi.

'Oil. I worked for BP for a year, now for Bayanoil.'

Bayanoil was Nescor's Mongolian partner. This was another of those ridiculous serial coincidences which no one would ever dare write into a film script or novel. Not only was he on the same train, he was in the same carriage, in the next-door compartment, and now we had spoken – evidence, surely, that driving through the dust of a wild ass brings good luck. There was more. Nasanbat was with a score of oil workers – some of them nodded at me through the compartment window. They were all disembarking in Sainshand, and heading for the Zuunbayan oil field.

'Can I come?' I said, after explaining my connection and interest.

'No problem. Truck will come from Zuunbayan. There is big room. This man will look after you.' Nasanbat pointed to one of the young men in a neighbouring compartment. 'He is interpreter with Americans.'

By the time the train drifted to a leisurely halt in Sainshand that night, we had travelled just under 500 kilometres in nine hours, which is not much slower than a jeep or a horseman used to take travelling flat out between relay stations. One should not complain. Having compared Mongolian saddles, jeeps and railway carriages, I was happy with the railway.

The truck that came surging out of the darkness certainly had 'big room'; it was precisely that, one big room, a cavernous six-wheel drive Russian army truck into which the twenty oil workers climbed. In the blackness of the giant metal cube, pitching through the desert, shouted conversation died under the roar of the engine. For two hours I lounged in a stupor on my pack, until lights passed the single porthole. I saw a gate, a compound, and a rambling wooden single-storey prefab, on which a sign proclaimed: 'Hotel California'. My designated interpreter took me inside along a corridor and knocked at a door. A rotund figure in long shorts and no top emerged, rubbing his eyes and scratching his head.

'Mr Daryl? Someone from UB.'

It was around midnight. Having materialized without warning and broken his sleep, I thought perhaps the time had come for explanations and apologies. There was no need. Mr Daryl remained bleary, but uncurious, and thoroughly amiable.

'Oh, sure, uh-huh. I'm wondering where to put you. Hell, come on through. You can sleep in my room. Shower's there.'

He led the way inside, pointed to a spare bed, and vanished beneath his covers.

'Turn the light out when you're done. Breakfast ends at 6.30, sharp,' said Mr Daryl. ''Night.'

Zuunbayan – 'Zee-Bee' to its expatriate inhabitants – was founded as one of the military bases for units of the Soviet and Mongolian army. The town was a fading and flaking collection of multi-storey apartment blocks, a single, potholed concrete road, abandoned barracks and a hospital. The oil camp – the Hotel California's bedrooms, offices and mess-hall, flanked by workshops and yards full of oil rig equipment – stood a mile away over sandy gravel. Further off, beyond a dozen storage tanks, a score of nodding-donkey beam-engines sucked up what remained in the wells the Russians had worked.

Daryl Lefevre, the camp manager, woke me and led me to breakfast, joining a dozen oil men, mostly American, in jeans and T-shirts. In a wilderness with nothing much around for 500 kilometres in any direction, I took my pick of eggs, fried, sunny-side up or over easy, pancakes, coffee and juice topped up with ice from the ice-maker. Fly screens and a fizzing mosquito zapper kept insects at bay.

Most of the Americans in the base were serving time, filling their scant leisure watching satellite TV; but one of them loved the desert. Dressed in overalls, wearing John Lennon glasses, he was middle-aged, with a grey beard, and super-fit. To escape the rigours of work, he liked to wander into the wilderness. He had been a rig electrician for over twenty years, mainly offshore. 'I got tired of offshore because of how complicated everything is.' He became tentative, as if embarrassed at the simplicity of his words. 'My job is just … very … complicated. I like coming back to land, because it was, ah, a little bit more simple? On a rig, if you want that simplicity, you have to run round the helideck or on a running machine, and there's lines of people waiting for the running machines. Here, it's just waiting for you.' His name was John Matthews, but everyone called him 'Gobi'.

'I like practising survival skills. I have stashes of water that I take out on my mountain bike, so a long run is not out of the question. I'm not comfortable with staying around the camp. It's pretty hard for my co-patriates to understand.'

I thought for a moment I was with a character out of *Deliverance*, some psychopathic loner, until I was won over by the gentleness in his soft speech and a thoughtfulness that suggested a man exploring not only the wilderness but himself.

'I liked the desert as soon as I saw it. It's sort of . . . in me. I'm from south Texas, and it's pretty dry there, though there are more bushes and mesquites and fences. This is sort of like south Texas as it used to be. Even today, you get the same feel from west Texas, if you go to Big Bend National Park or the Chihuahua Desert.'

The connection went deeper than a feeling for landscape. 'Gobi' was an American archetype, who by coming here had rediscovered roots that had become obscured by today's America and by the nature of his work. 'I believe I share with other Americans a feel for the Frontier. I believe my feeling is an extension of the frontier spirit that brought us all from Europe. Now there's no frontier, but the spirit is still there.'

This was not escapism. He had a wife and a son, whom he missed – 'I guess I'm more in love with my family than the desert.' It was just that he had a rare ability to turn a posting into something more than hard cash. 'Some of my copatriates, this job is real miserable for them. They count the days, they count the hours, and down to like a few days before we leave, they're counting the *meals* we have to go.'

To justify living in these remote and trying circumstances, many men find a higher purpose. 'Gobi' had his. Others built upon Nescor's intentions – to create a Gobi equivalent of a biosphere, a world apart from its surroundings, but which may, with luck, reform those sur-roundings in years to come. That aim inspired Friedline, and it inspired Daryl Lefevre. Wouldn't it be something, said Lefevre, downing his coffee, to kick-start an industry, to feed the local economy, in effect to save the people who would otherwise be stuck in a dead-end town?

This artificial world was underpinned in large measure by Sami, the Lebanese chef from Great Yarmouth. Sami, in his chef's white coat and white hat, glasses hanging round his neck, presided over a European–American mix of foods and equipment. His broad, unshaven features exuded a quintessence of wellbeing, which was a vital part of his professionalism. In this tight little world, with men working ten-hour days and thirty-five-day 'hitches' nonstop, everyone has to be friendly, and 'the only way you can get a worker to relax is give him good food, and have good relations, and have a joke'. He should know: he was used to living apart from the world, having been a North Sea 'tiger', a chef on an oil rig, for thirteen years. But the desert, he was at pains to tell me, was different from the North Sea. Sometimes there were eggs for two weeks, then no eggs for five weeks. Vegetables came rarely. Right now, he was out of Log Cabin syrup, which had to be imported from the States. There was always fresh beef and mutton – he bought the animals and had them slaughtered on the spot – but there was no milk. 'How to keep it fresh until it gets here? That is the problem. What I really miss, what I always used to love in Great Yarmouth, was to wake up to a nice cold glass of milk.'

What kept him going was the people. There was a problem with language, because everything had to be done in English, but the company ran a school, and the kitchen staff he was training were fast learners. 'These are very, very good people. I teach them so many things – they are willing, able, they work hard, especially the women. The women work harder than the men, and handle more responsibility. When you see their lives, you think how good they are. You been in Zee-Bee yet? It break your heart. Honest the truth.'

Among the staff was an English medic, Gary Parkinson, from Bude in Cornwall, who doubled as English teacher to the Mongolian staff. He too had been in the North Sea; and he too responded to the challenge, the novelty, the feeling of being on the edge, of planting the seeds of some future harvest. He and his interpreter, Gambat, were free. I could ride along with them and see the wildcat rig, the one that might, with luck, make a new strike of sweet, high-grade crude.

First, to get the feel of the place, Gary took me to the hospital. Started to serve the military base and the large Russo–Mongolian community, it had been languishing for years. 'This place has nothing,' he muttered as we approached the concrete hulk, with its boarded up windows and sand drifting into its compound. I was apprehensive, conjuring a picture of Third World suffering, with wards full of haggard patients, nurses shouting for drips and harassed doctors shaking their heads over yet another little corpse. But it became clear, as we entered, that Parkinson spoke the literal truth. The place had virtually nothing of anything: medicine, equipment, doctors, and at this moment patients as well, most having discharged themselves for the holidays. Built in 1985, it had been virtually abandoned when the Russians pulled out. The doctor who showed me round was a specialist in shock therapy, a useful talent perhaps, considering that he doubled for the ear, nose and throat man, who was on holiday, and also filled in as anaesthetist on occasion. Once, the hospital had performed two operations a day; now, one a week. Like the town itself, the hospital was on the brink of either collapse or regeneration, depending on whether the Americans found oil or not.

The road to Rig 101 was newly graded, making it an epitome of what had to be done to work with machinery in the desert. The day before, one of the first heavy rains of the summer had turned low-lying sections into quagmires. Within a day or two, the puddles would be gone and the dust begin to drift in from the saxaul-dotted plains, but to guarantee that work continued, a grader had ploughed away the mud and sand to reveal a hard base. A grader needed fuel, parts, maintenance, a world apart from that of the herders.

Ahead, the rig soared skywards for thirty metres from a base of portable cabins and massive trailer-truck. It stood against an artificial sand dune, the result of site clearance bulldozed into a barricade against the shrieking winds of early summer. Competing with the thud of a generator, the senior fitter, Ralph Fettig, a powerful figure in jeans, T-shirt, peaked cap and dark glasses, yelled his reasons for being in this forlorn spot. From Kill Deer, North Dakota, Fettig had been on rigs for twenty-one years, in his home state, the Rockies, California, Oregon and Mexico. He liked it here. 'It's hard to drill a wildcat well anywhere else in the world right now. Just drilling where other people have been before, that's boring. This is a new, dangerous adventure.'

Fettig deconstructed the litter of equipment. The whole rig was designed for simplicity and reliability. Having arrived in bits by train, it was built to telescope down to fifteen metres on to a six-wheel drive base with fat sand-wheels that ran it straight out across the desert. From camp to site, it could be up and boring in a day. 'We have everything we need right here, or in camp, all the cross-over subs, our small drill plate, our drill-collars, all the bits, stabilizers for hole problems, cement unit for the casings, everything to take us down to 7,000 feet (1.3 miles). That's not deep for a rig, but it's deep for round here. The Russians never got that deep, because their equipment weren't no good. I know because you can see it lying out there in the desert, broke down.'

Amidst the litter of sun-blackened, windblasted bits of metal, the decaying barracks, the sludge of polluted sand, the Russians did leave behind something of value. Nearby, they had built a runway for military aircraft, made of top-quality reinforced concrete slabs thirty centimetres thick and six metres across, a mile-long sheet of motorway paving the shifting desert. A dozen of those slabs created a platform fit for an oil rig to stand on. (No one, though, has found a use yet for the underground bunkers and storage chambers that made some of these forward bases proof against practically anything but a direct A-bomb strike.)

The real challenge here was the need to develop self-sufficiency. There was no room for the Russian attitude – 'Run it till it breaks, then throw it away and order another.' To order anything from the US – and it all had to come from the US – took a minimum of six weeks, twelve weeks to be safe. Small items they ordered in the States when they went on leave, hand-carrying equipment of up to 300 pounds. It will be harder for the Mongolians, when they find themselves on their own. Theirs will always be a world apart, because the equipment will always have to come from the US. They will always have to work in English – to understand instruction manuals, order new items, and maintain the equipment.

It seemed to me Zuunbayan was a town that reduced to two letters: IF. Everything depends on the finding of oil. If there's good, sweet oil, Zee-Bee will be an oil-rush town; men will realize their dreams; Mongolians will build new lives. If not, the gravel plains will once again become as empty and silent as they were fifty years ago.

To the Blue City

I left Zee-Bee by train. Ever since the Russians were here, there has been a branch line linking the town to Sainshand. It is not on any map that I saw, probably for now-outdated security reasons. The men on the two coaches wore jeans and cotton T-shirts, the women smart blouses, the children sneakers. There was not a deel in sight. As we clicked slowly into Sainshand through an industrial litter – a power station, an overhead crane, concrete prefabs, marshalling yards – it was clear that this whole region was a community that owed its very existence to external forces: the military, oil, the railway.

In Sainshand, trains from Ulan Bator and China meet. Slowly, as the heat of the sun died and night fell, the quarter-mile platform filled for the big event. Women and children hefting panniers of dumplings and soft drinks hawked their wares. Finally, with great breathy blasts, the eighteen carriages of the northbound train pulled in. It moved slowly enough for me to become a trainspotter: M62YM (006) glided to a halt, stately as a liner, green paint made bilious by the platform's widely spaced sodium lights. Minutes later, another series of blasts announced the arrival of the southbound train, mine. It drew up on the second line, beyond train No. 006.

For a few seconds I feared I was on the wrong platform. But there was only one platform, for two trains. I assumed the trains would engage in a slow-motion ballet, one heading on north, while the other shunted to the platform. Then all became clear. Those crowding the low platform moved forward and began to infiltrate between, *and under*, the carriages of 006. I stooped, and did likewise, abandoning the platform's lighting for a tunnel of darkness, edged with the silhouettes of wheels, the private parts of railway carriages, stooping figures and scavenging dogs. Something wet dripped on my neck, and I scraped my backbone on obtrusive metal.

Beyond, in the gap between the two trains, I stood for a moment, rubbing my back and allowing my eyes to get used to the gloom. This was time well spent, for between the two tracks ran a drainage trench several feet deep. On either side of the trench were banks of diggings. Troglodytes emerging from beneath the carriages and mountaineers descending from the train met in a slow confusion, all permeated by the hawkers of soft drinks and dumplings.

I knew my carriage number, knew I had to be in the right carriage, because the trains divided at the border, and I risked going to Beijing rather than Höhhot. The darkness and the acute angle made it impossible to read the little number placards set high on the cliff walls of the carriages. I clambered along the train, until a reassuring sign proclaimed 'Ulan Bator – Höhhot'. I climbed, and found home: an empty compartment, a bunk-bed set out with sheets and a thin duvet, and hanging on the window a plastic vase of red plastic roses in plastic earth.

Later, I was awoken by two cheery Mongolians. We exchanged greetings in snippets of our common languages, Mongol, Russian, German and English. One had been to Brandenburg, for reasons I was too tired to grasp. I fell asleep to one of them singing, 'Good morning to you, good morning to you,' to the tune of 'Happy Birthday'.

Dawn revealed grey gravel to the horizon. At the end of the corridor, a wood-fired water-heater was bubbling, exuding good cheer, and a young attendant invited me to help myself. Sipping tea, I watched the sun, turned into a red beachball by cloud, emerge above the flatline horizon. At walking pace, we drew into a toytown station, with pillars and an intricate yellow steeple, with scallops and semicircles and triangles outlined in red like children's bricks.

'Where are we? Is this China?'

'Zamin Uud.'

We had been travelling through the night, for six hours, and had covered no more than the 250 kilometres to the last town in Mongolia.

Officials inspected tickets and passports. Customs people came with dogs, and made much of checking baggage.

Three hours later, the train, with frequent stops, pulled slowly through the frontier, overtaking horses, trucks and jeeps lined up at two office buildings. Others were in the process of being built, an indication that trans-border traffic was increasing. A sign in English proclaimed that this was a joint Japanese–Chinese–Mongolian project.

The frontier itself was marked by a well-maintained two-metre wire fence, at right angles to a paved road, which led southwards between an avenue of trees and bland buildings to the Chinese border town of Erlian. In Chapman Andrews' day, Erlian was a couple of buildings and an occasional ger. Now, it is a boom town of tens of thousands, with a station of white brick, and neat courtyards squared off with ten-metre trees.

Here, the train underwent a change that marked the final break between Mongolia and China. Mongolia, having been drawn like a wandering moon from the orbit of China into that of the Soviet Union, inherited the consequences of a decision taken far away and long ago. When Europe began to industrialize in the early nineteenth century, most countries accepted the standard British gauge of 4' 8.5", including those, like China, whose railways were developed by imperial powers. Russia, however, opted for a wide gauge of 5'. Usually when the two gauges meet, people and goods change trains. In two places, through-trains receive new bogeys. One is Brest-Litovsk, on the Polish–Belorussian border. The other is Erlian.

When everyone else got off, I stayed aboard, and became flotsam in a mechanized stream. Weaving through cross-currents of overlapping tracks and piled-up debris of bogeys, the train shunted into a long shed, with backwaters of sidings clogged with more of the four-wheeled sets of bogeys. Squat metal pillars at each corner of each carriage revealed themselves as jacks. I would have thought that to change a train's wheels would require an army of men in oily overalls, but this was done as smartly as a set-change in an opera by young workers in blue and yellow jackets, many of them women wearing make-up. With the carriages exactly separated, a few deft turns released the old bogeys, which were whisked away by an overhead crane rumbling back and forth above the carriages. New ones were hooked from the sidings, swung into place, guided onto the track, and rolled under the carriages. In half an hour we were done, and rolling westwards.

The train pulled into Höhhot late at night. I pushed through a crowd, to the exit, and stood, baffled as a yokel by the noise that burst around me. The forecourt was dense with manoeuvring cabs and surging crowds. Drivers pushed forward, some touting for custom in English – 'You want hotel? Which hotel, mister?' What I could see of the town heaved with new building and quivered with neon, in Chinese characters, Latinized Pin-Yin and old Mongol script. From beyond the station came the roar of traffic and the ringing of ten thousand bicycle bells. This was the 'Blue City' of the Mongols, famous from its foundation in the seventeenth century for its Buddhist temples and lamaseries. Now, the name has been transliterated into a meaningless sequence of syllables – Hu-He-Hao-Te – and the Mongolians have been swamped by a million Chinese. Around me, in an area the size of the Sacred Mother mountain, lived a population five times that of the whole Gobi.

For months, I had seldom been with more than half a dozen people together. More than once, I and two companions had been the only ones in the whole circle of the horizon, three people in 1,000 square miles.

I picked up my pack, glanced at the town map, saw precisely where I was, and struck out through the lonely throng for my hotel.

BIBLIOGRAPHY

There is no book on the Gobi as a whole in English. There is not even one other than this, on the whole Mongolian sector. Most of those with 'Gobi' in the title (like *The Gobi Desert* written by two stalwart missionary ladies Mildred Cable and Francesca French, published in 1942 and reprinted in 1984 by Virago) actually relate to the Gobi borderlands of Inner Mongolia or Djungaria.

Books (in English):

Roy Chapman Andrews: *Across Mongolian Plains* (New York, London, 1921). An account of his preparatory trip in 1919.

    The New Conquest of Central Asia (American Museum of Natural History, New York, 1932). A classic, now virtually unobtainable. If you see one, buy it, for the fold-out panoramas, for the record of a great adventure, for the feel of the wilderness, for a superb account of science in the making. Of the eight volumes in this series, it is the least specialized and most appealing to the general reader.

Charles Bawden: *The Modern History of Mongolia* (Keegan Paul International) provides the best historical account of Mongolia from the late 17th century.

Charles Berkey and Frederick Morris: *The Geology of Mongolia* (American Museum of Natural History, New York, 1932). Another of the superb series that came out of Andrews' expeditions. Though specialized and dated, it contains timeless gems not included in Andrews' own book. Some of the pictures are the same, but the maps are treasures.

Sandor Bökönyi: *The Przhevalski Horse* (Souvenir Press, 1974). A historical survey.

Zofia Kielan-Jaworowska: *Hunting For Dinosaurs* (Cambridge/London, 1969) is a brief account of her Gobi discoveries.

Peter Matthiessen: *The Snow Leopard* (Harvill, London, reprinted 1995).

Judith Nordby: *Mongolia* (World Bibliographical Series, No 156/Clio Press, Oxford, 1993) includes a number of Gobi references.

Michael Novacek: *Dinosaurs of the Flaming Cliffs* (Doubleday, New York, 1996). This brings Andrews up to date, with a full survey of the finds and their status. Combining top-level expertise with an easy anecdotal style, it is far wider in range than the title suggests.

Donald Rayfield: *The Dream of Lhasa: The Life of Nikolay Przhevalsky* (Paul Elek, London, 1976) covers the explorer's time in the Gobi.

Joseph Wallace: *The American Museum of Natural History's book of Dinosaurs and Other Ancient Creatures* (Simon & Schuster). A good survey that includes the Gobi. Other US books that cover similar ground are: John Noble Wilford: *The Riddle of the Dinosaur* (Knopf, New York, 1985), Don Lessem: *Kings of Creation* (Simon & Schuster) and David Spalding: *Dinosaur Hunters* (Prima, California).

Papers (in English): An Introduction

Anthropology: specialists include Caroline Humphrey and David Sneath, of the Mongolian Studies Unit, Dept. of Social Anthropology, Cambridge; and Robin Mearns and Jeremy Swift, of the Institute of Development Studies, University of Sussex. Other specialist papers are published by the United Nations Development Programme.

Wildlife: The best general introduction to Gobi wildlife, as well as to Mongolian wildlife as a whole, is *Mongolia's Wild Heritage*, published both in English and Mongolian by the Mongolian Ministry of Nature and the Environment in 1996, edited by Chris Finch. It is in full colour, with maps of all the national parks. Richard Reading's *Biological Assessment of Three Beauties* is masterly, with a detailed specialist bibliography. Snow leopard literature is available through George Schaller and the International Snow Leopard Trust, in Seattle, Washington, USA. L.V. Zhirnov and V.O. Ilyinsky: *The Great Gobi Reserve – a Refuge for Rare Animals of Central Asian Deserts* (USSR/UNEP, Centre for International Projects, GKNT, Moscow, 1986) is a superb overview in English, if you can find it. On mammals, the best overview is David Mallon: *Mammals of the Mongolian People's Republic* (*Mammal Review*, 15, 1985). 'Przhevalski Horse' is a twice-yearly journal published by The Foundation for the Preservation and Protection of the Przhevalski Horse, Rotterdam, Holland.

Palaeontology: The finds are well documented in science journals – *Science*, American Museum *Novitates*, *Scientific American*, *Nature*. Names to look out for: Michael Novacek, Perle, Mark Norell, Luis Chiappe, James Clark, Barsbold Rinchen, Dashzeveg, Amy Davidson, Malcolm McKenna. The finds are summarized for the non-scientist in Novacek's book (see above).

Geology: Main contributors in English so far are Brian Windley and W. Dickson Cunningham, University of Leicester; and Lewis Owen (formerly Royal Holloway, University of London; now University of California, Riverside). Other names: J. Badamgarov and D. Dorjnamjaa, Paleontology Centre, Mongolian Academy of Sciences. The 1957 Gobi earthquake is assessed by I. Baljinnyam and others in the Geological Society of America bulletin, 1993, and by Bayarsaykhan and others in *Geology*, July 1996.

INDEX